Aces, Airmen and the Biggin Hill Wing

Leading Aircraftsman David Raymond Davies, RAF Biggin Hill, 1941.

Aces, Airmen and the Biggin Hill Wing

A Collective Memoir 1941–42

Jon E.C. Tan

Pen & Sword
AVIATION

First published in Great Britain in 2016 by
Pen & Sword Military
an imprint of
Pen & Sword Books Ltd
47 Church Street
Barnsley
South Yorkshire
S70 2AS

Copyright © Jon E.C. Tan 2016

ISBN 978 1 47388 169 3

Typeset in Ehrhardt by
Mac Style Ltd, Bridlington, East Yorkshire
Printed and bound in the UK by CPI Group (UK) Ltd,
Croydon, CRO 4YY

Pen & Sword Books Ltd incorporates the imprints of Pen & Sword
Archaeology, Atlas, Aviation, Battleground, Discovery, Family History,
History, Maritime, Military, Naval, Politics, Railways, Select, Transport,
True Crime, and Fiction, Frontline Books, Leo Cooper, Praetorian Press,
Seaforth Publishing and Wharncliffe.

For a complete list of Pen & Sword titles please contact
PEN & SWORD BOOKS LIMITED
47 Church Street, Barnsley, South Yorkshire, S70 2AS, England
E-mail: enquiries@pen-and-sword.co.uk
Website: www.pen-and-sword.co.uk

A Dedication

To my grandmother, Lily Davies and those many unknown women that devoted much of their post-war lives to the care and support of returning servicemen, indelibly marked by their experiences of war.

Per Ardua Ad Astra

Contents

Acknowledgements

This book has been many years in the making. In many ways, my grandfather was the instigator of the project through the stories he told me of wartime places and people. The Second World War is now only just within living memory and fading fast. So as history and its events race past us, sometimes we have to catch hold and ride along, becoming custodians of the memories of our ancestors. I approached this work with this sentiment in mind, asking how I might best represent Raymond's experiences and those of his comrades. It has felt both an honour and a great responsibility.

The sources used within the work are numerous and varied in type. The introduction provides a summary of these while discussing some of the challenges associated with their use. History, at its best, offers an interpretation of the past and attempts to cross-reference the recall of events, its 'evidence', in order to establish its perspective. In assembling what is essentially a case study of the Biggin Hill Wing 1941-42, using my grandfather's memoirs and service as a chronology, I am indebted to many people.

First and foremost, this work would not have been possible without the support of the veterans of Biggin Hill 1941-42. They were always generous with their time and shared so much with me in our conversations, audio-recorded interviews and written correspondence, sometimes memories that were deeply personal and challenging to revisit. Sadly, many of them are no longer with us, but I hope that in some small way the work presented here contributes a lasting memorial to them, their experiences and the sacrifices they made.

Flight Lieutenant Sir John Alexander Atkinson, DFC, CB, KCB.
Wing Commander Eric G. Barwell, DFC & bar, MID.
Squadron Leader Percy Beake, DFC, MID
Air Commodore Sir Peter M. Brothers, CBE, DSO, DFC & bar.
Squadron Leader Neville F. Duke, DSO, OBE, DFC & two bars, AFC, FRAeS.
Mr Ted Hayes (Fitter IIE).
Squadron Leader Walter 'Johnnie' Johnston.
Colonel Aviateur Raymond Lallemant, DFC & bar.
Lieutenant Colonel Ervin L. Miller. AM with 3 Oak Leaf Clusters, BSM

The Right Honourable Sir Tasker Watkins, VC, GBE.
Squadron Leader Geoffrey H.A. Wellum, DFC.
Group Captain Allan R. Wright, DFC & bar, AFC.

The families of a number of veterans that figure significantly in my grandfather's memories of Biggin Hill must also be thanked for their time in providing insight and understanding and primary research material. In particular, I am forever grateful to Helen, 'Tish' and Robert Kingaby for their immense support throughout the years of this project, and for their permission to draw upon the unpublished manuscript written by Wing Commander Donald E. Kingaby, DSO, AFC, DFM & two bars, DFC (USA), CdeG (Belg). Don was the first pilot of 92 Squadron that my grandfather worked with and he became one of a select group of regulars that he supported while the squadron remained with the Wing. He always had fond recollections of Don and, along with 'Johnnie' Johnston, his memories of Biggin and Gravesend in 1941 often involved mention of him. I must also pay gratitude to Martin and Helen Johnston for ongoing support following their father's passing. I had a great connection with 'Johnnie' Johnston, and our times together in Cornwall often would extend to many hours recalling the events of 1941 and shared experiences on and off duty.

I would also like to thank Mrs Lesley Kingcome for her discussions about her late husband, Group Captain Brian Kingcome, DSO, DFC & bar, MID, and for her permission to use his published work in my research. Brian was remembered fondly by all who I interviewed, often referred to as the greatest leader of 92 who was never officially appointed CO! Talk of great leaders also reminds me of the support and encouragement given by Squadron Leader John D. Barwell, AFC, particularly in our discussions of his father's crash in August 1941, while air-testing Spitfire Vb, W3365. The photographs that John was able to provide show how severe the accident was. Similarly, I am grateful to Mr Michael Stanford-Tuck for his words of support regarding my writing about his father, Wing Commander Robert R. Stanford-Tuck, DSO, DFC & two bars, DFC (USA), MID. I would also like to thank Mr Hamish Milne for his great assistance and encouragement in my writing about his father, Wing Commander R. M. 'Dickie' Milne, DFC and bar.

Much encouragement and often extended sessions of tea drinking and cake eating were provided by Mrs Barbara Wright, Mrs Patricia Miller and Mrs Eve Beake. Always so supportive of my visits to see Allan, Ervin and Percy, I cannot thank them enough for the warmth of their hospitality over the years of my research.

Special mention must be made to Ms Charlotte Atkinson. I will always remember with great affection the times Alec, Charlotte and I would spend together. From our first meeting, Alec and I seemed to have a great affinity and understanding. In Alec's later years, our meetings and excursions were possible because of Charlotte's unwavering support for him. You both offered me so much encouragement and showed such faith in my work. It is a friendship I will continue to cherish.

A number of authors, researchers and organisations must also be thanked for their contribution. In particular, authors Norman Franks, Philip Caine and Peter Caygill gave important support and access to materials: Norman Franks kindly supplied letters from Group Captain Raymond M.B. Duke-Woolley, DSO, DFC & two bars, DFC (USA) to help with my research about Operation Fuller. Philip Caine was of excellent help in developing the research for 133 Squadron's time with the Wing. Peter Caygill was instrumental in my initial contact with 'Johnnie' Johnston, who was very much a key associate in my grandfather's memoirs.

I would also like to thank Alan Thomas of the Air Historical Branch who assisted with my research of 'Dickie' Barwell's accident. Similarly, staff of the National Archives, Kew, The Royal Air Force Museum, Hendon, and at the Imperial War Museum's Duxford, Lambeth and photo archive facilities have provided valuable guidance along the way. I am grateful for the support and permissions given by a number of veterans' associations: The Eagle Squadron Association, The Canadian Fighter Pilots' Association and the 92 Squadron Association.

Special mention must be made of Jim Earnshaw AE, formerly of the 609 Squadron Association and a veteran of the squadron. Jim offered me great encouragement and assistance in working through the squadron's paper and photographic archives. He was a tenacious researcher with a great eye for detail. I am indebted to him and the association for their support and permissions to draw on the archive in this work.

With my grandfather's service providing the spine of this account of Biggin Hill's operations during 1941-42, I was conscious of the need to capture a ground crew's perspective as authentically as possible. I am thus grateful to my former work colleagues and friends Bob Mitchell, Peter 'Gerbs' Jeffrey, Tony Smith and the late Brian Brown. In particular, I would like to thank Bob and 'Gerbs' who, as former engineers with the RAF's Battle of Britain Memorial Flight (BBMF), did much to help me understand the specifics of working on Spitfires and Hurricanes. Many years since our work together for the Real Aeroplane Company, I think I still remember how to reassemble a Merlin camshaft, to do undercarriage retraction tests, radiator repairs, engine pre-oiling, pitot-static leak testing and how to prepare the aircraft for a Flight Release Certificate.

'Gerbs' Jeffrey, Paul Blackah and Mark 'Arnie' Arnold must also be thanked for making possible my access to Spitfire Vb AB910 with BBMF at Coningsby; and Paul Campbell at the Biggin Hill Heritage Hangar for access to Spitfire IX

TA805. It is incredible that both of these Spitfires survive and are still flying. It is wholly down to the expertise, dedication and creativity of their engineers that they are. Both of these aircraft were associated with my grandfather's service: AB910 at Dieppe with 133 Squadron; and TA805 with 183/54 Squadron in 1945, the squadron that Ray served with throughout the liberation of Europe and with whom he returned to RAF Chilbolton, Hants.

Many thanks must also be extended to my publisher Pen & Sword. I always have considered them to be one of the best and most respected of military publishers. To have their support in this project has been most welcome and rewarding. In particular, I would like to thank Laura Hirst and Barnaby Blacker for their enthusiasm, encouragement and hard work throughout.

Of my friends, there are some that deserve special mention for their ongoing support, interest and encouragement. They are: Steve Teasdale, Stephen Spencer, Derek Wheeler and Flight Lieutenant Terry Clark DFM; Christine Allan, Karen Davis and Janey McGoldrick; Justin Willis, Frank Morgan and Andy Smith.

Finally, but with most heartfelt gratitude and love, I would like to thank those family members and close friends without whom this work would not have been possible:

My grandfather and grandmother, Ray and Lily Davies
My father and mother, Chen and Jacqueline Tan
Jo Dixon
Derek Wilkinson

Thank you,

Jon E.C. Tan, 2016

Foreword

Aces, Airmen and the Biggin Hill Wing is a most captivating work as it approaches fighter operations during 1940–42 from a new and refreshingly different angle; that of those who toiled day and more often than not night, to keep their Spitfires in the air and flying at peak performance.

It is rather with a sense of humility that one is reacquainted with the lives of this good-humoured, loyal and hard working body of men, the ground crews. The confidence their pilots had in them, their dedication and their work was total. They were nicknamed the 'Erks'. It is no exaggeration to say that without them our country might or indeed would not, have prevailed to such an extent in those early and critical days of World War Two.

As a young fighter pilot then, you could not fly a Spitfire of 92 Squadron out of Biggin Hill during those days of 1940–1942 and expect to forget about it. Memories stay with you forever. This most welcome book brings back those memories very vividly indeed. It provides the reader with a valuable reminder of the extreme demands made of those airmen when servicing the Hurricanes and Spitfires of Fighter Command, Royal Air Force.

This work deserves, and I wish it, every success.

Squadron Leader Geoffrey H.A. Wellum, DFC

A Few Words from Sir Alec Atkinson

This is an important book. It is the only book I have read that properly recognises the role of our ground crews, to whom, as pilots at Biggin Hill, we were completely indebted. The author's extensive research brings back very vividly what it was like to serve at Biggin Hill in 1941–42 and to be operational with the Wing. I believe that the author's grandfather's experiences in the Second World War are well worth putting on record.

I was very pleased to see the references to Tom Lund. I respected Tom greatly and so did all the other members of 609 Squadron who knew him. I was at Kingswood School, Bath with him for several years and went up to Oxford University with him. Tom and I were both stationed at Biggin Hill. I shall never forget him as a dear friend and a fellow pilot.

Flight Lieutenant Sir John Alexander Atkinson, DFC, CB, KCB

Introduction

LAC David Raymond Davies and the Biggin Hill Wing:
I cannot remember when Ray Davies, my grandfather, started to tell me of his wartime experiences in the RAF. All I know is that I was very young and excited enough to listen. I also must have been rather impressionable, as I can remember how vivid these stories were to me and how they sometimes made it into my drawing in art classes in primary school. I am certain that my teachers must have worried: a boy of five years old graphically illustrating granddad in a foxhole, sheltering from strafing Messerschmitts and Focke Wulfs! A place called Biggin Hill figured significantly in all of this, as did the names of people that I could recite as if they were close members of the family. Ray talked a lot about Don Kingaby, of Jamie Rankin and Bob Tuck, I knew of 'Sailor' Malan, 'Dickie' Barwell and Brian Kingcome. There was a 'boy' called Wellum and someone called Tommy Lund, who Ray knew as 'Nobby'. For one so young, it was perhaps startling to hear me recall the names of public houses such as The Bell in Bromley, The King's Arms at Leaves Green and the Seven Stars at Chilbolton. By the age of twelve I had squarely lodged in my own consciousness these memories from Ray. I grew up knowing these stories, hearing them again and again, until I could tell them as if they were my own.

It was not until late in the 1990s, when I was in my thirties, that Ray and I started to revisit these memories more systematically. The catalyst was my giving to Ray a copy of Norman Franks' biography of 'Sailor' Malan. Normally quite a slow reader, he read it in about two weeks, phoned me up and said, 'Hello boy, when are you coming down next?' I made the trip to Wolverhampton a week or so later and there he started to tell me his own stories of practically everyone named in the book, including ones of 'the Sailor'. Having professional research experience by then, I asked Ray about us starting to document and record his memoirs. I am so glad he agreed. Yet, it was not without its challenges.

The first challenge was to establish a chronology for his RAF service, the squadrons he served with and the RAF stations to which he had been posted. Next was to place each of the individual stories somewhere along this timeline. Amazingly, once we had done this, and after many visits to the National Archives at Kew, the timeline served to jog his memory even further, resulting in other stories that I had not heard before. Perhaps also recognising my adult understanding and sensitivities, Ray now began to talk to me about the more difficult experiences of the time, of war and of loss. Talk of those pilots that he had known and that had been lost on operations during his time at Biggin Hill led me to another challenge: the search for any of those that might have survived the war and were perhaps still alive. I found a good number and am indebted to them all, along with their families. So began my writing of what amounts to a collective memoir of the Biggin Hill Wing 1941–42, with Ray's timeline as the backbone of the work.

Advantageously, weaving the recollections of others around those of Ray's has helped in piecing together the historical record with some degree of certainty. Sometimes this has enabled stories that existed as fragments in one person's recollections to be reassembled by drawing on other fragments from another's memory that completed the picture. A good example of this is the 'Bromley and the Bomb' story: Ray remembered some of the details (e.g. the name of the public house, borrowing a wagon from the Station Armoury and picking up Kingaby and Johnston; and being reprimanded by Jamie Rankin). 'Johnnie' Johnston was able to fill in the other bits!

Probably the greatest challenge has been the way to tell the story, with so many different sources of information. At one level, there were official documents, such as those RAF station and squadron operational records books held in the National Archives at Kew. These were useful, but of variable quality, their content being largely dependent on the person put in charge of making the daily entries. Pilots' individual flying logbooks were an interesting and important resource, but again they had to be considered carefully. As many aircrew recounted, they often gave their log over to a member of their ground crew to fill in, sometimes at the end of the month! Moreover, not all operations would be recorded: Those 'spur of the moment' and last-minute changes to operations and pilot availability sometimes resulted in personal logbooks not corresponding with the squadron's operational diary.

A significant amount of material has been published over the years, some of the most interesting being written in the 1950s and 1960s, when one might argue that the memories of those consulted were still fresh. Later published works have expanded the written account, offered new insights and analyses, and yet have sometimes replicated the errors of earlier works. Consulting surviving veterans is also not without its difficulties, particularly as one moves further away from the events themselves. Yet, I was amazed at how accurate and consistent their recollections could be, once I had started to cross-reference accounts with earlier ones committed to paper nearer the time (e.g. diaries and letters) and with other verbatim accounts and documents. Don Kingaby's unpublished and incomplete memoirs are a good example of this. Made available to me by the Kingaby family, it took me much time in cross-referencing the manuscript with other sources (including interviews with Ray and Johnnie Johnston, and with Don's logbook) in order to place the events more accurately in time. Whilst significant dates and events stood out immediately, others required careful interviewing and various means of stimulating the conversation and jogging memories. Sometimes the mere mention of a name would do. Other times it would be prompted by my bringing along an artefact (e.g. a period item of flying equipment), or simply reporting on a trip I'd made. When I chatted about my first visit to RAF Kenley, it was then that both Ray and Eric Barwell started to talk to me about 'Batchy' Atcherley and about walking up the hill from Whyteleaf Station.

Perhaps the most important part of telling the story is finding a voice, rather than simply recounting dates and events. After a number of 'false starts', I found that, along with a familiar pattern of descriptive narrative, interspersed with quotation of verbatim transcripts and documentary evidence, I was wrestling with the difficulties of trying to convey a sense of being there. To this end, at times I have adopted a more 'of the moment' narrative, bringing together a number of pieces of information and representing them in a way to bring a feeling of how the events were being experienced and the likely conversations that took place. I hope this helps the reader in gaining further insight into the operational experiences of those involved.

One last word must go to two of the major contributors to the 92 (East India) Squadron aspects of the book, my grandfather, Raymond Davies and Walter 'Johnnie' Johnston. In partnership with Don Kingaby, Ray and Johnnie shared a number of operational and social experiences during their time at Biggin Hill. Sadly, none of them are with us now. Don passed away in 1990, long before Ray and I began this work. I am so grateful to the Kingaby family, particularly 'Tish', Robert and Helen for their continued support. Before Ray and Johnnie died, they were able to read and comment on approximately two thirds of the manuscript, including all of the material relating to 92 Squadron's time at Biggin Hill. Having waited until he was almost on the last chapter I had given him, and eager to know how he felt about what I'd written, I interrupted Ray's intense concentration on the manuscript. 'Granddad,' I said, 'since I gave you that, I haven't been able to get a word of conversation out of you!' He replied, 'that's because reading this is me reliving my life.' Johnnie's approval was twofold: Firstly, he told me, 'I read it often, it sits here on the table next to me.' Secondly, he began to tell me more stories! I miss them both dearly.

Jon E.C. Tan, 2016, York.

Chapter One

To Volunteer

Nelson, Mid-Glamorganshire 1940:
For the first time that Raymond could recall, his father sat across the table from him in The Royal Oak quietly supping a half-pint of beer. There was something new, something rather comforting to see Dad this way. It was, of course, well-known in the village that Charlie Davies, lay preacher and miner, would drink now and again. Yet to Raymond, Charlie now seemed a little closer – not just as a caring father, or as a loving husband to Caroline Jane Davies his mother, but as a person. It was turning out to be an exceptional day, one that Raymond would remember for the rest of his life.

The day before, he had approached his father, telling him of his intentions to go to down to Cardiff the next day and volunteer for service in the Royal Air Force. It had not seemed like a difficult decision. The war was real enough, even here in the Valleys. At night, Ray and his youngest brother Leighton had lain awake listening to the bombers droning around in the blackout, sometimes hearing the distant crump crump of the explosions. It was usually the docks, but with the concentration of heavy industry in the area there seemed a number of prime targets for any enemy bent on destroying Britain's manufacturing capacity to wage war. Sometimes Ray and Leight' felt excitedly that things were getting a little too serious when closer explosions had been heard, in the direction of Caerphilly. But why would Hitler want to destroy this sleepy market town? 'To make the cycling club outings up the valley more exciting,' offered Ron, one of Ray and Leighton's elder brothers.

In all there were six of them. Glynn, the eldest and tallest of them. Ron, who would, with ever-present humour, never fail to greet anyone without making a joke or telling the latest 'tall' story. Eric, whose mischievous eyes would shine out from behind the coal-dust with a hint of the dramatic. Howard, strong, dependable and always with his head in a book. It was Howard who had taught Raymond to read, a skill that had allowed him to enter school at age four rather than the statutory five. Leighton, still the baby of the family really, and fair game in the many pranks with which they entertained. And Raymond? Well, Raymond was almost twenty and had avoided the usual career that saw sons follow their fathers into the pits, into some of the deepest coalmines in Britain.

Up until his decision to enlist in the RAF, he had been forging a promising career in the grocery trade, working in Cyril William's shop. It was one of those 'sell everything' shops that were the heart of the community. As was the norm, he had started there running errands, but, after leaving school at fourteen, Cyril had taken him under his wing with Raymond's younger cousin Donald becoming the junior. It was a better, safer trade than the pits, even now with the pithead baths in place – Charlie had campaigned for those. In fact, it had been the comparatively poor rates of pay in the South Wales coalfields that had prompted Eric and Howard to go to work in the Staffordshire mines. They had moved up there in 1938, after a family friend had returned from the Midlands, telling them of at least three times the rates of pay for miners in England. Much better to risk one's life on a day-to-day basis and forget the warmth and light of the sun for three times the pay.

Nelson was a small village then. Though small, a number of public houses watered the population. Near the handball court there was The Nelson Inn and the Wellington. The Royal Oak stood on the entry to Station Road, and the Working Men's Club on the main street through the village, opposite Thomas and Evans' grocer shop. Then there was the Dynevor Arms. The first of these public houses was named after Lord Nelson, who, reputedly had stayed there with Lady Emma Hamilton. To the Royal Oak, Raymond would run to get his Grancher Denham from his seat in the pub's doorway when it was time for his tea. The family had now moved up to 'The Wern', a large house on the Ystred Mynach road which gave a little more room in comparison to the old house in Donald Street, where Ray had been born. The Watkinses still lived in Donald Street. Raymond remembered Mrs Watkins cleaning Mrs Beddoes' front doorstep until its black-leaded surface shone brilliantly. He remembered because he was invariably sent round with a half pound of cheese in payment for the service. He also remembered Tasker Watkins, their son. Tasker was a few years older than Raymond – about Howard's age – and it was with Howard that Raymond most often encountered Tasker. But in Nelson, like so many other villages in the Valleys, the community was very much an extended family. So it was common for Mrs Watkins to ask Raymond in, for her to talk across the gate with his mother. Young Raymond, as he was often called, was also sweet on one of Tasker's sisters and had walked her home a few times.

The war however touched everyone. Raymond was conscious that his father had put down his glass and was now speaking quite deliberately. Something about taking care, about understanding his motives to volunteer, and about getting through it. Tasker had volunteered as well, but for the army, and so was soon to be posted to the Welsh Regiment. Billy Portlock, one of Raymond's best mates, was also joining the army. 'The army … couldn't do that,' thought Raymond as his father continued to speak. Firstly, he didn't see himself as fit enough. Secondly, the thought of the experience: fighting, hand-to-hand combat, deadly combat. Even though the idea of survival provided some sensible justification, could you really *kill* another human being? Rats and mice were one thing, they were commonplace in the mining communities. But another man? Face-to-face? No, that was too much to consider.

Though pleased to see his son volunteer for service, Charlie was fully aware of what difficulties and experiences lay ahead. He too had been a volunteer in 1916 and had been at the Somme as a horse driver in the Royal Field Artillery. He had seen the terrible costs that war brought to ordinary people, how it had wasted so many lives and made nervous, quivering wrecks of men once strong. So too it had affected families far beyond the boundaries of time set by the beginning and end of hostilities. It was hard to let a son step into this known landscape of uncertainties. There were 'knowns' in that even a cursory glance at history told of the heavy price of all wars. The uncertainties were in how flesh, bone, mind and soul would or would not endure. Raymond remembered some of his school teachers: ex-services, their minds indelibly written upon by their wartime experiences. They had ruled their classrooms with a sadism borne of living on one's nerves. Yes the war touched everyone, and just as young men still at home found themselves offered the 'white feather' in 1914–18 (an accusation of cowardice in being slow to join up), Raymond too found that the sideways glances and the talk in the shop of 'when's your Raymond going?' were now getting on his nerves. There was a pressure to go, and the RAF seemed the best option, or the least bad.

It was obviously that the Royal Air Force would need him in such pressing times, wasn't it? Every day the news documented how the youngest of Britain's armed services was maturing into a formidable, modern fighting force. The might of the German Army had thrown the combined forces of France, Belgium and Great Britain into the sea. With typical Churchillian spirit, the evacuation from Dunkirk had been turned into a victory of sorts but it really had been disastrous. Now it was the RAF's turn to carry the beacon of freedom and to demonstrate that Britain really would 'never surrender'. Whilst the south coast of England was now the greatest arena of aerial conflict, the sight and sound of aircraft climbing through the morning haze to patrol all areas of the country were becoming common experiences. High above the valleys of South Wales the recognisable silhouettes of Spitfires and Hurricanes, drawing their condensation trails across the skies, indicated the presence of these guardians of a nation's security.

The bus passed through Pontypridd and as Raymond looked out through the windows he thought of the weekly shopping excursions of Jinny (as his mother was known) and his aunts Eadie and Gladys. He smiled to himself, thinking of how his mother would, when he was a child, brief him to wail like a baby so to have Eadie buy him something that Jinny couldn't afford. It would be hard to leave the Valleys. What would he remember most? The dance rink at Treharris would definitely be up near the top of the list. Three or four times a week, and more if possible, he would go to the rink where he had a reputation as an exceptional dancer. He and his cousin Nancy would make up fancy routines and steps as something a bit special to wow the onlookers. He'd probably even miss the shop and the little strategies he'd employed to increase profits. Laughing with Donald when positioning the overhead fans so that they created a downdraft on the weighing scales in an attempt to recalibrate them! Oh and playing the spoons to accompany cousin Marcel's guitar playing. Then there was Leighton's Grail-like quest for the secret passage in the cellar that all the brothers had convinced him led underground all the way to Caerphilly Castle. Raymond smiled to himself as he remembered Leighton's excitement when he found a covered doorway in the cellar, and his astonishment when he finally surfaced again, no further than the middle of the lawn in the garden. Yes, wonderful times. Wonderfully youthful times.

With a little apprehension, Raymond ran a comb through his hair and shook his father's hand. Charlie smiled, saying that he would wait, hoping that his nearness would lend some support. The demeanour of the duty clerk at the front desk exuded a calm efficiency while conveying some of the seriousness of the undertaking. 'Good morning Sir, can I help you?' asked the clerk. 'Yes, I'd like to volunteer for the Royal Air Force,' replied Raymond, suddenly becoming conscious of the sound of his own voice. 'God, I'm nervous,' he thought, wondering if it showed. 'Not attempting to dodge a call-up for the army, are you, Sir?' questioned the clerk. He had a rather amused look in his eye, but Raymond was a little too nervous to notice at first. Drawing himself up a little, he replied rather seriously that no, he was here to volunteer for the RAF and if possible could he see the appropriate person in charge of recruitment. The clerk smiled and asked for some particulars. 'OK Mister Davies, please take a seat over there and there will be someone with you shortly,' said the clerk. 'Mister Davies,' Raymond thought to himself, 'all quite proper and polite, the RAF.'

A group of leather-covered armchairs stood in a regimented row against the back wall by the window, as if at attention. Raymond sat down, catching sight of the little speckles of dust floating in the sunlight that streamed through the tall window. He was not long sitting there when an officer appeared round a door. The clerk passed him the forms that he'd filled out on Raymond's arrival and the officer then took a few paces towards the parade line of chairs. 'Mr David Raymond Davies?' enquired the officer. 'Can you come this way, please?' With thoughts of his father's volunteering in 1916, Raymond followed the officer through the doorway into a large room with a number of curtained partitions. As they walked, the officer explained that it was here that he would have a number of medical examinations and told him to report to the duty clerk when complete. The first doctor waited at the first cubical, his hand holding open the curtain. With a nervous smile Raymond entered and began to listen as the doctor talked him through the procedures and tests.

After what seemed like an age, Raymond stood buttoning the collar of his shirt, thinking of how thorough the examinations had been. They had certainly put him through his paces. He'd never really seen any doctors before, not anything serious at least. Now he felt like he had seen enough to last him a lifetime! As he slipped his braces over his shoulders, a nurse brought his jacket and led him to the door and out. Reporting to the clerk, once again he found himself waiting, now with a few other young men who shifted agitatedly on those leather seats. He glanced at the large wooden-cased clock that hung on the opposite wall, wondering how long he had been in with the doctors. It must have been a couple of hours. One by one the other prospective recruits were called into the examination room and Raymond was just watching another getting up from a chair when the officer turned and said 'Oh Mister Davies, can you follow me, please?'

It was a short conversation and as Raymond recounted the day's experience to his father he felt a little unsure of where things now left him. 'A1,' repeated Charlie as they made their way back to the bus station. Yes, it was true. The seven doctors, after all their prodding, their hammering, and the lists of instructions that they seemed to trot out at a rate of knots, they had passed him fit for active service. Yet the officer had said that they would be in touch shortly, and as those words had hung in the air, Raymond had started to feel a little uncertain of what would be the next step. 'I suppose I must be in the Royal Air Force,' he thought, but really didn't feel any different.

The Waiting Game:
It took a few weeks for a letter to arrive. It was characteristically laconic. There was a little about the results of the medical and then a little more about instructions to report to Padgate for interview and some further tests. He found Padgate with some difficulty on one of Eric's old maps. It was up near Warrington, Cheshire. 'England,' said Raymond to himself, 'now this really was something different.' He had not ventured out of Wales before. Cycling up in the Brecon Beacons had been possibly the nearest he'd got – being able to see England in the distance. There was English blood in the family, through the Denham line. In fact through the Denhams the family was linked to the great film studios in London. Smiling to himself, Raymond thought of an Englishman he'd once encountered. While walking back towards Nelson one day, a car had pulled up a little way in front, the

driver beckoning to him. Winding down the window, the driver asked in a rather clipped English accent, 'Excuse me, I'm afraid I'm a bit lost. Could you direct me to … err …' – his voice became very deliberate, slow and searching – 'Whystrad Mineknatch?' Raymond, usually quite helpful in these situations, stood puzzled and pushed his cap back on his head, trying to decipher the man's words. 'Whystrad Mineknatch,' came the voice again, this time with an upwards and questioning intonation. Raymond puzzled further, having no clue whatsoever as to the place to which the man was attempting to refer. 'I'm sorry, there's no village by that name around yer,' said Raymond, now conscious of his own Valley's tones. 'Here, it's here,' replied the driver, now pointing with a gloved finger to a location on his map. Raymond began to smile as he focused on the place where the man's finger rested. He couldn't help himself and before he knew it he was laughing. 'Whystrad Mineknatch, you say?' he giggled. He corrected the man's pronunciation of Ystrad Mynach and began to direct him. Flustered and somewhat embarrassed the man drove off in a hurry, leaving Raymond laughing uncontrollably at the side of the road. There would be many Englishmen at Padgate.

While the thought of Padgate perhaps signified to Raymond the real beginnings of his RAF career – that is since the volunteering at Cardiff had become rather insignificant – the reality was something different again. Once more came the nervousness and the barrage of tests, this time coupled with the thrill of being actually on an RAF station. Padgate was one of the largest stations in the North West, with its own railway station and its well-proportioned architecture. Everything seemed so purposeful, as Raymond was escorted around with other new recruits. The tests were harder and more academic this time. More like school, he thought. Moreover, they were mainly like the bits of school he was not that good at, and he could hear the words of his schoolmaster's reports, 'Raymond must try harder,' as he attempted to work his way through the arithmetical exercises. Now History would have suited him. Why couldn't they have asked him some History? He had always taken an interest in that, being able to recite the important dates: 1066, Battle of Hastings; 1805, Battle of Trafalgar; 1815, Battle of Waterloo. Sometimes it seemed like we had always been at war with someone, somewhere.

The tests didn't go very well but Raymond still found himself being accepted. He stood to attention amongst the other recruits, all gathered in a large room. The officer at the front asked them all to raise their right hand while they swore allegiance to the Crown, to his Majesty King George VI. Yet, while his heart raced a little as a sense of pride came over him, the welcoming speech by the officer in charge was once again a little confusing. He said all the usual salutary and rousing things about King and Country, about the challenges ahead, but they – the Royal Air Force, Raymond presumed – didn't have any uniforms or rifles and so they were sending this excited group of young men back home! Raymond was rather shocked. At such a serious moment in a nation's existence, we didn't have any rifles and we could afford to go home and wait! There was nothing for it but to obey orders and return to Nelson, wearing an RAF Volunteer Reserve armband to denote that he *was* now doing his bit, but that His Majesty's Royal Air Force was not ready for him yet. It was like being first at a dinner and dance – the music had started, he was eager and prepared but they were still setting out the tables and chairs!

Goodbyes and Reunions:
As the months dragged on, it was as if the RAF had forsaken him. Raymond watched as autumn painted its sienna hues amongst the trees, reaching high into the valleys. Then the frosts came to harden the ground and to make a skating rink of the quarry lake. The Battle of Britain, as Churchill had so eloquently labelled it, had passed and the threat of German jackboots walking through Whitehall now seemed a rather hollow one. The aerial war, as far as Raymond saw it, had become clandestine and underhand. Infrequent now were the deadly ballets of opposing air forces acted out high in the blue arena of daylight. Darkness was the enemy's shield, his cloak of malevolent intrigue. And from this cloak came a dagger of seemingly indiscriminate bombing – the Blitz. No longer did the Luftwaffe seem bent on destroying Britain's war machinery. More so were the nightly bombings of the Capital and major cities. It had become as much a civilians' war as one for those now in uniform. Then, just when the immediate pressure on the RAF seemed to have eased, there was a letter on the doormat of the Wern. Jinny picked it up and placed it on the mantelpiece for Raymond to see when he came in from work. Somewhere within her she knew that he would not be long at home.

For Raymond, though the emotions associated with leaving home coursed deep within, they were tempered by an indecipherable excitement. Perhaps it was that sense of urgency that seemed to pervade everyone's day-to-day existence – that purposefulness that added the definition to the blur of activity, to the quickened pace. Raymond saw it in the ways in which people took time to ask about an absent loved one, a friend or relation. It was in the way the wireless was no longer sometimes only 'something on in the background'. And it was in the regularity with which his father wrote to Eric and Howard, the two of them now living in Wolverhampton.

'How far is Wolverhampton from here?' asked Raymond, now standing in the guardroom of his new home, RAF Bridgenorth. The duty sergeant looked up from the paperwork generated by the new intake and replied, 'Oh not far, 'bout fifteen miles, why d'you ask?' 'I have two brothers living there,' said Raymond, thinking that he must have sounded homesick already. 'When did you last see them?' continued the sergeant. 'Oh some time now, must be about three years,' replied Raymond, counting through the intervening years in his head as he spoke. 'Mmm,' muttered the sergeant, 'can't be having that.' He got up from his chair and disappeared into an adjoining room, returning after a few minutes, smiling. 'Listen, you're not due to report in until Monday morning and I've cleared it with the officer in charge. There's a wagon going into Wolverhampton later this afternoon, so here's a pass. Get yourself off, I'll see that your stuff is OK.' Not only was the RAF polite, Raymond thought, it was nice enough to organise reunions with relatives! He didn't need to be told twice, and was quickly rearranging some things in a bag ready for the journey.

Arriving in Wolverhampton later that afternoon, Raymond caught a tram out to Wednesfield, the small village where Eric, Howard and their families were living. Not too sure of his bearings he got the attention of a young girl and asked whether she knew of a Hyde Road, telling her of his surprise visit to his brothers. To his amazement, the girl, Beatrice Hollinshead, knew them well, being a neighbour. She offered to take him round and as they walked they began to talk freely about how Raymond had come to visit and how she knew of his relations. Both being somewhat adept at the art of conversation, the time went quickly and soon he was standing at the doorway, waving to Bet (as she liked to be called) as she went on her way. His knock on the door prompted the sound of footsteps in the hallway. The latch opened and there stood Rhoda, Eric's wife. She stood there silent for what seemed like an age. 'Good God, it's our Raymond,' she exclaimed, embracing him with a force that took his breath away! Rhoda then grabbed him by the hand and, before he could gather his thoughts, there he was standing in the front room with an equally astonished Eric and Howard shaking his hands, smiling and laughing. 'What you doin' here then, Boyo,' asked Eric, excitedly? 'Joined the RAF, been posted to Bridgnorth,' said Raymond, starting to explain.

In the hustle and bustle of the reunion they managed, without too much persuasion, to walk the odd half mile to a quite spacious public house, out beyond the red-bricked utility houses in more homely countryside surroundings. The Albion Inn stood as quite an impressive building on the Lichfield road, at its junction with Stubby Lane. Here, in amongst the cigarette smoke and the horse brasses, the three brothers reacquainted themselves with one another. For that brief night, they were together again and the war and the RAF were but a faint and fading impression on their consciousness. They drank and talked well into the night, beyond last orders, beyond the closing of the blackout curtain across Eric's front door and the first call from upstairs of 'come on, let our Ray get some sleep!' And as he drifted off to sleep Raymond thought how he would hold on to this night in times to come.

Slow Marches & Square-bashing:

There were wooden barrack rooms at Bridgenorth. The winter sun barely pierced through the regimented lines of windows and picked out the narrow iron beds and diminutive lockers that stood at equally regular intervals along the length of the room. In the centre stood a stout stove, the only form of heating in the whole place. It was difficult to comprehend that these austere surroundings would be home for the next six weeks. Was this the reality of service life, thought Raymond as he stood in the doorway? Yet, living with such frugality was not a stranger. No unfamiliarity could be found in the necessities of making do, of tightening one's belt. For most families that had lived through the uncertainties of 1930s Britain there was nothing new in austerity. At least, Raymond thought, he'd have his own bed, thinking back to the times when he and his brothers had slept six to one! There were further benefits also in having three meals a day. Yet, still he would miss the times when his mother would borrow large cake tins from the village baker and make hefty loaf-sized cakes.

Raymond took to the regime of service life in other ways. While there was the usual intensity of physical activity and tests of endurance, the necessary formalities of drill instruction were something that he enjoyed. He had, quite advantageously, been somewhat rehearsed by his cousin Marcel, who had been recently discharged from the Royal Corps of Signals with severe dermatitis. Marcel, though clearly disappointed by his early exit from the serviceman's war, had done his bit by teaching Raymond all of the finer points of the different salutes, of rifle drill (using a broom handle) and of different marches. One day on the parade ground he was brought out of the line by the squad sergeant. 'Davies,' came the shout, 'get out front, here!' Coming smartly to attention, he snapped out a compliant 'yes sergeant' and took a few paces forward. 'Now everyone,' continued the sergeant, 'Davies will now demonstrate how to *properly* execute the slow march … not like your shameful efforts, you lot of half-witted ballerinas!' It was a bit like being the centre of attention at the Treharris rink again. With the precision that Marcel had taught him, he pulled off a perfect example for the whole length of the line, then a smart right turn to face the squad, before a crisp halt to attention. There were a couple of grins from his assembled comrades, mainly from a chap with slick black hair named Campbell, standing in the front row.

Norman Campbell was from Darwen, Lancashire. He stood a little taller than Raymond and wore his jet-black hair slicked back with a mixture of Brylcream and paraffin – the latter of which made it shine. He and Raymond were fast becoming friends, both withstanding the rigors of their initial training with a sense of mischief. Already, they had both made the assessment that there was a lot of 'bull' – as the RAF called it – a lot of red tape; a lot of things that had to be learned and endured to keep out of trouble. Yet there were also ways round things, and they had begun to separate the 'duff' from the 'pukka gen' (a slang for incorrect and reliable information respectively). They tried to steer clear of those that seemed to generate or pass on the 'duff gen', and those that were susceptible to 'bull' were often the butt of their jokes and wind-ups. There were others from his squad with whom Raymond would talk, but it was 'Cammie' that he felt he could trust. Sometimes in the barrack block they would sit chatting about their homes and families, and Campbell would rib Raymond about how he had managed within the few short weeks they had been at Bridgenorth to get a letter off back to Nelson. But for Raymond, letters seemed one of few, now tenuous connections with home. It was as if that duty sergeant had known how precious and important that last visit to Eric and Howard would be.

As Raymond stood on the parade ground on that final day at Bridgenorth, he did so nervously and somewhat excitedly. Twenty years of age, the enormity of the task that was to be set before him seemed daunting to say the least. Yet, as he looked around at rank upon rank of RAF blue there was a real sense of being in it together; that the purpose that now organised their daily lives stretched far beyond that of the individual. He now answered to the name of 'Davies' rather than Raymond. In return he would call himself '692 Davies', and had written this – the last three digits of his service number – on his kit. So on that cold February afternoon in 1941, Davies felt proud to be a member of His Majesty's Royal Air Force, and was certain that now his part in the war was really beginning.

Chapter Two

To War and the Bump

Arrival and the Biggin Hill Wing, February 1941:
The train pulled into Paddington Station in the early evening of 18 February. The necessary blackout seemed to blot out all London, even at this ground level. It was sad to see the Capital in this way. Cold and damp with snow in the air, the winter conditions made the welcome even drearier. Yet as Davies gathered his things together any feelings of being a long way from home were tempered by his excitement. It had been with him ever since Bridgnorth when he had been told of his posting to 11 Group Fighter Command.

> *There were six of us who were detailed to go to Biggin Hill, Kent and the sergeant told us what a famous station Biggin Hill was in as much that it was the leading station in 11 Group, Fighter Command … And stationed there then were two or three of the squadrons that had fought in the Battle of Britain. We six were extremely privileged and excited to be posted there.* (LAC Raymond Davies, interview)

While clearly excited about their posting, these six new recruits were fully aware of the consequences of being at Britain's premier fighter station:

> *I shall never forget it. We were sorting out the postings and a corporal named us six and said 'you blokes are going into action, you six are going to Biggin Hill … from now on you'll be at war.'* (LAC Raymond Davies, interview)

Apart from the weather, the Luftwaffe had also pulled out all the stops for Davies' welcoming committee. On arrival, London was under attack.

> *We got into London and, of course, bombing was taking place and none of the Underground was in action because the population – those who could – went down to the Underground railways for shelter. We had transport to pick us up to take us from Paddington to Victoria Station … got across to Victoria and then down to Bromley which was the nearest town to Biggin Hill. There was a vehicle waiting there for us … There was bombing going on but, of course, the drivers had to face*

this … they had to get us to Biggin Hill as soon as possible because they needed every personnel that they could … We left Victoria and arrived at Bromley and there was a vehicle to take us out to Biggin. (LAC Raymond Davies, interview)

On arrival at the main guardroom, the six were shown to their billets in the permanent brick accommodation at Biggin's north camp. By comparison with other accommodation that Davies was to encounter later in the war, Biggin's airmen's quarters were luxurious. In amongst tree-lined tarmacadamed roads nestled these spacious, solid buildings, characteristic of the 1920s and 1930s RAF stations.

The billets were lovely, the ones we were in. We had good showers and baths. And we did have a hose-pipe for anyone that wouldn't bloody bath! … We didn't mess about. There was one bloke, we had to hose him down 'cos he stank. The billets were so many beds one side, and so many the other … a proper barracks. I was right on the end, by the door. (LAC Raymond Davies, interview)

At intervals sat the squat reminders of war – the earthen banks of the air-raid shelters. Other reminders were more immediate:

The first night Biggin was bombed and there were eleven bombs dropped on the airfield. When we arrived, we were sitting around the stove there, and there was an airman who had been in [the RAF] since before the war started. Of course he was telling us all sorts of things – things that everyone knew was shooting a line. I shall never forget because the Germans came over and started to bomb and this chap jumped up quick and he says 'ay up, let somebody run who can run!' but we were dead tired after the travelling and so stayed put. We slept through the whole thing. (LAC Raymond Davies, interview)

The light of day allowed Davies and his comrades to take in the realities of being on a front-line RAF station. Biggin was a shambles. The raid of the previous night had put some craters around the airfield, causing some damage. While none of the accommodation blocks had being hit, an air-raid shelter on north camp received a direct hit and all occupants were killed. Yet for Biggin, this raid was the latest in a long history of being 'at the sharp end'. Throughout the summer of 1940, and into the autumn, the station had witnessed the might of the Luftwaffe on many occasions. The worst raid had been on 30 August 1940 when sixteen 1000lb bombs had been dropped, killing 39 personnel and wounding a further 36. By October 1940 practically no building on the camp remained unscathed. Barrack blocks, workshops, MT buildings, station headquarters, the operations block and all hangars were severely damaged if not totally destroyed. Operations had been moved off-site into a shop in Biggin Hill village and, later, to a requisitioned country house at Keston Mark, some two miles from the airfield. In fact the then station commander, Group Captain Grice, had taken the unprecedented decision to demolish the only remaining hangar at Biggin on 4 September, with the idea that the Luftwaffe would have nothing visible to bomb and thus might leave the station alone. While raids after November 1940 were sporadic, the damage to Biggin remained into the New Year. A new pilot posted to Biggin in the April after Davies' arrival was Neville Duke. While the damage was self-evident, for him so was the *esprit de corps.*

Poor old Biggin is in a pitiful state – not a hangar standing, nearly all windows smashed, walls spattered and oceans of mud. But under all the stinking mire of war is the old Biggin I knew on Empire Air Days. (Pilot Officer Neville Duke, quoted in Franks, 1995, p. 6)

What also amazed Davies was the way in which life went on, and how Biggin returned to operational status so quickly after such raids cratered the dispersals and landing fields. It was a tribute to the organisation of the RAF war machine, and the ability of the personnel to just '*get on with it*'.

I always did admire the way the RAF was run … the planning was so detailed, they'd thought of everything. [After a raid] we wanted to get in and help with the clear up but they didn't want us. We weren't geared up … the personnel that they had were experienced in clearing the 'drome up and within a matter of hours you didn't know that a bomb had dropped. That's how efficient the machine was, and it didn't interfere with aircraft getting off. If you tried to interfere, you'd get told to 'hop it' and you soon learned not to get involved and get on with your own job. (LAC Raymond Davies, interview)

In the morning of 19 February, Davies and his five comrades reported to 3034 Servicing Echelon (SE) as armourers' assistants. 3034 were the resident servicing echelon at Biggin Hill during 1941–42, their work involving the assistance of squadron personnel with the maintenance and equipping of the resident aircraft. At the time of Davies' arrival three squadrons were at Biggin: 74 'Tiger' Squadron, 609 'West Riding' Squadron, and 92 'East India' Squadron, the latter having just returned from Biggin's satellite airfield at Gravesend. On the first day, however, the weather conspired to keep everyone grounded. As the station operational records book (ORB) reported.

Surface wind – w/sw. 10/15 mph. Weather – Cloudy with fog, rain and snow until 1000, then cloudy with snow showers. Cloud: 8/10ths to 10/10ths at 200/600ft until midday. Lifting and breaking 1000/2000ft. Visibility 1000–4000 yds.
(Biggin Hill, Operational Record Book, 19 February 1941)

Having reported to 3034 SE's headquarters, Davies was assigned to 92 Squadron. Their reputation throughout Fighter Command – if not the whole RAF – was one of fighting hard and playing hard. Their motto '*aut pugna aut morere*' (either fight or die) seemed to apply to both their operational flying and their 'sorties' into London or to the White Hart at Brasted. Once they had been known as the RAF's playboy squadron, sporting colourful silk scarves and long hair, and having a liking for fast cars that they ran on 100 octane in light of petrol rationing. Squadron Leader J.A. 'Johnnie' Kent AFC DFC had attempted to bring the squadron into line when appointed as their CO. His assessment of them (after scrutinising them for the first month of his command without saying a word) was uncompromising:

I have been CO of this squadron exactly a month and have several comments to pass on to you all. My NCOs are slack and slipshod. They have allowed the men to get lazy and out of hand. The Station Warrant Officer has complained to me that they are blatantly arrogant and so conceited that they refuse to take orders from anyone but their own officers…. I have studied my officers' behaviour with concern and frankly I think it stinks.

You are the most conceited and insubordinate lot I have ever had the misfortune to come up against. Admittedly you have worked hard and got a damn good score in the air – in fact a better score than any other squadron in Fighter Command – but your casualties have been appalling. These losses I attribute to the fact that your discipline is slack; you never by any chance get some sleep; you drink like fishes, and you've got a damn sight too good opinion of yourselves …

It appears that you have turned the living quarters which were allotted to you to provide a certain amount of security and rest into a night club. It also appears that you ask your various lady friends down to spend weekends with you whenever you please … Your clothes – I can scarcely call them uniform. I will not tolerate check shirts, old school ties, or suede shoes. While you are on duty you will wear regulation dress. Neither will I tolerate pink pyjamas under your tunics.

(Squadron Leader Johnnie Kent, CO 92 Squadron, in Wallace, 1957, p. 207–8)

While such a dressing down had almost caused a mutiny amongst 92's officers, Kent's prowess in the air won them over (shooting down the squadron's 100th enemy aircraft). Likewise, the squadron too made its mark on him, and he began to take on some of 92's spirit. As Flight Lieutenant Brian Kingcome – the squadron's 'A' flight commander – surmised:

Truth to tell, Kent's remarks about 92's lack of discipline were both misinformed and unjust. The squadron's discipline in the air was immaculate. It had proved itself to be the most efficient killing machine in the Battle of Britain; as the air attack unit longest in the firing line, its record of success was unmatched.

On the ground an outsider might have thought there was a lax air to be detected amid the general discipline, but the laid-back attitude was superficial, a front: the usual small irregularities and assertions of individualism – silk neck-scarves and longish hair. But 92 Squadron had stronger bonds of loyalty and solidarity, a fiercer pride in itself than existed in any other unit I came across before or after. Outsiders, as they sensed this, may well have felt excluded, but the only way for a new CO or flight commander to penetrate the protective wall of pride was to show he had qualities the squadron could respect. Leadership by example was the best method of winning such regard, rather than nit-picking with a copy of King's Regulations laid open at the elbow ...

It was not Johnny who changed the squadron but the squadron that changed Johnny. Almost without being aware of it he absorbed 92's unique spirit and, in a few short weeks, matured from being a chippy colonial into a relaxed, respected commanding officer. In our eyes he had certainly needed to do a little maturing, and, to be fair, he caught on quickly. (Flight Lieutenant Brian Kingcome, in Kingcome, 1999, p109–10)

A similar feeling of unease was at hand when Kent was succeeded by an officer from Training Command in April 1941, Squadron Leader James Rankin. Throughout 1941 Rankin, like Kent before him, would prove himself to be a worthy commander of 92.

The other two squadrons that made up the Biggin Hill Wing had also been in the thick of the fighting. The last time these three squadrons had met had been above the skies of Dunkirk in May 1940 when they had covered the evacuation of the British Expeditionary Force. Since then they had endured the raging battle above the south coast of England throughout the intervening eight months.

609 Squadron was an auxiliary squadron formed at Yeadon, Yorkshire in February 1936. During the Battle of Britain it had been one of 10 Group's leading squadrons and had been resident at Middle Wallop and Warmwell. As Davies had felt, 609 too were honoured to now be posted to Biggin Hill. With the departure of Squadron Leader 'George' Darley DSO in September 1940, the squadron was

now under the command of Michael Lister Robinson. If there was one person to make 609 shine as bright as the other two Fighter Command stalwarts, it was Mike Robinson.

Their prowess was unquestionable. During the Battle of Britain they had been credited as one of the top-scoring squadrons, with eighty-seven enemy aircraft claimed destroyed. In October they had become the first Spitfire squadron of Fighter Command to achieve one hundred victories when Frankie Howell, Sidney Hill and Flight Lieutenant Fieldsend had shared the destruction of a Ju88. On moving to Biggin Hill, their respect for their fellow squadrons was evident, Mike Robinson issuing the following words of advice:

> *It's not the sort of place any of us would be advised to start shooting lines in …*
> *when you get there, wait to speak until you are spoken to.* (Squadron Leader
> Mike Robinson, quoted in Ziegler, 1971, p171)

Alongside 92 Squadron, the 'Tigers' – 74 Squadron – were no less formidable. Up until the beginning of February they had been led by the legendary 'Sailor' Malan. Malan had joined them during peacetime, in November 1936, and had risen through the ranks to become CO in August 1940. Now in February '41 his personal score stood at twenty-nine, and he had collected both DSO and bar, and DFC and bar. A keen eye and an expert shot, 'Sailor' was a natural fighter pilot. His coolness in the heat of battle, and his firm but fair manner made him a born leader and tactician. During a short period of rest in the autumn of 1940 he had written his '*Ten rules of air fighting*' that were now distributed amongst Fighter Command and had become somewhat of a fighter pilot's bible. One of his comrades in 74 was Roger Boulding.

> *I flew as his number two on some of the sweeps across the Channel and found that*
> *there was no going back with him until we had done all that could be done – not*
> *that he took foolish risks but he was always full of determination – his aim was to*
> *get so close behind his target that he couldn't miss. We in 74 Squadron knew him*
> *to be a tough and determined and generally hard man to fly with. His demeanour*
> *was quiet and very cool. He seemed to have himself very much under control and I*
> *don't remember him ever getting excited on the ground … We all, I think, held him*
> *in very great esteem and had great confidence in his leadership, even if we were not*
> *always too keen on his methods of stirring up trouble.* (Roger Boulding, quoted
> in Franks, 1994, p95)

Now in late February 1941, Malan had been made leader of the Biggin Hill Wing, becoming the second of these new appointments in Fighter Command. Douglas Bader had been given the first to form at Tangmere in 10 Group. The command of the 'Tigers' passed to the 22-year-old John Mungo-Park who had been with the squadron since Dunkirk. On Davies' arrival, 74 Squadron were operating from Manston as an advanced base, and later from Biggin's satellite station at Gravesend.

Chapter Three

Spitties, Cannons and Learning a Trade

The Spitfire Vb & the 20mm Cannon:
It was with the first of these squadrons – 92 East India – that Davies began his operational career. For men of his trade, armourers and assistant armourers, it was to be an important time. To date, the standard armament for British fighter aircraft had been the Colt Browning .303 calibre machine gun. Both the Hurricane, and the Mark I and II Spitfires, had been fitted with eight of these guns. Capable of delivering 1,100 rounds per minute, these weapons could be very effective, especially at close range. However, the fitting of heavier armament had been sought, arguing that an aircraft so equipped would be able to deliver an equal, if not greater weight of shot in the short time that a target might be in its sights. At the same time a heavier weapon might be able to deliver the knockout blow at a greater range. To this effect a larger 20mm calibre weapon had been fitted to some Spitfires in 1940 but with little success.

The 20mm Hispano cannon originated from a Swiss design of an engine-mounted gun built by Oerlikon. In 1932 the Hispano-Suiza Automobile Company, who had developed a 37mm that saw service in the First World War, purchased some of the Oerlikon 20mm cannons for use with their HS.12x aero-engine. Problems with this combination led them to design a more suitable weapon that became known as the Hispano-Suiza '*Moteur Cannon*'. The success of this gun attracted much attention and in 1935 the British Air Ministry Gun Section advised its adoption in light of there being no British design available. After a demonstration visit to the Hispano works in Paris, an order had been placed for a batch of six guns for evaluation. Successful tests ensued and after considerable negotiation the Hispano-Suiza Company agreed to form a subsidiary manufacturing base in Britain.

Manufacture was one thing. Getting it up to operational status with the RAF's aircraft proved fraught with difficulty. The Spitfire's thin wing, accommodating the larger dimensions of the Hispano 20mm was problematic in itself. Even with the compact size of the .303 Brownings, Davies remembered having to wriggle them into place and many a pinched finger and grazed knuckle bore witness to the limited room available in the gun bays. To fit the 20mm into the Spitfire required the gun to be mounted on its side, with the bulky drum magazine feeding from above. These drums, holding only sixty rounds, imposed further limitations on the airframe as they required large blisters both above and below the mainplane. This increased drag and thus impeded performance.

The aircraft had to be modified with blisters around the magazine and, of course, the two blisters held up the aircraft in manoeuvring and everything. The magazine had to fit into the side of the gun, and it [the magazine] had to be mounted at one side in order to feed in. Then there was the added weight. The guns weighed just over 100lbs, so that was 200lbs (one each side) plus the ammunition. (LAC Raymond Davies, interview)

While 19 Squadron had taken part in some operational trials with the two-cannon configuration in their Spitfire Ibs in 1940 (the suffix b denoting an armament of two cannon and four .303 Brownings), the guns had proved unreliable and were effectively withdrawn from service. Those Spitfire Ibs operated by 19 Squadron had eventually found their way to 92 Squadron and they had soldiered on with these during the hard winter months of 1940 and 1941 with similar frustrations. Until February 1941 the standard eight .303 armament had continued as the standard armament to be fitted to the Spitfire Is and IIs that were now the main models operated in 11 Group.

However, towards the end of that month 92 Squadron became the first squadron to receive the new Spitfire V, with its up-rated Merlin 45 engine. With the need to combat the ever-increasing effectiveness of enemy armour, the squadron also saw the return of the 20mm armament. Records state that 92 Squadron became the first to become operational with the Spitfire Vbs in February, but throughout these early months of 1941, the term 'operational' masked continuing problems with the Hispano 20mm armament. Similarly, no true Mark V Spitfires had left the production line at this time, and the squadron was reliant on the modification of their existing Mark Ibs with the fitting of the up-rated Merlin 45 engine. This retrospective modification of existing airframes began in February, with small batches of 92's aircraft being flown from Biggin Hill to Rolls-Royce's factory airfield at Hucknall. Until this work was completed in April, the squadron flew Ibs and their refitted 'Vs', alongside each other.

On 7 April, Flight Lieutenant Wright and the new CO, Squadron Leader Rankin, returned Spitfires R6923, R7195, R6770 and R6908 to Biggin, completing the conversion programme. The better performance at height and the increased rate of climb that the new Merlin gave were welcomed by one and all. In terms of the aircraft's armament, the greatest problems in early 1941 were in the reliability of the ammunition feed mechanisms and the setting of the guns' recoil.

So significant was the need to find operational solutions that it was decided to assemble a specialist armament team to work exclusively with the cannons. To this team, Davies, his five comrades and a couple of armourers from 609 Squadron were assigned. The NCO placed in charge was 92 Squadron's Flight Sergeant Ronald Stewart. Ronald Stewart, known as 'Jimmy' throughout his service career, had been with the squadron since the beginning of hostilities. Owing to his work in getting 92 Squadron operational with the 20mm cannons, Stewart later became Chief Armaments Officer for 11 Group. Progress came from a mixture of dogged determination, trial, error, and ingenuity.

> *By Christ did we spend a lot of time on the butts! We used to have it [the aircraft] up on trestles, because the Spitfire flew two degrees nose down. So we used to put it up on the trestles and get the spirit level two degrees flying down. Then we used to have a big … heavy ball – it was specially made … one each side. We used to shove the rope over [the tailplane] and hang these, and then two of us blokes each side would hang on to the tail when we were on the butts. And with all that bloody weight – and especially when they got going – oh the vibration, the way it shook!! We had to hang on or it would have gone up in the air!!! (LAC Raymond Davies, interview)*

Getting the 20mm to fire smoothly without rounds causing jams, or stoppages as they were known, proved a major hurdle. While such testing was controlled by strict RAF discipline, members of the team began to gain expertise and respect for each other's competence.

> *We would be assisting the sergeant … even a corporal wasn't allowed to fire on the butts – only a sergeant. But Corporal Jones he was an expert and Sergeant Rains [of 609 Squadron] would say to him to get up in the cockpit, 'cos he'd want to check the vibration while firing…. And this was where we had to be careful in the experimental stage of not increasing the speed, the rate of fire – it could rip the wings off the aircraft. (LAC Raymond Davies, interview)*

Work as part of Stewart's team took place in addition to that required for operations and so Davies and his colleagues found themselves working round the clock. Often they were test firing through the night, much to the concern of the Squadron's CO.

> *I've seen us on the butts and CO would send a message out for us to pack it in, in the night 'cos we were keeping everyone up! It would be one single shot, and it would*

… BUMM … that was a stop. Then we'd get two out of it and it would bloody stop. Then three or four and it would stop again … and, of course they made hell of a noise. And the CO would send a message out to the site to pack it in … it'd be two o'clock in the bloody morning! After a hard days flying nobody could get any sleep. (LAC Raymond Davies, interview)

However disturbed was their pilots' sleep by these nocturnal trials, men such as Rankin, Robinson and Mungo-Park were aware of the necessity of these interruptions. It was only through these long hours of problem solving, theory and testing that progress was slowly made. Out of operational necessity, in these early months of 1941, some of this was made through compromise.

The problem of stoppages could be a combination of ammunition feed, the difficulties in getting the required amount of recoil off the gun, or sometimes the ammunition itself. The feed was a problem because we had to mount the gun on its side in the Spitfire, because of space in the wing … and the movement of the wings during combat might affect alignment and so cause stoppages. Sometimes ammunition would be badly positioned in the links, or an individual round might be faulty. So then we'd get a collapsed shoulder on the cartridge and the gun would not eject it properly. It would get stuck in the breech. But the biggest problem we had in those early months was that we couldn't get enough recoil from the gun in order to clear the chamber quick enough for the next round. I don't think we ever had the guns operating at their optimum of 600 rounds per minute at this stage. The only way we could get some reliability was by slowing it down. (LAC Raymond Davies, interview)

Throughout the spring, Stewart's team continued to make progress with the reliability of the 20mm armament. However, the problem of getting the correct recoil remained the main obstacle to trouble-free operation into the first days of summer. Firstly, it had been found that an accurate measurement of the recoil distance could be achieved by placing a piece of Plasticine on the end of the recoil piston. As this piston travelled backwards after firing, it made contact with the feed unit. The depth of the resultant indentation in the Plasticine corresponded to the amount of recoil distance achieved. Setting this distance required patience.

On the butts, it would be me and my mate Campbell on the tail, helping to keep it on the trestle. We'd fire one off and then Sergeant Rains would shout 'Another quarter turn off the recoil reducer, Davies'. So I'd go round to the front of the cannon, and I'd stand to the side of the barrel – just in case! – and make the adjustment with a special spanner we had for the job. Then we'd fire again and so on until we got the recoil working correctly and at a satisfactory rate of fire. (LAC Raymond Davies, interview)

Sergeant Ronald Rains was a pre-war auxiliary armourer with 609 Squadron. Known as 'Claude' after his famous namesake Hollywood actor, Rains was well liked by all.

Claude was a bloody good sergeant, and was always fair with us when he had to deal out some punishment for something we'd done. As far as I can remember, I don't think he ever put anyone on a charge. We used to joke that this was because he didn't know how to fill out the charge sheets! But he had his own ways of dealing with things and he would always give us something that would teach us a lesson, without taking us away from our duties. (LAC Raymond Davies, interview)

Work on the 20mm thus continued at a frustratingly slow rate. Now with the summer months ahead of them, and the likelihood of increased operations, the need to gain some measure of reliability from the Spitfire's primary armament was paramount. Working round the clock to achieve this serviceability required a dedicated team. Both Chiefy Stewart and Sergeant Rains welcomed the commitment and determination of their team, but were wholly realistic about what little progress was being made.

Duty Crew:
It was always a case of working 'dawn till dusk', and when not on operational readiness, the time was spent either in the firing butts or in the armament workshops carrying out various servicing checks at regular operational intervals. When on operations, the ground crews took turns to be on 'duty crew'. If the squadron was required at dawn, the ground crews would have to be at dispersal for first light.

We were dawn till dusk. You were in A or B Flight – I was always on 'A' flight and we'd have to be down the squadron ... if the squadron was on readiness, so we had to be down the dispersal at dawn. The kites were on readiness so we had to be there as well. Then on top of that we'd have to do a duty crew every third night ... we all used to wake each other up. It was a funny thing because my dad used to reckon that when I went to sleep I died! But when I had to wake at dawn, I'd wake at bloody dawn. We'd have time off to have our meals ... B flight would stand in for us, and then we'd stand in for them when they went. Then when we went down [to dispersal] the chiefy always had a chart and he would allocate … 'Oh Davies, you work with so-and-so today'. Or sometimes you wouldn't be assigned to anybody so you'd have to do general maintenance, cleaning the guns and so on. (LAC Raymond Davies, interview)

Across from the busyness of the ground crews waited the aircrews, they too being assigned different levels of readiness. Some would be on 'immediate readiness', sitting in the cockpit, just waiting for the order to take off. In the heat of the sun during that high summer at Biggin '41, this would be the most uncomfortable state. Others would have to ready for take-off in five minutes, and would wait with Mae Wests donned, and parachutes on the tail or mainplane of their awaiting aircraft. A further group would be on half-hour readiness.

At Biggin the pilots' dispersal point was out front and our armoury was just behind, at the back of them … and at the back of that was the hut where we used to do the parachute packing. 1941 … it was a marvellous summer and the pilots used to sit outside … because we were virtually always on readiness … they'd be on readiness, then it [the order] would come 'immediate readiness' and then 'scramble'. As soon as immediate readiness came of course everyone was then geared up, waiting for the scramble. The pilots used to lounge outside and try to relax but as soon as the 'immediate' came through they'd come alive and be ready for scramble. (LAC Raymond Davies, interview)

The relationships between pilots and ground crew were, as Davies suggests, necessarily separate to a great extent. Many of the sergeant pilots with the squadrons, such as 92 Squadron's Don Kingaby and Johnnie Johnston, were known to socialise with the airmen.

It was Don Kingaby's aircraft, QJ-V, that I was assigned to when with 92 Squadron. His full-time fitter was a chap called Thomas – another Welshman. So Thomas and I got to know each other very well working on Kingaby's aircraft. He [Kingaby] was a sergeant pilot then, and was one of the top pilots of the wing … I think he had about twelve confirmed already, and many more unconfirmed that he was sure of … [most] with 92. He was a great pilot and would often shout to us when we'd got a wagon into Bromley or Croydon and would jump in the back with us. He loved the squadron, and was always great with us. He wouldn't take a commission because he knew it would mean a posting away from 92. So he ended up with three DFMs – the only pilot to have three – before they forced him to accept [commission] and his own squadron. (LAC Raymond Davies, interview)

Other pilots, however, maintained a distance borne of rank and social class. Such a relationship was somewhat important to the maintenance of discipline within the RAF and in taking away the personalising of pilot losses, and unit movements.

However the respect and admiration in which the ground crews held these pilots was clear. They were young men, many just out of university or grammar school, and however great the social divisions between themselves and the 'erks' that looked after them, they were comrades in arms. They had a common purpose, perhaps not about winning the war, but just getting on with it – maybe even getting through it.

When our pilots took off, without any hesitation, I used to salute those men away. Because ... God ... it's no exaggeration of the guts that those lads, those men had. They were only the same age as myself – twenty years of age, just left grammar school, some of them ... entering university ... and having to dedicate their lives to fight and die for their country. (LAC Raymond Davies, interview)

Chapter Four

Leading the Way

On the Offensive:
During the spring and summer of 1941, Biggin Hill was a hive of activity with the start of offensive fighter operations. With tacticians such as Malan in residence, these operations became an important part of taking the fight to the enemy, probing its defences, while learning much about how to conduct an offensive campaign without incurring significant losses of both personnel and aircraft. As the Luftwaffe had found during the previous summer, striking a balance between losses and being seen to be on the offensive was a most elusive equilibrium. There were essentially two major components that sought to hamper these types of operations for Fighter Command.

Firstly, there were the problems posed by the limited endurance of the single-seat fighter aircraft that equipped the Command. Much as the Luftwaffe had found in operating the Me109 over southern England in 1940, the limited range of such aircraft severely compromised their ability to penetrate far behind enemy lines. Although the use of overload external tanks had been tested as early as 1939, the initial fighter operations into northern France were made without auxiliary fuel loads.

The second problem was that posed by operating over hostile territory and the subsequent loss of pilots. During the Battle of Britain, pilot losses had been minimised by the fact that, if shot down, many pilots who managed to bale out from their stricken aircraft lived to tell the tale, and – most significantly – to rejoin the battle. Now fighting over occupied Europe, those in similar situations most likely faced the duration of war as a PoW. Thus, on the offensive the loss of an aircraft equated most often with pilot loss as well. The early operations from Biggin and other stations of the south-east made aircrew and ground crew fully aware of these altered fortunes.

Most significant in the general offensive tactics adopted by the RAF at the start of 1941 was the operation at Wing, rather than the single squadron or section strength that had characterised fighter organisation throughout the first two years of the war. A Wing normally comprised of three squadrons, although Squadron Leader Douglas Bader in 12 Group Fighter Command had been allowed to experiment with five, during the later stages of the Battle of Britain. The three squadrons of a Wing, while retaining their individual commanders, were put under the overall command of a Wing Commander Flying, or Wing Leader as they were more commonly known.

At Biggin Hill, this responsibility had been given to Sailor Malan, and while there was no question of his abilities, the coordination of thirty-six fighters did not prove trouble-free. Throughout the early months of 1941, various ways of organising the Wing during operations were experimented with including the use of 'finger-four' formations, and 'pairs', as well as the textbook line-astern. During February, through to April, these first operations provided commanders such as Malan, Bader and Johnny Peel (leader of the Kenley Wing) with opportunities to develop these new tactics and hone their organisational skills across a range of operation types. Generally known as 'sweeps', such operations fitted broadly into four categories, each with its own code-name:

Rodeo: A sweep over enemy territory involving only fighters. This could consist of a single Wing operation of three squadrons, or a combined force of a number of Wings. The main purpose of 'rodeos' was to attract enemy fighters.

Circus: A sweep involving a force of bombers or fighter-bombers, heavily escorted by fighters. Rarely were any specific targets specified, the objective being to draw enemy fighters into an engagement.

Ramrod: Similar operation to a 'circus', involving fighters escorting bombers/ fighter-bombers, but with a specific target in mind.

Rhubarb: A freelance fighter operation to seek out targets of opportunity. Usually 'rhubarbs' consisted of a pair of aircraft – leader and No.2; most often flown in bad weather, where conditions would give cover, and could be used as a means of evading interception.

Weather conditions throughout much of February, March and early April had limited the scale and number of offensive operations, and much of 92 Squadron's time had been taken up by flying patrols. Typical of these mundane and often uneventful operations and aircraft movements were those immediately after Davies' arrival. On the 20th, Brian Kingcome returned from Manston in Spitfire X4847, landing at 1015 hours. Shortly after 1215 hours Kingaby, 'Tich' Havercroft and the CO, Squadron Leader Kent, landed in X4425, X4616 and X4057 respectively.

On the 21st, Kent flew his last sortie with the squadron, leading eleven aircraft on a sweep at 1550 hours. Flying X4425, Kingaby returned with the majority of the squadron at 1630 hours, having encountered no enemy aircraft. There were two late returns, Flying Officer Tony Bartley and Pilot Officer Mottram, landing just after 1700 hours in X4484 and X4723. Similar patrols continued on the 22nd when, in the morning, 92 Squadron were detailed to patrol the Tenterden area. All eleven aircraft returned safely at 1230 hours, having been airborne for one hour and twenty-five minutes without event. In the afternoon, Flight Lieutenant Kingcome led twelve aircraft of the squadron on a sweep with 66 and 303 squadrons, again with nothing to report.

While the changeable weather conditions seemed to confound any chances to take the fight across the Channel, the Luftwaffe confined itself largely to night operations, resulting in the unenviable readiness of detachments of ground crew and pilots throughout the hours of darkness. By this time it had already been recognised that single-seat fighters were unsuitable for night interception duties, lacking no electronic means of detecting intruders and requiring a heavy workload from the pilot. Yet in early 1941, the RAF's night-fighter force was under-equipped and without the large array of electronic devices that was to revolutionise night-interception in later years. Consequently, in an attempt to make up numbers, Spitfires and Hurricanes continued to be deployed alongside the two-seater Blenheims, Beaufighters and Defiants.

The Germans were mainly sending bombers over at night, up to London, Coventry and the industrial areas in the Midlands, the North, and South Wales, and so we'd have a couple of fighters on evening readiness. Sometimes this would be at Biggin, or we'd be sent as crew down to Manston or Gravesend to support the night-fighters such as 'Cats Eyes' Cunningham … We'd see him walking round dispersal, on the peri-track, with these dark glasses on, so as to train his eyes for the darkness. (LAC Raymond Davies, interview)

On the 26th, the Wing was on readiness from 0700 hours – Davies and the rest of those on duty crew being up well in advance in order to prepare the aircraft for operations. Down at dispersal, there was still frost on the ground and the aircraft stood waiting for their attentive crews. In amongst them stood Chiefy Stewart, quietly confident in his men and their ability to get the job done. Leaving his barrack block on North Camp, Davies made his way down to dispersal, reporting in at six o'clock.

Always watchful of his new boys, Chiefy Stewart went over to the chalkboard, where he had posted the day's assignments. 'Lads, you're on '425 today,' he said, gesturing down the peri-track. He then turned to reprimand a few late arrivals, sending them to their tasks – Stewart being more conscious of each man's contribution to keeping the squadron at full strength, rather than losing any to the guardhouse. As they wandered along to their aircraft, Davies and his comrades noted the hustle and bustle of the squadron as it stood to.

In the cold, half-light of the morning, each busied themselves with their tasks. Airframe fitters checked hydraulic and pneumatic systems for the undercarriage and gun operation, inspected control surfaces for free and full movement, coolant matrices for obstacles, and made sure the canopy was free-running so to aid escape if necessary. Engine fitters – plumbers as they were colloquially known – topped up oil and glycol coolant levels, clambering up along the nose cowling to check the latter (one coolant tank being located at the front of the engine, just behind the propeller).

Some members of 'B' flight sauntered past, now relieved from their duty crew of the previous night. They exchanged some banter, calling out, 'Don't drop anything down the Vee,'[1] to some engine fitters, and, 'Nice hand-bag, dearie' to an instrument fitter, clutching his diminutive tool kit. Then they were gone – back to their billets, maybe for some breakfast. As Davies passed the lines of aircraft parked up in their blast-pens, one of the more experienced squadron armourers pointed out whose aircraft was which. Then, rounding the corner of one blast wall, he said, 'This is yours – '425 – Kingaby's flying this today.' A bit further along, in the next bay, was Brian Kingcome's aircraft QJ-F (X4847). He would be leading the squadron again today.

Davies walked to the rear of the enclosure, to the corner where the entrance into the shelter was. A face appeared – another armourer. 'C'mon, help us with one of these magazines,' he said, placing a friendly pat on Davies' shoulder. The 20mm magazine was heavy and its metal cold to the touch. Davies and the armourer managed to lift it onto the trailing edge of the port wing, just aft and outboard of the open gun bay. The armourer then climbed up onto the wing, sliding along the walkway portion of the leading edge and then leaning forward over the magazine bay. Davies handed him the magazine and watched while he lowered it onto the two supports, and draped the securing straps over the drum. 'Now just have a look at that adjustment,' said the armourer, handing Davies a screwdriver. He did so,

---

1. If you dropped anything into the middle of the engine (i.e. into the V-shaped void between the two cylinder banks) it could be really serious. In worst cases if a tool or a loose spark plug got trapped in the bottom of the V it would involve taking the engine out and removing one of the cylinder head blocks.

crouching under the mainplane and finding the adjusters through the two holes in the lower fairing. They were OK and he nodded to the armourer to fix the magazine in place with the fabric straps. Closing the quick-release fastener, he gestured for the upper fairing panel saying, 'OK that's this one done. Let's get on with the starboard.' Davies carried the second magazine to the opposite wing, noticing how the armourer had slid effortlessly over the fuselage, passing some comment to Thomas who was cleaning the cockpit glazing. They repeated the operation, and secured the wing panels. Last of all, they slid covers over the cannon barrels and stuck red fabric patches over the apertures for the .303s. Job done.

Another airman plugged the trolley accumulator (or trolley acc.) into the receptacle on the starboard side of the fuselage, waiting to start the engine. The duty crews had been keeping them warm during the night, running them periodically.

When an aircraft was on readiness, we used to run them up to temperature every half-hour. In that way we could keep the oil temp and pressures ready for immediate take-off, if there was a need for scramble. When on operations, we would run all the kites up before the pilots arrived. (LAC Raymond Davies, interview)

Everything was ready by 0700 and a couple of pilots who were posted for immediate readiness came down to the dispersal to sit with their aircraft. With the majority of the preparation now done, Chiefy Stewart let a few of the crews off for breakfast. A NAAFI wagon rolled up some distance along the peri-track and at intervals Chiefy Stewart would let the remaining crews grab 'char and wads', while others covered their work. Across to the southern end of the airfield, Davies could make out the ground crews of 609 Squadron, similarly going about their tasks. At 74's dispersal, the scene was much the same. Davies and his comrades shuffled along the queue at the NAAFI wagon, chatting about the impending operation. Cupping their mugs of tea for some warmth, they knew little of what 'ops' were detailed for today.

As information went, the ground crews were often last to know the specifics of air operations, apart from those technical details that they needed for preparing the aircraft. Unlike the later operations of 1941 and 1942, little information could be gleaned from the type of ordnance or fuel capacities carried. The Spitfires at this time were operating without additional fuel tanks or external stores. Fuel was the maximum internal load of eighty-five gallons. Ordnance approximated 120 rounds of 20mm for the Hispano cannons (60 per gun), and 1,200 rounds of .303 (300 rpg).

After their briefing, the pilots started to appear at dispersal. Kingaby was one of the first. He was always one of the first. Davies watched him as he looked around the aircraft, trying to balance what he had heard about Kingaby with the person he now saw standing a few yards away. Donald Ernest Kingaby was a vicar's son from Holloway, North London. He had just turned twenty-one, seven months senior to Davies. His Irvin jacket he wore with the collar up as protection against the morning's cold, its bulk disguising his slim build.

He walked round the leading edge of the mainplane, saying something in passing to his plumber who was just securing the last fastener on the oil tank filler panel. As he talked he looked up towards the propeller spinner, and ran an inquisitive hand over the surface of a propeller blade, looking for cracks or dents that could signal weakness or failure. His eyelids turned down at the corners, giving him a rather doleful look, somewhat at odds with his reputation in the air. Kingaby was already an ace. Flying Spitfires first with 266 Squadron, and then 92, he had flown throughout the Battle of Britain and had been officially credited with some fourteen aircraft either damaged or destroyed. Most of these had been Me109s, and a few days before Davies' arrival he had shot down another. Throughout the squadron and in and around Biggin he was thus known as the '109 specialist'.

The early morning mist was now clearing and more pilots started to arrive. Most seemed to have cars of various descriptions, all of which seemed to have a liking for 100-octane fuel in these days of shortage. There was now a real excitement in the air, and pilots and ground crews alike went about their duties with a nervous sense of anticipation. It was now a mixture of ranks: flight lieutenants, flying and pilot officers, sergeant pilots, then LACs, AC1s and AC2s. Now united, working as a team with a common purpose.

They all dealt with the forthcoming operation in different ways. A few of the pilots congregated around an aircraft in the next E-pen, talking, sometimes laughing nervously, about the last 'op' while clarifying the details of the one in hand. Heights, formations, rendezvous points, ETAs. Some of the more experienced gave friendly advice to those under their command – fuel management, best cruise settings, enemy tactics. All the time the crews did last minute checks, going over tasks already completed just to be sure. Malan arrived with Mike Robinson and Brian Kingcome, dropping the latter at his aircraft before heading off to 609's dispersal. Malan would often 'do the rounds' before an op, clarifying details with squadron COs and flight commanders, and giving pep talks to the pilots.

Davies watched Kingaby climbing into X4425 and looking around could see other pilots doing the same at their respective aircraft. The airframe fitters stood on the wings, holding the harness straps ready for their pilots who, when ready, clipped the buckles into the quick-release boxes. Thomas offered up the side door to Kingaby who then latched it in the half-closed position to aid escape if anything should go wrong before take-off. Then a Very flare cut across the morning sky: the signal to start.

Across the field Davies could make out the propellers of 609's aircraft beginning to turn, the sound of Merlins breaking into life. A lick of flame from '425's exhausts and Kingaby's propeller started to rotate. Davies turned to avoid the rush of air, holding on to his forage cap that was now flapping around, trying to escape from under the epaulette of his battledress. All around the airfield the aircraft were starting to move, and Davies stepped further out of '425's slipstream as Kingaby signalled 'chocks away' and began to advance the throttle.

As Kingaby taxied out of the bay, Davies scrambled up the steep incline of the earthen bank that made up the wall of the blast-pen. On top, along with his colleagues, he stood in wonder at the spectacle that now unfolded before his eyes. This was the first time he had seen the Wing take off. Thirty-six aircraft. Three squadrons. His senses – sight, sound and smell – were all at once arrested. The Spitfires meandered in one long snaking line around the peri-track, moving characteristically from side to side, their pilots carefully eyeing the track ahead down the side of the long cowled noses. It was the only way to see forwards. In this tail-down attitude the long nose of the aircraft blocked out anything immediately in front. Looking out of the quarter-lights of the cockpit glazing, along the side of the cowlings, while taxiing from side to side achieved a modicum of forward vision.

From the top of the blast-pen, this panorama was the most exhilarating slight, and its effect on morale was unquestionable:

I remember the first time, seeing them off. I stood on top of this blast-shelter and looked out along the perimeter. The Spitfires, thirty-six of them, were making their way, taxiing and lining up for take off. It was incredible, like a lot of little ants, lines of ants crawling along. Boy, it was sight to see, I'll never forget it. (LAC Raymond Davies, interview)

The ground crews watched this almost balletic procession as it wound its way downwind, picking out 'their' individual aircraft. At the head of the line was Malan, his aircraft personalised with the codes AG-M, as was becoming the standard practice for Wing Leaders. A brief pause with Kingcome and his wingman beside him, Malan then straightened up, trimmed the aircraft and fed in the power. The other three aircraft did the same and in an instant the tailwheels were up, bouncing off the ground. Mainwheels now. A slight hesitance as they brushed through the grass. Then they were off. The pilots touched the brakes to stop the wheels vibrating in the wheel-bays, then tucked up the undercarriage as they cleared the boundary. Davies watched as they seemed to dip slightly, losing sight of them as the formation disappeared momentarily into the valley. He held his breath, wondering. Then the excitement returned as they reappeared and began to climb away. In groups of threes and fours the formations of Spitfires became airborne, Biggin Hill reverberating with the sound of the Merlins. Then all was quiet. It was 1215 hours.

The period between the Wing or squadron taking off and their return was an uneasy time for those left on the ground. The combination of not knowing and imagining what might be occurring, and what the pilots were experiencing, played on the nerves. While busying themselves with other daily duties and the routine of service life, there were still moments in every hour the aircraft were away when thoughts strayed to their comrades now climbing high into the afternoon sky.

Around the camp the atmosphere was thick with anticipation. Some managed to cut through it (or at least cope with it) with bravado – 'hope they bag a few today' – and this served a purpose in maintaining morale. Others remained quiet and just 'got on with it'. Whatever strategies each employed to see them through this time, they were united in their hope that all was going well and that all pilots would return safely.

Having climbed down from the blast-pen embankment Davies walked over to the squadron armoury, situated a little way back from dispersal in the trees. Like the others he had passed in his walk from the peri-track, he tried to think about other bits of work that he had been allocated – some general cannon maintenance and cleaning. Yet in the workshop, with the smell of paraffin and grease around him, his focus was elsewhere. Seeing the Wing take off for the first time was a magnificent sight, and it would have the same effect on his senses every time. But, probably like all ground crew, part of him was with the pilots, in those cockpits, perhaps now high over France, Belgium or Holland, looking out for any sign of the enemy.

Sometimes some images from the newsreels he had seen during the previous year pricked at his consciousness: dogfighting; aircraft trailing smoke, some during their final plunge to earth; parachutes; aircrew being rescued out of the sea; blazing wreckages. So too the vapour trails left by patrolling fighters that he had seen high above the valleys back home – perhaps even those of 92 Squadron's Spitfires when they were stationed at Pembrey. At the cinemas the newsreels invariably showed enemy aircraft being shot down, and the wreckage of some black-crossed bomber awash on a beach on the south coast, but the reality was that death and destruction was apportioned with cruel impartiality, and without any sense of the greater good. The paraffin and a shout from outside brought him back to the present.

Unbeknownst to the ground crew, the Wing had been given orders to carry out a Circus operation in the area of Calais. Escorting a force of a dozen Blenheims, detailed to bomb the dockyard area, the three squadrons of the Wing made rendezvous with the bombers high over the coast. Malan assigned 609 Squadron to provide top cover, with the brief of protecting the formation from any interceptions from above.

It was 609's first operation with the Wing and it had come as a bit of a surprise to Mike Robinson when Biggin's station commander, Group Captain Soden, had requested their presence the morning before. Equipment was still arriving from Middle Wallop and the squadron had not flown an operation together as a complete unit since the previous November. Coupled with the fact that his pilots had yet to try out their 'new' charges – 66 Squadron's bequeathed Mark II Spitfires – Robinson was a little apprehensive to say the least. At 28,000 feet, 609 held station. Below them Malan leading with 92 Squadron manoeuvred the Wing into position, keeping watch for any enemy fighters that might be tempted by the bait.

In this respect the operation proved to be largely uneventful. A few high-flying Me109s were spotted, but they remained some 10,000 feet above 609's altitude and were content to be spectators. The Blenheims bombed on time and overall the squadrons experienced some wildly inaccurate flak in the immediate target area. The only incident of note occurred when 609's 'Teeny' Overton lost consciousness owing to an oxygen system failure. The squadron looked on helplessly as he suddenly broke formation and meandered earthwards. Luckily Overton – a veteran of the squadron – regained consciousness at 10,000 feet and proceeded without further event back to Biggin.

At 1340 hours the Wing crossed the boundary fence at Biggin to the excitement of the awaiting crews. Hearing a call from outside and the sound of the Merlins as they roared overhead, Davies left his workbench and hurried out of the workshop. He eyed the gaggle of aircraft now in circuit and counted three, six, nine and yes, all twelve of 92's Spitfires as they passed low over South Camp. Now at the end of the downwind leg of the circuit, the undercarriages locked fully down, they began their turn onto final approach. Kingaby checked the green lamps of his undercarriage indicator once more and pulled the landing flaps lever to the down position, hearing the satisfying hiss of compressed air as the flaps extended. Now over the boundary and flaring gently, he put '425 down squarely on the grass. As they taxied in some of the ground crews ran out to their aircraft, both to guide their pilots in and to hopefully be first to glean any information about how things had gone. Kingaby brought QJ-V up to dispersal, spun the aircraft round and switched off. Davies ran to lend a hand, noting that the fabric patches over the gun ports still remained intact. No action today.

Chapter Five

Continuity, Change and More of the Same

A New CO with Ninety-two:

As February drew to a close, operations continued in much the same vein. Flying Officer Allan Wright and Pilot Officer Saunders closed the squadron's operations for the month with a dusk patrol on the 28th. Both took off at 1900 hours in Spitfires X4847 and X4419 respectively, and landed without incident at 1925 hours. Notably, the end of the month saw the arrival of the new commanding officer for 92 Squadron – Squadron Leader James Rankin.

'Jamie' Rankin was born in Portobello, Edinburgh in May 1913 and had received his commission with the RAF in 1935. His career in the RAF throughout the early years of the war had been somewhat varied, spending time both attached to the Fleet Air Arm, and as an instructor at 5 OTU until the summer of 1940. Until February 1941 he had been attached to 64 Squadron as supernumerary Squadron Leader at Southend so to gain some combat experience.

His promotion to CO of 92 Squadron caused some raised eyebrows amongst the squadron: a newly appointed squadron leader who had not flown operationally during the Battle of Britain and with little combat experience, posted to command one of the top units in Fighter Command. After all, the squadron had a reputation to maintain, particularly amongst its Biggin rivals of 609 and 74. His time with 64 Squadron had not been without success, sharing two Ju88s, one damaged and one destroyed. Yet this did little to stem the feeling in 92 that they had been given a CO from Training Command. As Allan Wright recalled:

I was 'B' Flight commander – only just appointed to the job – and the other flight commander, much more senior to me was Brian Kingcome. Brian ... took over from the CO temporarily, and, well we would have liked him to have become acting squadron leader and then CO. At the time it seemed most unfortunate that somebody of Jamie Rankin's background who had frankly no operational experience but was already a squadron leader was posted in to take over the squadron ... We hoped [Brian] would get the job ... and it seemed very sensible because he was properly experienced in fighting the enemy whereas we knew nothing about Squadron Leader Rankin. (Flight Lieutenant Allan Wright, interview 10/06/01)

Don Kingaby, however, had met with Rankin before and knew something of Rankin's skill as a pilot:

During this time we had returned to Biggin Hill [from Gravesend], much to everyone's delight, but our C.O., then S/Ldr Kent, was posted away ... and although we were pleased to hear of his promotion, we were very sorry to lose him.... The burning question in everyone's mind now was 'Who will get the Squadron?' We all hoped that one of the flight commanders in the squadron would be promoted as he had led us so well on so many occasions. But no, the news came through one morning that a S/Ldr Rankin was taking over. There was genuine disappointment in the squadron mainly because no-one had heard of him before except for myself. I said that I had known S/Ldr Rankin at training school and that he had been my instructor. I secretly hoped that 'Jamie' would make a go of it, and sure enough he did. Within three months he had become one of the best commanders the squadron had ever had, and had himself bagged over a dozen huns. (Sergeant Don Kingaby, unpublished memoirs)

Rankin was well aware of 92's reputation and was astute enough to allow the squadron to show him the 'form', until he felt it appropriate to introduce his own ideas and leadership. For his initial operations with the squadron he was thus contented to sit back, learn from their operational experience, and at the same time gain their respect by demonstrating his own abilities. As Allan Wright recalled, the way this transition occurred was very effective at an operational level, and it presumably had a similar positive effect on the squadron's acceptance of him in all respects.

We wondered if he would be up for the job before he arrived, but he was a very good CO. In fact what we did, with his full approval, was that Brian [Kingcome] led the squadron on operational flights and he [Rankin] would fly as number two to somebody – he wasn't too proud to do that. After a few operational flights he got to know the hang of things and said he thought he was then ready to take the job on operationally, and so he led us from then on ... it was the obvious way to do it. (Flight Lieutenant Allan Wright, interview 10/06/02)

As March opened, 92 and the rest of the Biggin Wing found it difficult to get the enemy to bite and so in between wrestling with the weather the squadrons flew a number of uneventful patrols and the occasional sweep over France. The first five days of the month were typical. On the 1st, Rankin led a patrol over Maidstone at 1210 hours, landing back at 1400 hours. Kingaby was once again in Spitfire X4425, landing a little later than the CO at 1445 hours, along with Sergeant de Montbron in N3125. The only incident was Sergeant Le Cheminant's forced landing at Manston. Later on that day Rankin, flying R6919, led a sweep across the French coast with Kingaby flying as his number two in '425. All aircraft landed back at base in the gathering darkness at 1650 hours. In the late afternoon of the 2nd, the CO sent Kingaby, Sergeant 'Tich' Havercroft and Sergeant Aston to patrol the vicinity of Manston, again without incident.

The following morning saw the squadron at early readiness, taking off at 0910 hours to patrol Maidstone at 15,000ft. Allan Wright led the first section of five aircraft in P9462, along with Kingaby in his usual '425. Rankin followed with a second section at 0945 hours, landing back safely at 1110 hours. For the morning of the 5th, Rankin staggered two patrols to cover a convoy movement in the Channel, himself leading the first at 0745 hours, followed by Pilot Officer Saunders, Sergeant Lloyd and Sergeant Le Cheminant at 0850 hours. A fighter sweep later on the 5th was significant for 92 as it was the first time that the squadron was able to use all MkVb Spitfires. With Malan leading, 92 and 74 completed a sweep over the French coast between 1255 and 1440 hours. The following pilots and aircraft of 92 Squadron took part;

Squadron Leader Rankin (X4257)
Sergeant Havercroft (R6923)
Flight Lieutenant Kingcome (R6833)
Sergeant Gaskell (R6919)
Sergeant Kingaby (R6882)
Pilot Officer Saunders (R6897)
Sergeant Lloyd (X4062)

Later, a standing patrol of six aircraft was detailed to cover the Dungeness to Hastings area, again making exclusive use of the squadron's 'Merlin 45 Spitfires'. 'Tich' Havercroft flew R6923, de Montbron R6919, Pilot Officer Mottram R6776, Pilot Officer Saunders R6897, Le Cheminant X4062, and Kingaby R6882.

On 19 March, Rankin had a narrow escape. Leading eleven aircraft in X4257, Rankin had been detailed to patrol Hastings at 36,000ft. At height, Rankin was confronted with erratic engine speed variations, owing to the failure of the propeller's de Havilland constant speed unit (CSU). The freezing of the oil supply into the unit had been encountered during trials by the Aeroplane & Armament Experimental Establishment (A&AEE) at Boscombe Down. With the severe decreases in temperature associated with high altitude flying, the automatic adjustment of the blade angles was thus lost, resulting in a loss of engine/propeller control. De Havilland's service manuals pointed to such problems, even under cold conditions at ground level:

> *It is also an advantage to expel as much oil as possible from the cylinder, as viscosity increases very rapidly as the oil cools, until in really cold weather, it may congeal to such an extent as to retard seriously the flow of oil through the ports of the governor … Until warm oil has replaced the cold oil in the cylinder, therefore, the airscrew will not respond promptly to governor control.* (De Havilland 'Controllable Pitch Airscrew Constant Speed Control Unit: Service Manual' p. 34)

Two other pilots, sergeants Le Cheminant (in R6897) and de Montbron (in R6776), had similar problems, both having to crash-land. However, to complicate matters, having left the formation, Rankin suffered an oxygen failure and passed out, only coming to in a dive at 12,000ft. With engine speed having passed the maximum permissible of 3,000rpm, Rankin was forced to crash-land the aircraft near Maidstone.

April continued in much the same vein as the previous two months with elements of the Wing operating standing patrols along the south coast. On the 2nd, Pilot Officer Neville Duke arrived from 58 OTU and was eased into the fold in the usual manner: dogfight and formation practice with some of the squadron's 'old lags', and the obligatory talks by the CO, Malan and the boffins. On return from his R/t course at Uxbridge, Tommy Lund took him up for some dogfighting.

> *[Monday, 7 April 1941] I went up after lunch with Tommy Lund to do some formation. Had a bit of a dogfight and he was apparently satisfied with my stuff. Went off after this in a Spit V. Wizard machine and seems to handle smoother than the Is – bags of power. Did a few landings to get things taped a bit.* (Pilot Officer Neville Duke, quoted in Franks, 1995, p. 9)

The mixed weather provided little opportunity for the Wing to operate at full strength and so 92, 609 and 74 all engaged in probing excursions into France, either as a single squadron, a flight or a pair of fighters. On 6 April, two pilots from 74 Squadron, Flight Lieutenant Tony Bartley – recently posted across from 92 – and Pilot Officer Spurdle, decided on a 'Rhubarb' from Manston. Pilot Officer Spurdle's combat report documented the opportunist, and hazardous, nature of such flights:

> *I was flying as Blue 2 in line astern on F/L Bartley DFC and we left Manston at 1630 hours. We crossed the Belgian coast at approximately 1645 hours near*

Gravelines and flying just below cloud 1,500 – 2,000ft. headed in the direction of St Omer. We crossed the 'drome and saw no a/c dispersed and no AA fire. There was little traffic on the roads and visibility was very limited owing to low cloud base. There was a little tracer stuff coming from what appeared to be an ammunition dump (separated buildings with blast walls). We came on a Me109 in a field; it appeared to have force-landed so we came low and machine-gunned it. I saw a big cloud of brown smoke go up after F/L Bartley had shot at it. I fired a few rounds but observed no further effects.

We climbed up under the clouds again and shortly after, heading NW, we were attacked by an E/A which we didn't see to identify. I received two cannon shell hits and four machine-gun bullets. I gained cover in the clouds, losing sight of F/L Bartley. My machine was shaking and control at low speeds was very poor. I tried to fly blind but my gyro instruments were upset so after about three minutes circling in cloud I came down to get a horizon and let them settle down. I came out of the clouds and saw a Me110 just in front and slightly to my left flying in the same direction at approximately 400ft. I opened fire and E/A turned left and crash-landed in a big field. The rear gunner got out and on turning back I gave him a quick 'squirt'. He fell down but I don't think he was hit. My machine was shaking heavily and I entered cloud and flew on course 280 degrees making landfall at Dungeness. I landed at Manston at 1740 hours. My port aileron controls were shot away and I had a cannon shell through my airscrew blade. (Pilot Officer Spurdle, Combat Report, quoted in Tidy, 1972, p. 103–4)

The month saw Rankin starting to apply his exacting standards of flying to his marksmanship. On the 11th, he and three other aircraft were scrambled to intercept a Heinkel He59 seaplane that was being towed back into Boulogne harbour. Having spotted the Heinkel on the water, Rankin led the formation into attack. Within moments it was enveloped in a writhing mass of waterspouts as Rankin's cannon and machine guns tore through the sea. Turning to see the Heinkel sinking, the formation was then intercepted by a detachment of Me109s from III/JG51. In the ensuing short engagement Rankin managed to damage one of the '109s before heading back to Biggin. Sergeant Gaskell, flying Spitfire X4062, did not return.

On the 24th, while flying a patrol in Spitfire R7161 (QJ-J), Rankin encountered an Me109 of 2/JG52. Again, Rankin was quick to react to the threat. With his number two, Pilot Officer Brunier, he shot it down. The pilot, Feldwebel Günther Struck, managed to jump from the burning aircraft over Broomshill Rye, Sussex, to become a prisoner of war. Neville Duke noted the action in his diary, along with the daily routine of readiness-action-celebration!

[Thursday, 24 April 1941] Up at 4.15 for dawn readiness this morning! Nothing doing until about 8.30 when heard CO and one of our Netherlands East Indies boys, F/L Bruinier, had shot down a 109 over Dungeness. It came down in flames, the pilot baled out and was taken prisoner. He evidently mistook our chaps for his friends as he made no attempt to duck into cloud and even waggled his wings to them! He was machine-gunning some town – Rye I think. Some people have all the luck. Went up at about 12.30 on a standing patrol over Maidstone. Took F/L Wright on leave in the Maggie and landed him in a field near Maidenhead. One hell of a party to celebrate the Hun! (Pilot Officer Neville Duke, quoted in Franks, 1995, p. 10)

On the 26th, Duke managed to damage an Me109F while flying QJ-Y (R6904). Earlier in the day he had been on a dawn sweep over the Dunkirk-Calais area at 32,000ft – up at 0730hrs despite having been on a sortie of his own the previous night that had started at the White Hart at Brasted and finished in Knockholt and the return to billets at 0400 hours. After taking off on the second sweep at 1230hrs, the squadron encountered some '109s.

After taking off, control vectored us on to some Huns that were about. Intercepted a flight of Hurricanes at 32,000. Saw five Me109s and tackled them. Got a shot at one from astern as he dived for the sea – flaming from his exhaust. Another Spitfire cut between us and I had to break away without seeing whether I got it or not. Ronnie Fokes got one down in the sea. Same one as I shot at? (Pilot Officer Neville Duke, quoted in Franks, 1995, p.11)

The following day brought the usual standing patrols, 609 sending eight aircraft in two sections. Pilot Officer Seghers provided the only entertainment by getting his aircraft caught up in a camouflage net. As 609's records indicated, he was seemingly making a habit of his interceptions of ground-bound obstacles!

Pilot Officer Seghers failed to get off the ground owing to getting caught up in a camouflage net. 2 days previous he had a similar difference with a NAAFI wagon. He thinks it is very strange that these things should get in his way. (609 Squadron, Operational Record Book, April, p. 5).

For 609 Squadron, the day culminated in a rather boisterous party in celebration of Sidney Hill's birthday.

Pilot Officer Hill's birthday provided as good an excuse as any for another 'party',
the intention being signified by a loud post-prandial beating of drums. A game of
snooker degenerated into hockey played with cues and billiard balls, and after
Pilot Officers Hill and Ziegler (Intell. Officer) had fought a duel with soda
syphons (clearing the bar like an old-time western saloon), the party adjourned
to Southwood, where after a while the birthday boy was found lying flat on his
bedroom floor. He was lifted into bed and his sole recollection is the sight of Flight
Lieutenant de la Torre (Intell.), cap reversed, shouting that he was the fire brigade,
and that all bombs and fires had been satisfactorily dealt with. (609 Squadron,
Operational Record Book, April, p. 5)

By the end of April, the three squadrons of the Wing had settled into a state of
friendly rivalry, each striving to be the most successful, while maintaining a healthy
encouragement and respect for the other two. 74 Squadron were still at Gravesend,
flying over to Biggin for early morning briefings when a Wing operation was the
order of the day. The 'Tigers' had seen some changes during these first months, and
some still were feeling the effect of Malan's departure as their leader. Mungo-Park
proved a largely popular choice for Malan's replacement, having been promoted
from 'B' Flight commander. Johnnie Freeborn remained as 'A' Flight commander,
having been pipped at the post for the CO's job.

'B' Flight was now led by Tony Bartley, formerly of 92 Squadron. Bartley had
been talked into the post by Malan who wanted him to take some responsibility
and calm his rather playboy existence. Malan had accosted him at a party, tarring
the rest of 92 with the same brush and demanding an answer by morning. Sobered
up, Bartley had taken stock. Friends were leaving 92 for promotions, so he sold
his beloved Lincoln Zephyr, adopted regulation dress and joined 74. However,
according to Bartley, 74 had lost some of their spirit, and having been in the thick
of the fighting for so long, were tired and battle-scarred.

The exemplary leadership of Mike Robinson had maintained the cohesion of
609 as a unit, and its officers tended to operate as such as much socially as they did
in the air. Thrown into the now offensive operations of the Wing, the squadron
still had little to show for its endeavours after its first two months in 11 Group.

Some of the squadron's 'old lags' were due to be rested but pressed on until the
'Doc' saw that they were posted for some well-earned time off from operations.
Some, such as 'Teeny' Overton, had been on 'ops' constantly since 1939. Similarly,
across on north camp, 92 Squadron could boast a number of veterans: Kingcome,
Wright, Kingaby, de Montbron, Mottram, Lund, Wellum, Le Cheminant, to
name a few. All continued on operations into the summer months of 1941.

For Davies and his five comrades, it had been an exciting introduction to the RAF; they were truly at war. Though the weather had, at times, confounded full-scale operations, the sight of the Biggin Hill Wing taking the fight across the Channel was burnt deep into their experience. Like those other ground crew with whom they worked, they felt justly proud of their contribution. As the summer unfolded, the partnership between air and ground crew would be further honed, and their strength and expertise continually tested.

Chapter Six

Chance, Risk and the Strongest Link

Opening Shots:

A brief glimpse of sunlight welcomed the crews of 92, 609 and 74 squadrons into May. Momentarily its rays stood proud against the gathering clouds as if to point the way to the stars. A little warmth accompanied its glow, but not yet quite enough as to take the chill off the walk to dispersal and the frostiness of the spanner or the bicycle seat.

The first days of the month saw a few chance skirmishes with Me109s and aircraft from 609 and 74 squadrons, but the most significant opening shots were called by 609 Squadron. For their first three months as part of the Biggin Hill Wing, 609 had little to show for their endeavours. True, they had been very successful during the Battle of Britain, but no real opportunities had arisen since their arrival on 'the Bump' for them to demonstrate their prowess.

Like all squadrons – particularly those that had been in constant action for many months – there had been some changes in personnel. Some had been dictated by operational strains and illness, others by the Luftwaffe. 'Teeny' Overton had been stood down as 'A' flight commander. Since his 10,000ft dive on 26 February caused by his blacking out through oxygen starvation, Overton had not felt right, and had been on and off the sick list throughout the following months. By April it was decided that he should be rested, and was consequently posted as an instructor to 59 OTU.

His replacement was Flight Lieutenant Paul Richey, brother-in-law to Mike Robinson. Even though the squadron had been in action only sporadically since February, two NCO pilots had also been lost. On 27 March, Sergeant MacSherry had been killed in Spitfire P7785, while attempting to land at Hawkinge. Flight Sergeant Bennett, who had been with the squadron since 1939, was posted missing, presumed dead, on 29 April, his Spitfire (P7669) shot down during an early morning skirmish with some Me109s over the Channel.

It was Rankin's birthday on 7 May and the whole of Biggin Hill turned out to wish him well. All personnel were out on parade for the event, ground and aircrews from all the squadrons, administrative staff, and airfield defence units as one happy crowd. 92 themselves had contributed to a portrait of their CO, this being presented to him during the parade. Rankin was clearly impressed by this show of respect, both in terms of 92's growing acceptance of their 'training command CO', and Biggin Hill as his new home.

The following day, it was Mike Robinson's birthday, and 609 along with the rest of Biggin celebrated in a rather more unusual manner that perhaps signified the better luck with which 609 might now be afforded.

Luck came in the form of the heavily contested rescue of a downed pilot in mid-Channel that became known at Biggin as the 'Battle of the Dinghy'. During the afternoon of the 8th, the squadron took off to patrol Maidstone at 15,000ft, having been at readiness since early morning. While 'stooging' around, control told them of a German airman, adrift in his life-raft, to whom an RAF motor launch had been sent in rescue. On arrival, Mike Robinson spied the launch and the dinghy, now with a number of Me109s circling like vultures. Leaving one section of four aircraft as top cover, Robinson took the remainder of the squadron in to rescue the launch. However it was too late and the launch was set on fire while the top cover was engaged and Sergeant Mercer (in P7734) hit.

Reforming, the squadron spotted a second motor-launch, also being set about by a further group of Me109s. The squadron attacked again, this time with Paul Richey's section remaining at height as top cover. The squadron's intelligence officer, 'Spy' Ziegler, documented the ensuing action:

Michael quickly shot down the nearest; Johnny Curchin sent a second into the sea and hit another, which David Hughes-Rees finished off. Two more were claimed in swift succession by Tommy Rigler, an NCO pilot who had just joined before 609's departure from Warmwell. Then Sergeant Palmer (called 'Goldy' because of his locks), who had chased two of the enemy to Calais, heard on the radio: 'Beauty Leader being fired on'. Michael, who after a long, lone pursuit had shot down a second quarry down beside the French cliffs, had suddenly been set upon at the moment he ran out of ammunition by a whole Staffel of enemy fighters (he counted nine), which attacked him all the way back across the Channel. It was then that this superb pilot, disarmed as he was, showed the mastery in the air that brought ground staff and other pilots out to watch each time he indulged in aerobatics. But this time it was to save his own life. With split-second judgement, again and again, he turned sharply towards each opponent at the very moment the latter opened fire, and – with some eventual help from 'Goldy', who shot one Messerschmitt off his tail just as he was being attacked himself – got home without a single scratch. (Pilot Officer Ziegler, 609 Squadron Intelligence Officer, quoted in Ziegler, 1971, p. 185)

At Biggin, news had filtered through from control that 609 had been committed to action. At 609's dispersal, the chat amongst the ground crews had reached fever pitch, all wondering about the squadron's fortunes and those of 'their' pilots. Clearly, Mike Robinson had been engaged, and had been fired on. Over at 92 Squadron's dispersal, word had also gotten round that there was an almighty confrontation taking place over the Channel.

Having been released from duties until the evening, a number of pilots had taken leave of the camp. However the squadron was detailed to fly to West Malling to take part in nocturnal patrols in support of the more suitably equipped Blenheims and Defiants. While readying the aircraft for these later duties, the ground crews began to receive rumour of their comrades' engagement. Meanwhile, the operations block was getting quite crowded as Malan, Rankin and the sector intelligence officer (SIO), 'Spy' de la Torre, listened in anxiously to the R/t conversations of 609's pilots, now embroiled in a deadly mêlée of whirling aircraft.

Having been told of his squadron's meeting with the enemy, 'Spy' Ziegler was down at 609 Squadron's dispersal, pacing uneasily as he waited for the first aircraft to return. If they had not heard the rumours yet, his demeanour spoke volumes to the awaiting armourers, fitters and plumbers. Just after 1745 hours Mike Robinson's aircraft, PR-B, appeared over the airfield and announced the squadron's successes with two victory rolls before landing. As Robinson taxied in the other aircraft began appearing in ones and twos, their wings seeming to quiver excitedly as the pilots brought them in to land. All at once, dispersal seemed to become awash with all manner of station personnel.

The ground crews, though conscious of their immediate post-flight inspections, sought out as much information they could from their returning pilots. Armourers started to bring re-arms, making a careful mental note of the aircraft that had fired their guns; most had their fabric patches shot through. It had clearly been a busy afternoon. As Mike Robinson flicked the magneto switches to off, pulled back the canopy and unlatched the door, Ziegler started his usual inquiries:

'Yes, I got two, Zieg.' He did not sound elated, and his voice was tired. 'The second one tried to force-land on the beach – I hoped he would – but he didn't make it. He crashed into the surf, and I felt sick – it might so easily have been me.' It was all I could get for the moment. He went over to greet Johnnie [Curchin], who limped in badly shot up, with a blocked aileron and windscreen daubed with enemy oil. He too had temporarily ceased to be his usual aggressive self, and wore a far-away look as if still living the few split seconds when he wondered whether his Spitfire would ever pull out of its dive. Contrast Tommy Rigler, whom I spied leaving his aircraft with confident gait [having shot down two confirmed in this, his first

combat]. (Pilot Officer Ziegler, 609 Squadron Intelligence Officer, quoted in Ziegler, 1971, p. 185–6)

After a most difficult debriefing, with a parade of pilots, the station commander and Sailor Malan greeting every returning combatant, the squadron's score was a most impressive six Me109s destroyed and a further two probables. Only two Spitfires had been damaged. The following day, a flight from 609 encountered more Me109s and managed to damage one. Sadly, Sergeant Mercer's Spitfire P7305, was badly damaged and while attempting a forced landing on the beach at St Margaret's Bay, Kent, it exploded, having struck a landmine. Mercer had been with the squadron since 1940.

From Squadron Patrols to Parading Wings:
On 16 May a number of patrols brought some frantic encounters with the enemy. Malan led the three squadrons on what was to become a sweep in the area of Dungeness–Dover. As 609 recounted, Malan's first intention was somewhat removed from the ensuing operation, but the change of plan had been motivated by the sheer impressiveness of the three-squadron Wing in formation.

> *Wing Commander Malan, DSO, DFC and bar, thought it was about time the Biggin Hill Wing got together for a little practice so, with himself leading 92 and 609, took off at 12:30 and met 74 from Gravesend over Base. The temptation to parade this monster show of strength before the Nazis was however irresistible, so they swept up and down the Channel, little pairs of 109s skipping out of the way in a fright.* (609 Squadron Operational Record Book, May, p. 5)

Being part of such a formation had positive effects on morale. As Alec 'Joe' Atkinson of 609 Squadron commented:

> *[Operating as a Wing] gave you a good feeling. I don't think that it made much difference to your own performance but to see all these masses of aircraft and you knew they were ours really was rather encouraging. It had a very good effect on morale.* (Pilot Officer Alec 'Joe' Atkinson, interview 28/03/04)

The squadron had been on readiness from early morning and Davies had made his way down to dispersal with Don Kingaby's fitter, LAC Thomas. Thomas was from Caerphilly, a small market town that lay some six miles south of Davies' own village of Nelson. Davies had good memories of Caerphilly, being a popular trip for his Sunday cycling club. Yet the war had brought other associations that he and Thomas shared.

> *When I was still in Nelson at the start of the war, I'd often hear the German bombers during the night. Sometimes, either when they got lost or were intercepted by one of our aircraft, they would come up the valleys and would jettison their bombs. Most of the time they seemed to drop them on Caerphilly Mountain, which was only a few miles away from us. So by the time I moved to Biggin I was used to the bombing to some extent.* (LAC Raymond Davies, interview)

Kingaby lifted Spitfire R6882 away from Biggin, gaining height with the rest of this incredible formation. Standing with Thomas by the peri-track, the two strained their eyes to catch the last sight of 'their' aircraft, as it quickly disappeared into the milky haze of the morning sun. With the usual good luck rituals they then went about their duties. Davies walked the short distance to the side of a blast-pen where a collection of 20mm magazines stood waiting. He checked a couple over, and marked them ready for re-arms if it should be required when Don came back. The waiting game started once again.

Thomas reappeared with a couple of mugs of tea, not being able to settle to do anything else while the kites were away. The two sat down, lying with their backs up against the earthen wall of the pen, and started to chat idly about some of the escapades of a few nights before. They had managed a good night in Bromley with Campbell and Healey, and had only just made the wagon pick-up time – not yet having the luxury of a 'sleeping out pass' that they would enjoy with later promotion.

Thomas, however, was set on seeing the air war from the 'other side', and had made an application to remuster as aircrew. Davies ribbed him, finding Thomas's real motivation not in a sense of duty, but in the need to access one of the pubs in Bromley that had an 'Officers only' policy. Others operated an '*Officers in the lounge, other ranks in the bar*' caste system that rankled with the sense of being all in it together and united against a common foe. Underneath, Davies admired his friend's courage and determination in this decision. The bantering was an expression of this.

Time seemed to pass quickly and before long aircraft started to reappear over Biggin, and clearly there had been some commotion. Kingaby returned just before 1400 hours and jumped down from the cockpit grinning from ear to ear. Clambering over the wing with the re-arms, Davies saw the beads of perspiration on Don's brow as he pulled back his flying helmet. Several 109s had been seen and he and Allan Wright had managed a good squirt at a couple. Don had fired on an

Me109F with both cannon and machine guns, and had observed a lot of pieces flying off it before it started to smoke. There was frustration in his voice as he recounted the engagement, having had to break off owing to the interruption of two other enemy aircraft. It was a 'damaged' at least.

Other pilots had been in action as well – Wright also claiming a probable – and it was clear that the Luftwaffe had decided to probe Fighter Command's strength. At Wing strength, they could not have picked a worse day. With refuelling and re-arming completed within the half-hour, R6882 was ready once again. Kingaby and a few others went to grab a quick bite to eat from the NAAFI wagon.

A call came through to 92's dispersal late in the afternoon, and before long the squadron was back in the air for the second operation of the day. Soon after 1600 hours the skies above the Channel were filled with the now characteristic sight of twisting and turning aircraft, and the chattering of gun fire. In what seemed like a split second the Wing's formation broke from the cohesive fighting machine, becoming a frenzy of individual actions. Number twos tried desperately to stay with their leaders, conscious of their duty to protect their tails. But soon it largely became an 'every man for himself' situation. There was no choice in these matters: either kill or be killed, '*either fight or die*'.

An Me109 flashed past Rankin (flying QJ-J, R7161), showing its pale blue underside. He gave it a burst of cannon and .303 and observed multiple hits. The enemy aircraft seemed to tip drunkenly, emitting an oily smoke that signalled a probable mortal wound. Allan Wright, in QJ-S (R6923), also managed to deliver a seemingly knockout blow to a 109 that got into his sights, but, like Rankin and others, he found it impossible to track it to make sure of its demise. Sometimes the temptation to follow an aircraft down was very great, but the experienced pilots knew that to do so could be fatal.

Kingaby spotted an Me109 diving towards France, trying to make its retreat. He dived after it, coaxing every ounce of power from his Merlin. The Spitfire reached 470 miles per hour in the dive and Kingaby eventually was able to catch up with the enemy at 7,000ft. Carefully squeezing the gun-button, he unleashed a withering barrage of lead from his guns. It was all over in a moment. The 109's starboard wing crumpled and the aircraft spun wildly. Kingaby watched as it plunged earthwards, the detached wing spiralling more slowly, showing its alternate grey-green and pale blue sides.

Mike Robinson, leading 609 Squadron, had been happily surprised as he led the squadron into attack. Despite the initial upset of losing one of the squadron's weavers, Sergeant Palmer spotted a gaggle of Me109s a few thousand feet below the formation, giving the Wing the advantage of height. Pilot Officer Sidney Hill and Pilot Officer Keith Ogilvie quickly shot down two Me109s at 1615 and 1620 respectively, but were unable to confirm as they disappeared into the haze below.

It took 'Spy' Ziegler the rest of the day trying to obtain proof of these successes, which were finally confirmed by the Dover battery of Balloon Command. Pilot Officer Hill had almost paid an impromptu visit to them when he had followed 'his' 109 from 20,000 to 1,000 feet before it disappeared into the heat haze, narrowly avoiding the balloons whilst pulling out of his dive. 'Vicki' Ortmans also managed to damage an Me109. In the meantime, Sergeant 'Goldy' Palmer wrestled with his badly damaged Spitfire P7602, having been bounced by a couple of Me109s during the initial engagement. He managed to force-land at Detling, and returned to Biggin in a Magister, much to the delight of the squadron.

The next day saw a similar pattern emerge. Malan led a high patrol of six aircraft over the Dungeness–North Foreland area at 32,000 feet. At 1250 hours while descending to 23,000 feet over Dover, Malan's keen eyes spotted a gaggle of six Me109Fs, some 3,000ft below. Having the advantage of height, Malan decided to have a crack at them and half-rolled after the unsuspecting enemy. The Spitfires fell in behind them but found the Messerschmitts' turn of speed enabled them to keep some 800 yards away. Less than ideal. Without any warning the enemy suddenly broke formation, four of the aircraft using the momentum they had gathered in the dive to climb steeply. Malan selected the other pair, but soon found himself outmanoeuvred. He considered the risks and chose to break off.

Heading back towards Dover he found another four Me109s, this time in staggered pairs at 18,000 and 20,000 feet. As the lower pair turned sharp right, Malan managed to get in several bursts at both aircraft. He observed hits around the cockpit and engine of one, losing a cowling and the canopy in the process. Copious amounts of black, oily smoke issued from the Me109, but Malan was unable to confirm its demise due to the attention of the uppermost pair, now joining the fight. They flew protectively around their crippled comrade and Malan was forced to disengage. The badly mauled party of Me109s retired towards France. Sailor's aircraft had too been damaged in the action and his engine was now vibrating badly. Not one to be caught out, he decided to land at Hawkinge, and returned to Biggin by Magister.

Malan was not the only one in action in the area. Alec 'Joe' Atkinson of 609 Squadron also ran into a group of enemy fighters over Dover, while flying as weaver to the flight. Without warning he was suddenly struck by cannon fire.

I was a fairly new pilot and I was flying along in a formation of about, I suppose a Flight. We were flying over Kent and all of a sudden a great hole appeared in my starboard wing! Obviously we'd been jumped by 109s but I never saw them.

I asked the flight commander what I should do and he said I should land at the nearest airfield. (Pilot Officer Alec 'Joe' Atkinson, interview 2005)

Atkinson lost a few thousand feet and found himself alone over Kent with his aircraft badly holed though still handling quite normally.

So I looked around and saw that there was an airfield at Rochester and I made an approach. I put the wheels down OK and I was making quite a decent approach. Then I put the flaps down foolishly and the flap on the side that the hole was didn't go down, but the flap on the other side did! The consequence was that the machine was very difficult to control because it wanted to sort of turn round on its head. So I hung on to the stick and needed all my strength to prevent it from going bouleversement. I careered off across the country and I saw that there was a very large ploughed field in front of me, so I thought that was the place for me! So I snatched my hand off the control column so long as I could take it, and pulled back the throttle. I landed with the wheels down in the ploughed field. Of course the wheels were soon taken off and I banged my head on the gunsight which made me bleed. I came to rest in a great cloud and there was a chap in the corner of the field who was hoeing turnips – he may have looked up but at any rate he went on hoeing his turnips! There was a road by my side where an RAF officer was driving along and pulled up his car, jumped out and came over towards me. I said to him 'turn off the petrol', and he said 'I'm awfully sorry, I can't because I'm an equipment officer'. So I turned it off myself and then a policeman who was passing in his car came along and offered me a lift back to Biggin Hill which I gratefully accepted. It was a frightening experience, I thought my last day had come! (Pilot Officer Alec 'Joe' Atkinson, interview 2005)

The other casualty of the day was 609's de Havilland Puss Moth, which had become a symbol of liberty and escape. Weather checks, leave taxi and armament shooting practice spotter, the Moth had given faithful service. Now damaged owing to brake failure with Mike Robinson and the adjutant on board, it was destined never to be repaired.

The month tailed off with a few more sporadic encounters with the enemy, and the loss of the squadron's first Belgian pilot: Rodolf de Grunne. A flamboyant character, of aristocratic blood, de Grunne had flown Me109s in the Spanish Civil War, and had served with 32 Squadron at Biggin Hill during the Battle of Britain. On 18 August 1940, de Grunne had been shot down during an encounter with Me109s of 7/JG26 while flying Hurricane V6535. He had managed to bail out, badly burned, but returned to operations in 1941. On 21 May, with Malan leading 609 Squadron as top cover to the Kenley Wing who had been assigned close escort duties, the massed formation of fighters (including most of 11 Group and elements of 10 and 12 Groups) swarmed around the seventeen Blenheims en route to Bethune's oil refinery. As the bombers left the target area, Me109s in groups of twos and fours attacked the Circus, now just coming out over Gravelines. De Grunne was flying a No.2 to Flight Lieutenant Bisdee when he was surprised by a 109F. At 1715hrs de Grunne was seen to bail out of PR–M (P7436) over the Channel. Goldy Palmer in PR–F (P7917) and Sergeant Boyd in PR–Z (P8098) circled de Grunne as he descended – Palmer leaving only when he saw his comrade enter the water. A rescue launch was sent out from Ramsgate but de Grunne's body was never found. Sergeant Boyd managed to force-land at Manston, while Palmer – also out of fuel – managed to put his Spitfire down in a field near Kingsdown, Kent.

Chapter Seven

Pea-soupers, Rhubarbs and Sweeps

Rhubarb and 'Blister' Weather:
With variable weather in the last week of May, the Wing operated infrequently, all squadrons bearing the frustration of readiness followed by cancelled 'ops'. The odd *'rhubarb'* into France was ventured by some, but these were characteristically hit and miss affairs. Having helped 'Titch' Thornton arm up Rankin's and Kingaby's aircraft on 25 May, Davies watched the two set off, accompanied by de Montbron and Duke – all hoping for some opportunist action. Rankin, in the company of Malan (flying 92 Squadron's R7346 and R6882 respectively), had already battled with the rain and strong winds earlier in the day for no result. As Duke recorded, there was little success in these excursions.

> *Monty and self left CO and Kingaby off Boulogne. Crossed the coast in cloud; Monty dived onto a hangar and I lost him. Prowled off on my own inland, in and out of cloud at 4,000ft. Nothing flying. Came out at Dunkirk – accurate AA fire. Not a shot at anything; 'O' feet next time. Anxious moments coming back, miles of sea, low petrol. Hit coast south of Harwich! Force-landed at Gravesend.* (Pilot Officer Neville Duke, quoted in Franks, 1995, p. 11)

Worsening weather in the afternoon of the 26th, and news of the *Bismarck* being hit after its sinking of HMS *Hood*, sent a number of pilots of 609 to London, their target being the Suivi Club. It was a long-drawn-out operation out of which Flight Lieutenant Richey, Pilot Officer de Spirlet and Flying Officer Ziegler were seen staggering at 0600 hours. The next day 609 received its first Spitfire Vbs, long overdue, having been promised at least six weeks prior. Mike Robinson took one up and declared it 'delightful'.

May's operational flying was brought to a close on the 28th, with all three squadrons being involved in a sweep with the Hornchurch Wing. A few 109s took the bait and inflicted damage on at least two of the Wing's aircraft. One of 609's Belgians, Pilot Officer Wilmet, found himself the focus of attention and his Spitfire (P7834) badly holed. Similarly, 92 Squadron's 'Wimpey' Wade was badly mauled by a 109, his aircraft receiving cannon and machine gun hits in the wings. Wade spun out of control for 15,000 feet, yet managed to get back to Manston.

Others such as Roy Mottram also landed at Manston, short of fuel. Sam Saunders coaxed his Spitfire as far as Gravesend, seemingly running on fumes. Frustrated, Duke had returned early having found that his oxygen would not turn on.

Persistent rain and general murk cancelled operations in the afternoon of the 28th and 609 was released from duties, a number of pilots making it up to London. Further rain and fog ended the month and grounded all three squadrons. Both 92 and 609 were stood down on the 31st and all manner of means were used to transport the gaggle to Edenbridge where Captain Cuthbert Orde, the war artist, threw a party in their honour.

The poor weather continued into June and, while it resulted in many operations being cancelled, it gave both air and ground crew some welcome time off. In the first few weeks it seemed that the most flying hours were notched up by the Lysander on weather recce flights. With rain and fog, the Lysander crew had the unenviable duty of periodic flights into the murk, groping around to give some report on the weather conditions, wind strength, the extent of cloud cover and other measurements. It was crucial information, but far too scientific for the likes of most personnel. More usually, a quick run across an ice-cold floor to the barrack room window, then a wipe of the condensation, followed by a rather sleep-laden peer into the gloom, was enough to declare it '*a real pea-souper*'.

During the day it gave ground crews time to do their usual checks, and to carry out repairs and routine maintenance on the aircraft. Duty crew still kept those squadron aircraft at readiness, prepared and warmed up for operations. Working on the aircraft at Biggin in 1941 was still made difficult by the effects of the considerable damage incurred during the summer of 1940. No permanent hangarage remained and, as associated maintenance services were usually built as part of the hangars, stores and workshop facilities had been similarly affected.

To compensate for the loss, a number of temporary constructions had been erected around the perimeter. Made of corrugated steel, these 'blister hangars' were open at either end, with canvas awnings attached. They accommodated one aircraft at a time, and so much maintenance still occurred outside.

Apart from the routine maintenance of the aircraft's armament, the reliability of the 20mm cannon still was questionable. Now with 609 and 74 squadrons so equipped, addressing this problem caused continued head-scratching for Chiefy Stewart, Sergeant Rains and the team. Stoppages were still occurring at an unacceptable rate during test firing on the ranges, and a number of pilots had encountered problems when on operations. If one cannon jammed, then the aircraft yawed violently with the asymmetry of the resultant recoil. At other times, rounds that became stuck in the breech then exploded, causing damage to the aircraft. Sergeant Johnnie Johnston recalled such problems:

With the Hispano it was not unknown for the extractor to fail and leave an empty case in the chamber. The HE shells we used were pre-set of course and if a new round was then fed into the chamber you had a situation where the shell could explode in your wing. Not long after I arrived at 92, I was flying behind Tich Havercroft when this happened to him and the panel came whizzing past over my head. The Hispano was not very reliable and I cannot remember ever emptying both drums, there was always a stoppage. (Sergeant Walter 'Johnnie' Johnston, interview 2002)

When operations were cancelled it allowed the team to work normal hours, putting in a full day's work on the firing butts without the need to be deployed down at dispersal. As the rain drummed on the top of the blister hangar, Corporal Jones and the team sat wondering whether 'Claude' would require them for another night. Rains and Stewart stood engrossed, talking over by the servicing bench where a 20mm lay with its breech laid open by an exploded round. Dealing with problems of this kind was becoming routine, which was in itself frustrating.

'Not much of a night, lads. Better get yourselves away,' said Rains, now once again aware of his surroundings. Campbell smiled and looked round. 'King's Arms or The Jail?' he questioned. Eddie Healey stood up and unbuttoned his leather jerkin – 'Yeah, come on, Taff, let's go find a dance or something.' 'Now, Cammy,' said Davies, 'you know I haven't a pass, and neither have you.' 'King's it is then,' replied Campbell, as the group made its way out of the hangar.

On a few occasions when they had not been able to get a pass out of camp, Campbell and Davies had managed to find a way out by squeezing through the fence that ran down behind the dispersal. The gap in the fence was sufficiently far along the airfield boundary to be the 'right side' of the picket post that marked the northern end of the Biggin–Bromley road. The road had been closed since the height of the Battle of Britain when 'tourists' from London would come down in open-topped buses to watch the station being bombed! Fear of Fifth Columnists and spies that could report on Biggin's remaining strength had prompted 'Groupie' Grice to have the road in front of the camp closed and a guard picketed at each end. Being the liberty-side of the picket post meant that it was then only a short walk to the King's Arms public house at Leaves Green.

Davies pulled up the collar of his greatcoat and tried to bury his head further into its comforting warmth. He walked briskly with Campbell, Healey, and Harry Woods, half-wishing that they had caught some transport in to Bromley with some of 92's erks. The rain rested in beads on the shoulders of the thick serge of his coat. 'Dad' Best spotted them on his way back to the billets. 'Dad' hardly ever came off camp, but relished in the stories that 'Taff' and 'Cammy' told on their return. 'C'mon Dad,' shouted Campbell, 'you'll be wearing out that armchair in the mess if you don't watch it!' But he was not to be persuaded. 'He'll get some stories tomorrow,' grinned Campbell, 'Won't he, Taff?' Davies nodded in agreement, thinking of the necessary collusion that usually followed these outings. Line shooting to 'Dad' had become something of a sport over the last few months.

The King's Arms was a small half-timbered pub that lay just off the main Bromley road. The small hamlet of Leaves Green boasted a few houses, a row of which nestled around the green just adjacent to the pub. It was warm inside, its smoky atmosphere being a combination of the open wood fire and the cigarette- and pipe-smoking clientele. The smoke clung to the low ceilings, amongst the horse brasses and mementoes. All around, in every nook, was the comforting sea of blue serge, and the glint of a buckle or a cap-badge as it caught the light. The sounds of laughter punctuated the murmurings of the RAF at rest.

It was largely an airmen's haunt, mainly due to its close proximity to the camp. Some of the NCOs, sergeant pilots and the like were also to be seen, but those with commissions and their own transport tended to reach further afield into Brasted, to the south, and up to Croydon and London, Davies hung up his greatcoat and before long had forgotten the rain, the damp and the fog of the previous few weeks.

Campbell returned from the bar with four half-pints, nodding to Healey about a couple of WAAFs that he'd seen over in the corner. Davies smiled, wondering whether this would be the start of some good line-shoot for 'Dad' Best on their return. Over the first few months, Davies and Campbell had, according to 'Dad', gained a rather notorious reputation for entertaining women. It was all 'bull', but after the first time the temptation to spin another yarn and watch Dad's wide-eyed reaction had proved irresistible. So it had become form, and much entertainment was had back on camp for all those in earshot when these stories were being recounted, punctuated by Dad's exclamations of '*never!*' and '*he didn't!*'

Davies lit a cigarette, the first of a new packet of Players that had been sent from home. He did not smoke heavily but this one was very welcome. A few days previously he had returned from dispersal and lay on his bed gasping for a cigarette. A full packet of twenty lay on the side cabinet next to its corporal fitter owner, so Davies had asked him if he could have a loan of one.

I never really smoked heavily, even though I'd started very early on, picking the dog-ends out of my elder brothers' pockets when I was no more than six years old! A packet would usually last me weeks, and later, during the invasion, I pretty much lived off my cigarettes by trading them for food etc. But there was one time at Biggin, I'd come off the flight and was gasping for one, and on the cabinet was a full packet that belonged to a Corporal fitter. I said 'excuse me, Corporal, would you loan me a cigarette?' He said no, and then told me that he couldn't lend me one because if he did, I'd have to have at least two to pay him back! So he said he'd give me a cigarette, rather than 'loan' me one. But it taught me a lesson that stayed with me throughout my life – never to be in debt to anyone! (LAC Raymond Davies, interview 2002)

After a more than adequate amount of beer the merry group made its way to the door. Outside the fog had rolled in even more, but the rain had abated somewhat. Healey stood adjusting his side-cap. 'It's OK, Eddie,' said Woods, winking at Davies, 'no officers on parade, tonight.' Healey was always smart, always ready to take the salute, always preening. He loved the service life, and was always looking to impress. Eventually Campbell appeared, having been accosted by a WAAF plotter who he had spent some time with in Bromley one night. 'Right O,' said Davies, 'better get back to it.' The four sauntered back, feeling their way through the fog that seemed to hang a few feet in front of their faces.

In the distance they could hear the sound of some crews running up a couple of Blenheims that had come up from Manston on night duties. Davies imagined their mood. On the one hand, there would be the optimistic thought that some brave enemy would venture into the murk and thus being at readiness was of important purpose. On the other, the ground crew would convince each other that it was all a waste of time because nobody in their right mind would fly in such weather. The gap in the fence appeared out of the gloom, and Davies caught a smart hold of Woods who had clearly forgotten about the need to steer the reciprocal clandestine course and was heading off in the direction of the picket post and the main gate! Along by Davies' barrack block, the four said their goodnights and disappeared, happy and contented.

Despite the inclement weather, usual patrols were attempted whenever possible. On 3 June, some of 92 and 74 managed a convoy patrol in the Thames estuary in cloud down to 800 feet. The ships added to their guardians' fun by complicating the 0–700 feet flying with the trailing of a balloon barrage somewhere in the cloud! There were no incidents and the eight aircraft managed to make it back to Biggin where the weather was clamping down.

The following day 609 Squadron lost Flight Lieutenant Curchin DFC during an escort duty to an ASR Lysander looking for a downed 54 squadron pilot, Flight Lieutenant George Gribble. Having detached Paul Richey's section to pick up another Lysander from Hawkinge, Mike Robinson and the remaining nine aircraft had continued to patrol at 2,000 feet when three Me109Fs were sighted directly above. Banking steeply, Robinson called up Richey to gain height over Hawkinge with the intention of surprising the enemy up sun. However, before this could happen, one 109 dived on Vicki Ortmans, who had been forced to lag behind the main formation with low oil pressure and rising engine temperature. Ortmans took violent evasive action causing the enemy aircraft to break up and fall into the sea.

In the mêlée, Robinson fought frantically with two very experienced pilots for at least ten minutes. As one came into attack, Robinson turned sharply and throttled back, managing to get a long burst at the 109 from astern. Smoking heavily, it turned on its side and dived to sea level. Another 109 darted between Curchin and Pilot Officer MacKenzie, the latter being unable to make an attack owing to getting into a spin. Tommy Rigler caught one in the climb at full deflection. Somewhere in all of this confusion, the CO saw an aircraft hit the water. It was John Curchin's.

A gap in the weather on 12 June allowed 92 Squadron to escort a roadstead of three Blenheims to attack shipping off the coast near Calais. The squadron patrolled between 1,000 and 4,000 feet to cover the bombers' return. Two Me109Es were encountered in a head-on battle over Dover harbour, and Rankin, flying R6890, managed to fire on one of the pair as it closed rapidly. The aircraft, from I/JG52, was later reported to have crashed into the sea; the pilot was picked up.

On Saturday the 14th, 92 took 609's place on Circus No.12 to St Omer as part of a large fighter force comprising of approximately 200 fighters from Biggin, Hornchurch, Kenley and North Weald. As part of this huge escort for twenty-four Blenheims, 92 and 74 squadrons patrolled the Calais–Boulogne area at 7–10,000 feet. Near Marquise, 92 ran into a number of 109s. Flying as Allan Wright's number two, Neville Duke chased after one.

I was with Allan Wright but got separated and attacked a 109 and went into small circles. Gave long bursts but no visible damage done. Came up behind a 109 flying straight and level, throttled right back. Almost overshot him at about 10–20 yards by 'swish-tailing'. Frantically pressing the gun-button but all the ammunition was gone. Daren't break away or he would have got on my tail so followed him about for some time. A horrible state of affairs – doubt if I shall ever get such a chance again. Eventually the 109 started turning and I broke away, screamed down out over Boulogne at 1,500 feet at +12 boost. About 320 mph. (Pilot Officer Neville Duke, quoted in Franks, 1995, p. 13)

Allan Wright was taken by surprise by an unknown number of Me109Fs, having found himself alone without his wingman. Duke had spotted a 109 and had gone after it without calling out any position. Leaving one's leader was strictly forbidden, but sometimes in the heat of battle, and with inexperience and excitement to wrestle with, it was bound to happen.

Wright cruised along until he was surprised by tracer shells whizzing past his cockpit and over the wings of his aircraft. Thinking it was Duke opening fire, he peered forwards looking to see his wingman's target. There was nothing and in that split second between quizzical thought and the realisation of the pursuing danger, he wondered what the devil Duke was firing at! Breaking away, his aircraft was hit by a small number of bullets but enough to place Wright in an extraordinary situation:

It was rotten bad luck. My aircraft was only hit by a few bullets – I think it was nine, or ten or even twelve – as soon as I was attacked I pulled the stick over to the right and the first bullet severed the wire that enabled me to pull the aileron down again, and the second bullet jammed it in that position. So looking out the cockpit out to starboard there was the aileron sticking up and there was nothing I could do about it. The immediate result was that the aeroplane began to roll and I had to use the stick to keep the nose up so that it didn't spiral downwards, and it seemed to affect the centre of gravity in that the nose also went up and down and it took quite a few moments to stop it going straight down towards the ground. Eventually I found that I could stop it rolling by having the stick right over to the left so that the port aileron was up, equal to the one on the right. In that position it was unstable fore and aft so if the nose came up and I pushed the stick forward to get it down again, then it would go down and even if I centred it it would go on going down, so I had to pull it back again to get it up. It was very difficult to control and I was over northern France so I had to struggle with the thing all back across a bit of northern France and the Channel before putting it down at the first available airfield which was Shoreham-by-the-Sea. It was not a very big airfield and I can remember being concerned whether to put the flaps down or not because if only one had come down because of the bullet holes, if it was the wrong one it would flick over and go straight into the ground. So I just had to come in at low level and use plenty of power, keep it at 145 mph – it seemed to want to roll over below this – and as soon as I got over the hedge I put it on the ground, closed the throttle, stick back and hoped for the best! I went right to the other end of the airfield and I thought it was going to go into whatever was there and so I put left rudder on and skidded sideways and fortunately stopped. When I got out I found that there was a ditch about six feet deep at the end of the airfield … usually an airfield ends for some reason otherwise they'd make it bigger … it's either a hedge or a ditch! (Flight Lieutenant Allan Wright, interview 10/06/2002)

After returning to Biggin, Wright tore a strip or two off the inexperienced Duke.

He saw something that I didn't see ... I think to his starboard and going down, and he obviously thought 'I'm either going now or never, and I must get the bugger' you see. Forgetting his duty. I know I gave him a terrific [rocketing] when I got back! ... He was a very keen fellow was Neville – and did wonders later on – but this was about his first or second operational flight with the squadron. (Flight Lieutenant Allan Wright, interview 10/06/2002)

The only confirmed victory for 92 was, characteristically, from Rankin, flying R6890. His victim was an Me109F of I/JG52 whose pilot managed to bail out into the sea off Dover.

While 92 and 74 had busied themselves in the skies above the Channel, Sergeant Rains and the team had spent the time with 609 squadron back at Biggin, the purpose being to allow the squadron to gain some experience of their newly acquired cannon armament. Like the other squadrons had found, the cannons were OK when they worked, but so often they didn't! Thus throughout the afternoon Davies and his comrades, along with 609's armourers, had the frustrations of a number of stoppages and the return of some equally frustrated pilots. The squadron's operations record book pointed to a pattern to these problems:

Owing to Circus 12 being at 06:30, before the return from Fighter Nights, 92 had to take 609's place, and had an exciting time. All the flying 609 did was to shoot off their new cannons in to the sea off Beachy Head, frequently finding that the port cannon didn't work. (609 Squadron Operational Record Book, 14 June 1941)

Chapter Eight

Sun, Sweeps and the Station Commander

Glorious Summer:

Favourable weather on 16 June saw all squadrons of the Wing deployed. In the morning, from 0500 hours onwards, 609 sent sections of four to cover convoys in the Channel before being released in the afternoon. After breakfast, the squadron was also encouraged by their 'spy' to attend some educational events including a film about the new dinghies that were to be issued to fighter pilots.

To date they had been reliant only on their Mae Wests, the speed of the motor launches and other passing seaborne traffic, and, of course, the grace of God. Now they were to be issued with a small one-man rubber dinghy that included survival equipment. By some miracle the boffins had also managed to fit all this into the space of a parachute seat cushion that would replace the existing one. Some of 609's pilots also received further education as to the dangers of sleeping out at dispersal in the now suddenly hot weather – a lesson learned through sore and tight-skinned faces!

As the sun baked a number of 609's pilots, over at 92's dispersal the ground staff were similarly trying to come to terms with the changed climate as they readied the aircraft for another sortie. Perched on the starboard wing of Kingcome's aircraft – QJ-F (R6908) – Davies watched the bowser as it picked its way amongst the gaggle of 'A' flight's aircraft that waited outside dispersal like a flock of thirsty sparrows. Periodically he would hear the shout from the attendant crews and then the chugging and clicking of the pumps as they dispensed another eighty-five gallons of 100 octane.

A fitter leaned over the nose and unclipped the earthing strap from an exhaust stub, handing it down to the bowser crew. He waved them away before using the L-shaped spanner to secure the brass filler cap firmly in place. The wings were hot from the sun; Davies could feel them through the seat of his overalls. As he shifted around he became aware of Campbell handing up a 20mm drum magazine. He turned and pulled it up over the leading edge. Though it was now somewhat routine, Davies made deliberate his checking of the drum and its fitting to the cannon. Sergeant Rains had taught them all to be methodical in their armament duties, and the 20mm seemed still to require that extra care in handling.

With the bulged panel in place, he glanced over to the other wing where the other two armourers were doing the same. Across the flight, a corporal fitter was signalling to someone to shut down an engine, spotting an oil leak blowing back from just behind the propeller. Perhaps a CSU (Constant Speed Unit) problem, he thought, smiling at his own attempt of a wider knowledge of things he had heard others talk about.

He pushed the screwdriver back into the side pocket of his overalls, alongside the small wooden-handled cocking spanner, and slid down from the wing. He ducked under the wing and made one last visual check that all the underside panels for the Hispanos and Brownings were secure. Campbell was now standing by the muzzle of one Hispano, making sure that the cannon's fairing was also correctly aligned and secure. 'Just have a look-see of this, Taff,' he said. The pair always liked to work a cross-check as a point of safety. Davies gave it the once-over, taking out a screwdriver to check the small screw at the underside of the barrel fairing where it joined the leading edge. As a last check, he inspected the ejector chutes for any foreign objects that could impair the discharge of empty cartridges and links. Across the peri-track other crews were now congregating, their work completed for the moment. Like other armourers there was now little to do except prepare re-arms for the returning aircraft, if a quick turnaround was needed.

Kingcome was one of the squadron's stalwarts. Indeed, many considered that Brian Fabris Kingcome *was* 92 Squadron. He had been posted to the squadron as a flight commander in May 1940 and had remained ever since, almost as a symbol of 92's enduring spirit in the face of adversity. Tall and lean, with a strong jaw and deep, piercing eyes, Kingcome was a commanding presence, noted for his dry and quick-witted sense of humour. In the air, there were few of his equal. Yet Kingcome was not one to keep score – it was not the point. The important thing was getting the job done, a team effort with common objectives. Trying to notch up a personal tally was inviting oneself to get distracted and perhaps follow an enemy aircraft you had damaged to make sure of the kill. That's when you got careless. So while some measured Brian's ability by the score they kept on his behalf – at least of the ones he bothered to tell about – it was his leadership that stood him apart from the crowd. For the squadron, Kingcome was held in deep regard both for his skill as a fighter pilot and a leader, and for his clear commitment to those around him on the ground and in the air. Irrespective of rank, if a person had earned Kingcome's respect, it was remembered and paid back in equal amounts. As Johnnie Johnston concluded:

The man that I would have flown anywhere with or behind was Brian Kingcome.
He was the best leader, not only in the air but on the ground. Brian was exceptional.

There was something about him ... couldn't have had a nicer man. Brian [was]
the daddy of them all. There was nobody like [him], I would have followed him
to Hell and back. I met up with him in later in Italy, I was a lowly squadron
leader, he a group captain. He introduced me to a group of officers – none under
Brian's rank – as Squadron Leader Johnston, 'better known to me as sergeant pilot
Johnston' ... and he meant it: it was the best way. We'd been together on three
units when I was commissioned but he remembered me better like that ... from the
same squadron. (Sergeant Walter 'Johnnie' Johnston, interview 14/9/2002)

There was also a new face down at the dispersals – the recently appointed station
commander, Group Captain Philip Barwell DFC. 'Dickie' Barwell was something
of model commander amongst operational pilots, having been at the 'sharp end'
since the start of hostilities in September 1939. Unusually he had received his
flying training while with an operational squadron – No.19 – rather than being
first posted to a training unit, and had been considered so highly as to have flown
at the Hendon Air Pageant of 3 July 1926, before officially receiving his wings.
This temporary award, on this occasion secured with pins, was made permanent
two months later.

His periodic flying assessments bore witness to his prowess, with eighteen
of the twenty-three being 'exceptional'. By 1939 he had risen to command 46
Squadron and earned one of the first DFCs of the war after a number of successful
operations, notably that of 21 October when they had downed six enemy aircraft
for no loss, Barwell himself claiming one and one shared destroyed. After further
promotions and postings he finally had arrived at Biggin on 2 June 1941.

It was unusual for those of his rank to take an active flying role in operations
but from the start 'Dickie' proved himself to be no ordinary station commander in
this and every other respect. His commitment to operational flying came from the
belief that this kept him tuned in to the experiences of those under his command.
However, this brought him into conflict with the AOC of 11 Group, Air Vice
Marshal Leigh-Mallory. While Leigh-Mallory considered station commanders to
be too valuable to risk their loss on operations, Dickie and others, such as Victor
Beamish at Kenley, argued that it was only through continued experience that
they could adequately represent their pilots and speak authoritatively at tactical
conferences. As Dickie's younger brother, Wing Commander Eric Barwell DFC
recounted:

Leigh-Mallory told him that he didn't agree with station commanders flying on
operations and my brother argued with him and said 'well if I'm not flying on
operations how can I raise my voice at all at conferences?' He saw it as absolutely

essential to do so, and others like Victor Beamish thought the same. So although he refused to lead the Wing at any time, he nearly always flew number two to the Wing leader. (Wing Commander Eric Barwell, interview 27/6/2002)

So now the station commander was already becoming a noticeable presence around the peri-track, and the air of confidence that he brought to Biggin influenced all: pilots, officers, NCOs and other ranks alike. Whether you were the wing commander flying, a squadron leader, a sergeant pilot or an AC2, Barwell was generous with his time. Before long he would be known and liked by all at Biggin. Starting on 16 June he began to take time away from flying a desk to 'keeping his hand in' in the broadest sense of the term.

The battles of 16 and 17 June were hard fought with a number of encounters with the enemy. As was becoming routine a number of light bombers were escorted into France with the docks at Boulogne and Cherbourg being the targets on these two days. Drawing up heavy opposition, Fighter Command – including the squadrons from Biggin – managed to beat off repeated attacks by gaggles of Me109s. On the first day 92 and 74 accounted for five destroyed and a further four probables for no loss. Rankin caught one unawares but was unable to see its demise, though of this he was certain. Kingcome too had been successful and, lighting a post-op cigarette, cheekily remarked to Davies and Chiefy Stewart, 'all this without one stoppage!' Over at 74 Squadron, John Mungo-Park counted two Me109Fs destroyed.

The following day 92 Squadron were detailed as top cover while 74 and 609 flanked the group of Beauforts as they made their way to the target. Spotting a group of eight Me109Fs, Malan took a section of 74 Squadron into attack but they half-rolled away below 10,000 feet. A number of individual combats ensued with subsections of the Wing. Banking sharply left after attempting to swat an Me109 off the tail of another Spitfire, Malan caught another in the turn. With two short bursts of cannon and machine gun fire the Messerschmitt's port wing crumpled and the aircraft gyrated feverishly in palls of black smoke. Ninety-two Squadron came face to face with twenty Me109Fs. Allan Wright and Jamie Rankin both claimed probables. The boys at 609 were kept equally busy, claiming three destroyed off Le Touquet at around 1930 hours. The drinks were on Keith Ogilvie, John Bisdee and de Spirlet that night.

For a month that had started slowly, June was now becoming a hot time in every sense. Dawn till dusk, the hours seemed to pass like an express train. While early mornings saw preparations in full swing by first light, one or all of the squadrons of the Wing were at various states of readiness throughout the day and evening.

As Davies found, punctuality could ensure a properly digestible breakfast first thing in the morning, but as the day progressed the usual breaks for lunch became more snatches of 'char and wads' courtesy of the NAAFI wagon. In amongst seeing the aircraft prepared and re-arms at the ready, work now began to be pushed into the evenings. For Davies this still meant firing at the butts until the early hours and spending time maintaining the guns in accordance with the required periods of inspection. For others, the airframe and engine inspections and repairs lasted long into the night. Uppermost was the need to keep the kites on line, and the commitment of the crews to this duty saw them working round the clock when that little bit of extra effort was needed for tomorrow. They could explain their commitment in many ways but most often they did it for 'their' pilot, their squadron, and for Biggin on the Bump.

As June ran out its last ten days the pace never eased. With the improved weather, late sunsets and Greenwich's clocks at double BST, there was ample opportunity for the Wing to fly as many operations as daylight would permit.

The 21st proved indicative of the days and months to come. It started early with the usual convoy patrols in the tepid air of the morning. By midday the temperature had risen steadily and the crews at readiness tried to relax and keep cool as best they could. The armchairs were pulled out of the flight hut and in and around them the pilots lounged in their shirtsleeves. Some tried to read. Others lay out catching the warmth of the sun, with silk scarves, newspapers and whatever else that came to hand draped over their faces to afford some protection.

Out at the aircraft, working in this heat was similarly uncomfortable. Regulations were out the window and the airmen worked steadily to complete the turnaround for the afternoon's operations wearing their overalls undone and tied at the waist. The flesh was at the mercy of the oil, the grease and the glycol, and the ragged, unseen locking wire – but at least they were able to work. Between jobs they rested under the wings of the aircraft or in the shade of the blast-pens and workshops.

In the early afternoon the Wing flew as part of Circus 16 against the airfields at St Omer/ Longuenesse and Fort Rouge. As the aircraft landed in, the ground crews rushed to prepare them for the next operation. Circus 17, an escort for six Blenheims of 110 Squadron to bomb Desvres airfield, was scheduled for 1600 hours. Time was tight.

It was probably on this day – or one like it – that Davies and the Wing Leader met eye-to-eye for the first time. Malan landed and taxied quickly towards 92 Squadron's dispersal. Davies, having checked re-arms for the returning aircraft, stood watching as Malan taxied straight into the bay, swung round and switched off. As the propeller swung to a stop, Malan pulled back the hood, dropped the door off its latch and beckoned to Davies:

I'd been delivering some re-arms for the 20mm cannon and Sailor Malan came back off this sortie where they had been escorting bombers. They'd all been up at altitude and Malan had used up his oxygen. Well he came into the bay, turned round, and I was there on my own … and he shouted 'change my oxygen bottle, airman … immediately. I want to get off as quick as I can'. Well, I'd never changed an oxygen bottle and thought 'God, what am I to do?' He didn't get out – he sat in the cockpit waiting. There was always spare ammunition and oxygen that we stacked in readiness for quick turn-around. I'd seen the riggers … the airframe fitters change a bottle. I thought I dare not say that I couldn't do it, so I managed to get the panel off and got the old bottle out, and I was just about to put the new one in when the rigger came. He said 'what's up Taff?' I said that he'd ordered me to change the oxygen and I was determined to do what I could. 'Great' he said and took over but showed me how to do it as he completed the job. So in the future I knew what to do. It was all a matter of minutes cos with Sailor, he knew how long it [a job] should take and if you weren't on the ball, he wouldn't put you on a charge, but he'd give you a right [rocketing]. Boy was I relieved when that fitter came! (LAC Raymond Davies, interview 28/12/2001)

At 1555 hours the Wing took off on Circus 17, reaching the target area around 1630 hours. Stacked up in fours between 15 and 18,000 feet, the Wing readied itself for the oncoming Me109s. Malan, with Pilot Officer Sandman of 74 Squadron as his wing man, attacked an Me109F as it headed for Boulogne. Closing to fifty yards, he delivered a hail of cannon and machine gun fire at his adversary. The enemy aircraft immediately burst into flames with oil and debris flying back at Malan's own aircraft. A moment later, he engaged a further aircraft at 12,000 feet off Le Touquet, again closing to fifty yards to deal an equally telling blow. Covering the return, 609 squadron's afternoon was as eventful.

On approaching the French coast, return journey, between Hardelot and Le Touquet, Yellow Section saw 4 Me109F flying parallel. As they converged, leader (Flying Officer Ogilvie) turned head on and fired, this starting a general dogfight. Ogilvie got behind one e/a and brought it down to Le Touquet aerodrome 'in full view of the ground staff' as the papers added. The pilot baled out. Sergeant Boyd fired at another which overshot its dive, this spiralled down from 3,000 feet to crash in a field – Sergeant Boyd's first victory, and a popular one. Pilot Officer Ortmans, after shaking a 109 off his tail, sighted another in a dogfight with a Spitfire. He delivered two beam attacks, and the e/a dived at 45 degrees streaming black smoke. Finding his engine vibrating, he broke off, thinking there was another e/a behind. Meanwhile Flying Officer Ogilvie, starting for home, was attacked by another 4 Me 109F which was very fast and could only be shaken off by violent evasive action. After being hit in the wing by two bullets, he spied what he thought was Dungeness, then found to his horror that it was Boulogne. Crossing the sands at 1,000 feet, he met his friends again and only got rid of them by making use of the sun and the welcome haze over the sea. All this time he was in effect without ammunition, as he couldn't make his guns work. 'I made a slight error in compass reading', he said, 'and gave those Luftwaffe boys entirely the wrong impression'. The only other pilot to be engaged was Blue 4, Pilot Officer Offenberg. Flying at 15,000 feet inland of Boulogne, he saw an Me109 streaming glycol, and another (F) flying parallel with him below. He chased this one to Le Touquet and back, skimming the treetops, and once they met head on, both firing. Eventually with petrol and ammunition running low, he dodged back to England when e/a wasn't looking. (609 Squadron Operational Record Book, 21 June 1941)

Further north, a lone Hurricane pilot from 257 Squadron was jumped by three Me109s. Taking off at 1330 hours on a routine patrol, Bob Tuck, ex-flight commander of 92 squadron and now CO of 257, had steered a course that took him one hundred miles out from the coast. Without warning cannon shells ripped into the wings and fuselage. In those agonising seconds between panic and survival instinct, he was convinced that his time had come. All the chances and luck that had been with him throughout Dunkirk and the Battle of Britain had now been used up.

Hurling the aircraft round, a 109 passed close underneath him and, pushing the stick forward, Tuck managed to get a bead on the enemy's canopy. A quick squeeze of the gun button and the Me109 seemed to rear up before plunging uncontrolled towards the sea. There were others and in the turn Bob locked onto another of his assailants. With his vision greying out and g-force pushing him down into his seat, they were now less than fifty feet off the water. As the enemy eased off his bank, Tuck gave him a two-second burst of 20mm and sent him straight in – the Hurricane flying through the resulting spray. Head-to-toe now with the remaining Me109, Tuck coaxed the last of ounce of tenacity out of his charge and sent the enemy trailing glycol back towards the French/ Belgian coast.

The Hurricane's engine was now missing badly to, at times, the point of complete stop. There was no throttle control, the temperatures and pressures were climbing and the airspeed was dropping steadily. Drenched in glycol and oil, Bob undid his harness and reluctantly took to the silk. A coal barge out of Gravesend picked him out of his dinghy a few hours later. Two destroyed and one damaged.

The 22nd June was equally contested, with significant claims for the Biggin Hill Wing. During the escort of twelve Blenheims to the marshalling yards at

Hazebrouck (Circus 18), Blue leader of 609 Squadron (Flight Lieutenant Bisdee) spotted nine Me109Fs flying down the coast from Dunkirk. Of these Bisdee shot down one at point-blank range with machine guns, and Sergeant Rigler brought a second down, both of these aircraft failing to make any evasive manoeuvres. Jean Offenberg, flying as Red 2, damaged an Me109E during a zero-feet chase across the sand dunes off Gravelines before needing to evade the attentions of an Me109F.

Yellow section was bounced crossing the coast while covering the withdrawal. Pilot Officer de Spirlet was shot down but baled out at 1,000 feet. His rescue proved somewhat eventful, having managed to fall out of his dinghy twice and then being competed for by both Royal Navy and RAF launches – the latter finally being successful much to de Spirlet's disgust as they had run out of rum! It was, however, Tommy Rigler's day, having destroyed a further two Me109Es to add to his 'F' after a frantic exchange with seven.

Circus 19 was flown to Choques/Bethune in the early afternoon of the following day with significant successes achieved by 92 Squadron. Flying close escort, Kingaby watched apprehensively as first the English, then the French coasts disappeared in the haze behind them. With no auxiliary fuel, thirty miles inside the French coast usually called for some creative throttle management and gauge watching, followed by landing at a forward base such as Manston. Bethune was fifty miles inland. At just after 1400 hours the squadron encountered numerous Me109Fs around the Bethune area.

Leading the squadron into attack, Rankin sent a first down in flames, followed quickly by a second. As the engagement tumbled into terse gyrating actions, Rankin severely damaged a third – though personally he felt it was a 'cert' – Kingaby's cannon shells ripped the wing off another Me109, and Phil Archer sent a further enemy aircraft spiralling earthwards. Neville Duke, flying as Blue 2, saw an Me109 coming head-on and succeeded in scoring hits with cannon and machine guns. The enemy's aircraft passed over Duke's head belching black and white smoke from the engine. Duke claimed it as 'damaged'. Sergeant Bowen-Morris went to the aid of another Spitfire but was himself shot down. As Kingaby recalled:

It was in this scrap that I lost the first of my sergeant pals – he saw a 109 on the tail of a Spitfire and went down to get it. The Spitfire got away OK but Bowen was left with five other 109s to deal with. After a stout fight he was badly wounded and was shot down. It was tough break to buy it after helping an unknown comrade out of trouble. I am glad to say that he was repatriated …, and still retains the spirit that made 92 tick. The show concluded successfully on the whole – all the bombers were brought back and the day's score showed a ten to one profit against the Huns, of which 92 had bagged five. I pushed off on leave that afternoon, but felt very sorry that I had lost such a companion as 'Bowie'. (Flight Sergeant Don Kingaby, unpublished autobiography)

Rankin landed in at Biggin to much celebration. As the propeller milled to a stop he jumped down from the aircraft to his awaiting ground crew. Kingaby, Archer and the other pilots joined him and soon the air was filled with adrenalin-fuelled excitement and illustrative hand movements as each told his part of the interlocking jumble of encounters. For a moment all work halted as ground and aircrew alike revelled in the successes of the day. It was as much a victory for those on the ground as in the air. Victory, however, was edged with sadness as they all tried to piece together what had happened to 'Bowie', his crew clinging to the hope that perhaps he had cheated death and was now a PoW.

Later in the evening, the Wing Leader led 92 as part of yet another operation – Circus 20. Crossing the French coast at 2020 hours, Malan climbed the Wing into its position as high cover at 27,000 feet. At this height, even during the summer months, it was bitterly cold, and the pilots all adopted various ways of dressing to combat the unforgiving climate. Many, like Malan, flew with sea-boot stockings as well as long knitted tubes that stretched up over the thighs. Three pairs of gloves were the norm: a silk inner, knitted outer and a final leather gauntlet.

Chipping the frost from the inside of the windshield, Malan caught sight of a formation of fifteen to twenty Me109s below at 20,000 feet, coming out of Boulogne. Radioing the squadrons into attack, Malan wheeled over into a dive, his keen eyes immediately selecting one of the formation of black-crossed machines. A quick burst of cannon and machine gun fire and the enemy aircraft simply disintegrated and Malan collected some damage to his port wing from the debris. Rankin and 92 Squadron hurtled down alongside the Wing Leader and Sergeant 'Chem' Le Cheminant caught another of the enemy formation. Malan selected another that was climbing up sun and delivered a characteristically knockout blow from fifty yards. So ended 23 June, with 92 Squadron claiming five destroyed, two probables and one damaged, and Malan claiming a further two destroyed for the Wing. Bowen-Morris was the only loss from Biggin.

Further successes by the Wing on the 24th – including two destroyed for 92, three and one probables for 609 and 74 respectively, and one destroyed for Malan – were followed by yet more sweeps to Hazebrouck (Circus 22) and St Omer/ Longuenesse airfield (Circus 23) on 25 June. An early briefing and breakfast saw the Wing off at 0910, flying its usual position as high cover at 30,000 feet.

The sun's radiant heat had yet to warm even the lower altitudes as Malan led Biggin's squadrons towards the French coast. Tucked in as number two to Mike Robinson was Group Captain Barwell, flying one of 609's newly allocated Spitfire

Vbs (W3365). At height 609 saw very little: a German convoy, but no enemy aircraft. In a curved approach over the target area, Malan brought 92 and 74 down to 28,000 feet and spotted two Me109Fs 3,000 feet below.

As he brought his section into attack two more Me109s came in fast but Malan was quick in the turn and managed to latch onto the rear of the pair. He opened fire with cannons but found his reflector sight malfunctioning. Keeping with one of the enemy he eventually managed to open up with machine guns, making the Me109 smoke heavily before having to break off due to the attentions of another. As this third Me109 flashed past Malan saw an explosion to his left and about a mile away – it was his first assailant. Allan Wright and Neville Duke dived on a couple of Me109Fs over St Omer, Allan getting hits on the enemy's coolant system before it crashed into the ground. Later Duke became embroiled in a dogfight and gave a burst of cannon and machine guns to an Me109F from astern. His combat report was as follows:

> *Combat Report for 25th June: Time 1245 hours off Dunkirk:*
> *When at sea level flying west of Dunkirk, I looked back and saw six Me109s having a dog-fight with two Spitfires. I turned and joined in and managed to get on the tail of one Me109F which was on the tail of a Spitfire. I opened fire with cannons and machine-guns and gave him two bursts and closed to 50 yards, when I had to pull away as I got into his slipstream. I came back on top of him and saw the pilot sitting quietly without looking around or up and proceeded to go down in a gentle dive from 2,000 feet, and hit the ground just east of Dunkirk and blow up.*
> (Pilot Officer Neville Duke, Combat Report, quoted in Franks, 1995, p. 16)

Another Me109 fell to 92 Squadron during Circus 23, flown in the late afternoon/early evening. It was largely uneventful, with only sporadic encounters with the enemy. In view of the great efforts that were being made at Biggin, the squadrons were stood down at 1930 hours for a well-earned evening off.

Some maintenance continued after dinner, as the Wing was required for duties in the morning. At 1135 hours the Wing crossed the coast at Mardyck, Malan climbing 92 and 74 squadrons as target support between 17,000 and 20,000 feet, with 609 perched high above Gravelines at 27,000 feet. As was becoming routine, the Me109s were waiting for them. Rankin counted twenty-four coming from St Omer as he led 92 in amongst them. Momentarily blacking out as he brought the Spitfire over into a dive, Rankin came to a few hundred yards behind an Me109E, diving towards the coast. Opening up with cannons and machine guns, he watched as the enemy machine first showed a plume of glycol, then turned over on its back before smashing into the ground some ten miles inland of Dunkirk–Gravelines.

Allan Wright too brought 'Satan III' (W3265) to bear on an Me109E and saw it go in somewhere near Dunkirk. All told the Wing accounted for three destroyed and two damaged – all good old ninety-two's. Dickie Barwell was amongst the celebrants once he too had landed in from the operation.

The routine of the day-in-day-out operations did little to prepare Biggin for 27 June. The morning had started with a rather brief roadstead, with 609 and 92 protecting a handful of Blenheims that were detailed to bomb shipping off Calais. When it became apparent that Circus 25 was to be an operation against a steelworks at Lille, the mood was black. Lille was far inland – too far on eighty gallons as some of 609 protested – and thus stretched the Spitfire's capability to the limit. Further inland meant watching your fuel gauges and making prompt decisions to disengage from combat. Further inland meant further to come back. To make matters worse, the Luftwaffe continued to harass the squadrons as they withdrew, knowing full well that they would be now short of petrol. As Alec 'Joe' Atkinson of 609 Squadron recalled:

We regarded Lille as a bit far. Managing fuel wasn't very easy because you'd get to Lille and then you'd go back towards the coast. Then you'd hear them saying '100 plus bandits over the coast', and you looked at your petrol gauge and there was not much left so it wasn't very funny. On a number of occasions I landed at a forward airfield, Hawkinge or Manston with very little [fuel] to spare! (Pilot Officer Alec 'Joe' Atkinson, interview 28/03/2004)

Whether such factors contributed to any uneasiness during the operation or to its disastrous outcome cannot be known. Yet the returning pilots were clear that this had been one of the toughest.

The greatest blow came in the loss of three popular and able pilots from 74 Squadron. At their dispersal the crews waited for news that perhaps they had managed to get down at Manston or the like, or had just dead-sticked into some field on the south coast somewhere. As the time wore on, there was no hope left. Pilot Officer 'Sandy' Sandman – who had flown as Malan's number two on many occasions – along with Sergeant Clive Hilken had both failed to return. The CO, Squadron Leader John Colin Mungo-Park DFC, was also missing presumed killed. He was twenty-three.

The final days of June saw more sweeps across the Channel of a pattern that would be repeated for many months to come. The Wing had achieved some phenomenal successes during what was to be the start of one of the most hectic periods in its history. As the operation to Lille had shown, these incursions into enemy territory were hazardous and often costly affairs. To take such undertakings in one's stride was to brace against a whirlwind: it only took a moment's lapse of concentration, one second away from living at the edge of your wits, and you could lose everything. And there was only so much that one could endure. The ground crews fought long and hard throughout the night to get as many aircraft serviceable for the next day. In those closing days of the month, operational losses and damage began to take their toll and sometimes the squadrons flew at less than full strength. On the 28th, 609 could only muster nine for Circus 26. On another, 74 Squadron could find only six. But for those at Biggin – like so many other fighter stations on that south coast – there was to be no let up. Not now: the summer of '41 was really only just beginning.

Chapter Nine

Keeping Up the Pressure

Through Adversity:

The loss of Mungo-Park weighed heavily on the morale of 74 Squadron and the whole of Biggin Hill. John had been with the squadron since the beginning of hostilities. He had flown cover over Dunkirk, attempting to ward off the hordes of enemy aircraft that were trying to get through to the beaches to prevent evacuation. Throughout the Battle of Britain, he and 74 had been in the thick of the fighting and they had acquitted themselves well. He had been a popular successor to Malan as the squadron's CO, despite now being somewhat tired and long overdue a rest from operations. A bar to his DFC was gazetted weeks after his failure to return from the Lille operation on 27 June. For Biggin, it was the loss of its first squadron CO since Fighter Command had gone on the offensive. By and large, Biggin had been very successful in the first half of 1941 and the development of the tactical uses of Wing formations were in no small way down to the likes of Malan, Rankin, Robinson and Mungo-Park.

Kingaby returned to Biggin on 1 July, having had a well-earned seven days leave. The squadron was away with 609 on what turned out to be an event-free sweep between Gravelines and Étaples but returned by midday. In the afternoon, they were released, giving Don time to catch up on the events of the last week.

Later some of the crews made it round to the 'Old Jail' at Downe, a small, welcoming pub along one of the winding lanes round the east side of the airfield. Like the Kings Arms at Leaves Green, it was a popular haunt for airmen and NCOs. At first visit you had to be a bit of navigator to get the correct course as the lanes looked much the same as each other around this side of Biggin, and the trees reached their boughs across the roads as if in a protective embrace.

In the summer, cycling along under these verdant canopies you could lose yourself watching the light pick out the holes in the cover and dance merry patterns on the ground below. In the evening with the blackout, returning from a watering sortie at the Old Jail called for precise dead reckoning as one dicey navigator could put you on the way to Cudham, or on a long convoluted route back to camp through Leaves Green – that was if you did not try the cross-country route.

Time off was so much like another life. One played out in stark contrast to the 'hours on' when you stood face-to-face with fear, with sadness, and with death. So too for the ground crews who could one minute be sharing a joke, a chat, and with some pilots a pint and a cigarette. Then to be easing them out of their shattered cockpits, cold, fatigued and in pain – the colour drained pallid from their face by an agonising wound they had nursed back from mid-Channel. As Brian Kingcome commented, it was:

> *The strange double life, each one curiously detached from the other. One moment high above the earth, watching a sunrise not yet visible below, killing and avoiding being killed; and the next chatting with the locals over a pint of beer in a cosy country pub as casually as though we had just stopped off the six o'clock from Waterloo after a day in the City. Occasionally a local commenting critically on the aerial activity he had witnessed that day as though he were discussing his local football team. And the next morning back to the unreal world and the twisting smoke trails at angels two-five … Of course there were intensely sad moments as well as intensely exciting ones. I lost many old friends as well as making new ones, and the worst part was watching them die, spiralling down with a smudge of smoke, or breaking up, watching for the parachute to blossom, the relief when it did, the sickness when it didn't.* (Flight Lieutenant Brian Kingcome, quoted in Kingcome, 1999, p. 185)

On 2 July, the Wing returned to Lille as escort cover to twelve Blenheims on yet another Circus (number 29), a power station being the target. Malan led with the 'Tigers', with Rankin and 92 following, and 609 in their usual place as top cover. Communications from control indicated that the Blenheims were five minutes early and so Malan attempted to close the gap. However both Rankin and Robinson misinterpreted the signal to mean that *they* were early and thus instructed their respective squadrons to ease back on the throttle.

As the familiar sight of Dunkirk came into view Malan received a further communication that the bombers were now seven minutes early and that the cover wing should proceed with all speed to give support. By this time the three squadrons had become separated, with 74 reaching with haste towards the target area, 92 lagging but attempting to make up the distance, and 609 proceeding with similar urgency but somewhat remote from the others.

Then the Me109s came down in pairs and fours, making use of their speed in the dive to punch repeatedly at 74 and zoom climb back to height in preparation for another. So critical were these timings that Malan and 74 were largely alone in this whirling dogfight, attempting to stay covering the bombers and repeatedly turning on each incoming attack. Five miles to the rear, Rankin and 92 Squadron could do little other than catch the peripheries of this action but soon became engaged as they covered the withdrawal. Kingaby, flying W3249, was quick to react:

… I had one of the luckiest shots at a Hun I have ever had. We were just crossing the French coast on the way home when two aircraft dived down in front of my section. I thought for a moment that they were Hurricanes and let them go. Then I realised that they were 109s and that they formed part of the Hun's old decoy trick. I looked above me and sure enough there was a small bunch of 109s with another two diving down in front of me to try it again. I knew that if I dived down after them the rest would come tearing down on my tail, but I decided to take a chance this time, and took a squirt at the first one. I broke away and climbed immediately to throw the 109's pals off the scent without looking to see what had happened to him. I hadn't expected to hit him, as it had been such a hurried shot, and I was amazed when my No.2 called up on the R/t to say that I had got two of them. Apparently I hit the first one and the second one had collided with him. I looked down and sure enough there were the two parachutes and then two great splashes in the water far below as the remains of their machines hit the drink. When I returned to base and checked up on my ammunition I found that I had only given a three second burst of cannon and machine gun to get the two Huns! (Flight Sergeant Don Kingaby, unpublished memoirs)

Two other sergeant pilots from 92 returned with victories confirmed. Both Sergeant Dave Lloyd and Sergeant Pietrasiak claimed an Me109 each. The squadron's luck was holding and they had continued to have the greater successes of the three squadrons of the Wing. Now at the beginning of July, 92 Squadron were credited with approximately 165 confirmed enemy aircraft destroyed. Seemingly, though, the frequency of losses tempered these successes.

On 3 July, during Circuses 30 and 31 to St Omer and Hazebrouck, another two pilots were posted missing: Flight Lieutenant Xavier de Montbron from 92 and another from 74. For the second day running Davies saw Kingaby back in at Biggin with his gun canvas patches shot through, claiming a probable. Over at 609's dispersal, Mike Robinson had drawn first blood of the month for the squadron, having ripped the wing of an Me109F with his cannon fire. Malan too had been in action.

There was one last sortie of the day: one hell of a party down at the Old Jail. Under its low beams vast quantities of Pommard were consumed and 609's Pilot Officer MacKenzie was allegedly debagged by four women. 'Vicki' Ortmans took the party out into the beer garden by riding through it on a carthorse and disappearing into the night. He arrived the next morning somewhat the worse for wear but with a hare that he had managed to shoot.

The following day – 4 July – 74 lost another pilot. This time it was during a return operation to Choques. Biggin reverberated to the sound of the Merlins as the three squadrons lifted off the grass and across the valley, climbing into the afternoon sun. Davies stood with Campbell and Woods watching the light glinting off the Spitfires' wings as they gradually disappeared into the heat haze.

The three sat down in the grass, feeling quite relieved to see the squadron get off OK. Davies lay back, feeling the grass under him as he stretched out. As he closed his eyes he could have easily drifted off to sleep. What with being on since first light and the late nights he and the team had been spending on the firing butts, he only been grabbing a few hours. Now with quiet returning to Biggin and the warmth of the sun it was so tempting to slip under some shade somewhere and get some kip. Still, the kites would be back soon.

Healey sauntered over asking if anyone had any 'shrapnel' – loose change – as those wonderful NAAFI girls were on the way round. Davies sat up and rifled around in his overalls for any coins, fancying one of the small cakes that sometimes accompanied the great mugs of tea. He accompanied Eddie over to the E-pen where the van had pulled up and joined the queue. There was the usual idle chatter – the debriefing of the previous night's 'ops' to the Kings Arms, the Old Jail, the Queens Head and the Bell in Bromley. Others made comment about the 'old man Groupie' and the regularity of his 'local' flying.

High above the French coast, Barwell was once again 'local flying' as number two to Malan, as the latter led the Wing as escort cover to twelve Blenheims bombing the Kuhlmann chemical works and power station at Bethune. He had been with 'Sailor' on the previous day when Malan had damaged two Me109Es, sticking to Malan's every wild and yet calculated manoeuvre. Now, on the 4th, the situation was every bit as intense. Barwell's combat report details the actions that took place, and how easy it was to become separated from your leader:

On the 4th July in the vicinity of Bethune while flying as No.2 to W/C Malan, who was leading the Wing, we attacked some 109s. As W/C Malan was engaging one 109 another passed beneath him and climbed away from us to our right. I turned for this E/A and got a quarter deflection attack from underneath with about a 2-second burst at a range of approximately 300 yards. The 109 emitted black smoke and petrol vapour and went down in a dive. I lost sight of the A/C, as I concentrated on reforming into my position behind W/C Malan, but he confirmed that it was probably destroyed.

Shortly after this, while still in position as No.2 to W/C Malan, and while he was turning to port to attack another 109, I sighted a 109 almost behind us and slightly to starboard diving and opening fire. I had no time to warn W/C Malan but turned toward this E/A which then turned and dived away. I then found I had lost sight of W/C Malan and could see no other friendly A/C. My height was then about 8,000 ft. and I proceeded to weave my way home. (Group Captain Barwell, Combat Report, 4 July 1941)

Barwell was wise to weave his way back to Biggin, keeping a watchful eye on his rear quarter. Before long he became the attention of numerous enemy aircraft.

On the way back I was attacked on numerous occasions, firstly by single 109s and at one point as many as five. All I was able to do was to turn very quickly towards the attacks just before they got within firing range, and open fire myself with a short burst. I saw no results from my fire except in one case where I saw my bullets strike the E/A and a few small pieces break off. I had no time to watch for any further results.

Between Bethune and Gravelines my height varied between 8,000 ft down to 5,000 ft. At one time when I was rather hard pressed I managed to hide in cloud for a short time. I saw no friendly A/C until I was about 5 miles from Dover, when I had just been attacked for the final time from behind by a 109. (Group Captain Barwell, Combat Report, 4 July 1941)

Barwell claimed one probable and a damaged. Malan, having to fight his way out of similar 'scraps' managed to shoot down two 109s and damage a third. Flying as rear cover, 609 had equally intensive engagements with the enemy. Both Mike Robinson and Paul Richey claimed Me109Fs as damaged, but the squadron lost Flying Officer Keith Ogilvie over the target area. Ogilvie's loss was badly felt by 609 and Biggin, lightened only six weeks later by the news of his status as a prisoner of war announced in one of the usual gloating broadcasts of Lord Haw-Haw.

The usual unpopularity greeted the operations of 5, 6 and 7 July owing to the extreme ranges at which the Wing was required to fly. While the bomber groups involved in the circuses now, on occasions, saw the use of four-engined Short Stirlings with their increased bomb-loads and fuel capacities, the fighters still operated without any auxiliary fuel supplies. Thus for Circus 33 on 5 July, Biggin sent its squadrons to Lille as target support and caused much worry back at base when, after two hours, the ground crews still waited nervously for their comrades to return.

Usually they would see the 'kites' start to appear over Biggin after ninety minutes. Fuel shortages saw most queuing to land in at Detling and Manston. Circus 35 in the afternoon of the 6th – again to Lille – was a similarly close run thing, and on the 7th the long haul south to Albert was compounded by the bomber force being six minutes late, thus causing the fighters to waste precious petrol. Watching the gauges was critical, and even the veterans of the Wing were sometimes 'caught out' owing to the need to keep the Merlin at 'full chatt' during prolonged combat manoeuvres. On the afternoon of the 7th, while returning from the Kuhlmann works (Circus 38), it was Paul Richey's turn. As 609's Operational Record Book recalls:

> *Flight Lieutenant Richey had the misfortune to suffer his engine cutting in mid-Channel owing to lack of petrol. He glided in to Hawkinge, but had to make a forced landing owing to several Hurricanes coming in at the same time.* (609 Squadron Operational Record Book, July 1941)

The week was also 74 Squadron's last on the Biggin Wing, and it was with much sadness that the 'Tigers' departed. Lifting off from Gravesend in their replacement aircraft, the squadron made one last fly-past over Biggin Hill before disappearing northwards, bound for Acklington and 13 Group Fighter Command. So ended one of the busiest periods in their history. For their replacement – Desmond Sheen's 72 Squadron – there was no time for bedding in, and the 'new boys' had been re-equipped with 74 squadron's relinquished Spitfire Vbs. Operations continued as normal.

Gauge-watching & Bail-outs:
The experiences of one pilot of 92 Squadron during this period serve as a good example of the rapid introductions that many pilots had to their new squadron, particularly for those now on the offensive into France. Pilot Officer Percy Beake was posted to 92 on 27 June – the day of Mungo-Park's loss – having enquired about '*seeing some action again*'. As he recounts:

> *I was with 64 Squadron at Drem in Scotland and we had a squadron party … and I was sat next to the CO and I said 'oh God when are we going to get down and see some action'. I probably had had a fair bit to drink at that time, and the next day he called me, he said 'Beakey, you were talking to me about getting down and seeing some action, were you sober?' 'Well', I said, 'well yes I think so' and he said 'well where would you like to go, Biggin Hill or Manston?' I said 'Oh er … Biggin Hill I should think', and I was sent off there and then! I always remember*

that the chaps were saying 'Oh well, Beakey, you know you're going to take a dead man's shoes' and I said that I knew that, and I got my rail ticket and it happened to be number 0013 – I thought 'that's a good start!' Anyhow I was fairly tired by the time I got Biggin and I saw the CO. It happened to be Jamie Rankin and he had been supernumerary CO with 64 squadron when we were at Hornchurch, and he said to Don Kingaby, 'Oh he's all right, Don, put him in.' And I very soon found myself climbing into a Spitfire V that I hadn't flown, fitted with cannons that I hadn't seen, and I was off on an op! And I was asking the ground crew who were strapping me in, about the various knobs and tits! That's how I arrived at Biggin on the 27th June … My log book says the 26th was my last flight at Drem, and on the 27th I was on a circus operation over Lille at 29,000 feet. (Flying Officer Percy Beake, interview 2003)

Though an experienced, ex–Battle of Britain, pilot, once in the thick of the action, Beake also found it difficult to keep with his leader – on this occasion Brian Kingcome.

I lost Brian. He took me as his number two and I got a bit of a wigging when we got down, he said 'you must never lose me, you know' … but God knows what he did! I don't know but he disappeared somewhere! (Flying Officer Percy Beake, interview 2003)

Then eleven days later – now on 8 July – the 22-year-old Beake found himself grappling with his dinghy mid-Channel after a savage encounter with the Luftwaffe during Circus 39 to Lens.

We were doing an escort cover wing at 15,000 ft for four Stirlings bombing Lens and we were attacked by 109Fs on the way back just off Gravelines. My radiator was hit. The CO shouted 'break' but I think it was a little late or I was a bit slow to react maybe – I don't know. Anyhow, he got my radiator as I'd turned to the right, but I think seeing all the glycol pouring out he broke off the attack. So I was left there then having to basically decide whether I should turn back and chance landing in France … I was at 15,000 ft and did have a bit of height and so I decided that I'd get as far away from the French coast as I could and chance to my parachute and dinghy, which we had only recently been issued with dinghies … and it wasn't as comfortable as the cushion it replaced and I didn't care for it much until this occasion – then I never wanted to fly without one! I kept the engine going for a bit but it was getting very hot and so I throttled back and started gliding down. I kept looking at the water below, and it didn't look all that inviting, but happily it was early on a July morning and so I started giving m'aidez signals.

Now my first CO of 64 squadron had said that the best way of getting out of a Spitfire is to put the little flap down (the side door), stand up on your seat, sit on the flap and roll over. So I thought that's what I would do, so I took off my helmet so not to strangle myself with my r/t leads etc and put my flap down but I couldn't seem to stand up – I don't know if my legs were a bit rubbery or what – but anyhow I thought 'I've got to get out somehow' so I inverted the aircraft but didn't fall out at all cleanly. The cockpit was pretty small and I seemed to be jammed in by my parachute and so I kicked away with these rubbery legs and I must have put my hand on the rip cord because I can't remember feeling for that. I eventually kicked free but I think I pulled the rip-cord at the same time, rather than counting three as one had been taught so as to be clear and I thought 'Oh God, I must have been caught up on the tailplane or something' as I was brought up with a jerk. But no, I could see the aeroplane going down and everything worked OK and the canopy opened.

I hit the quick release box just as my feet touched the water and there must have been a slight breeze that blew the parachute away – that was another thing that sometimes happened, you'd get into the water and come up under the parachute and jolly well drown because you'd get all mixed up in the nylon lines and the parachute itself. But I had no problem and I found myself with the dinghy. I unrolled this as one had again been instructed to and very slowly opened the compressed air bottle so that the dinghy gradually took shape but what I didn't do was clamber in at the far end – at the other was a canvas box with a hole in it which filled with water and acted as a counter-balance to the body climbing in. I tipped the thing up and inverted it, then righted it and got in the prescribed way and quickly looked around for leaks. It was sitting very low and so I got out the hand pump and pumped away until it was nice and plump and then started bailing out all the water that I'd shipped! When you're down in the drink like that there are no markers to see any progress you might make or where you might be going, but it was fairly early morning and I could see the sun coming up in the East, so I pointed the dinghy away from that knowing that I wanted to go west to get to land and I started paddling just with my hands. I'd hoped that I was making a little bit of ground, but mainly it was to keep warm and avoid hypothermia. But I wasn't awfully careful doing this and scooped quite a bit of water into the dinghy, so I alternated between paddling and then scooping out any water.

I heard then Merlin engines and there were a couple of Spitfires who'd obviously come out on a search but the difficulty was that, being a July day, with the sun there was quite a haze over the sea, and there was no signs of recognition before *they withdrew. Then, looking west, I eventually saw two little white streaks. First they were going north, then they changed and came south, and I realised that these were two high-speed rescue launches. One I could see was going to be far too south for me, but the other I thought there might be a chance. Spirits rose and then every time it turned away I thought 'Oh my God, no'. I carried out stupid, imaginary conversations with it. We didn't have distress flares in the dinghy then and the whistle I had seemed of very little use. Eventually it approached and as it got nearer I was waving madly with anything I could. It was a wonderful feeling when you saw that you had been recognised. I was pulled aboard, my wet clothes were stripped off, I had a good rub down and was then issued with blue overalls, a sweater and a blanket to wrap round me. I was picked up eighteen miles east of Dover and headed there. I was really unscathed and almost leapt into the ambulance and was driven to Hawkinge, then back to Biggin Hill.* (Flying Officer Percy Beake, interview 2003)

The sight of Hawkinge brought welcome relief to Paul Richey of 609 Squadron, who had nursed a rough engine back from the target area; with its temperatures soaring off the clock and pressures dropping, Richey was closely protected by his section as he dropped down through the bomber formation and headed back to England. As Richey slid down from the cockpit, an attendant fitter removed the small oil tank panel from the port side cowling and did a contents check – less than a gallon!

Sergeant Hughes-Rees chased after a couple of Me109s and attacked one from astern. He had just enough time to watch it flick onto its back and then explode before he was subjected to heavy fire from another enemy fighter that had latched onto his tail. Mike Robinson was quick to react and shot at the Me109 as it crossed in front of him. Severely damaged, the Me109 broke off the attack and dived away. Hughes-Rees' oil pressure dropped to zero and over the French coast at 9,000 ft his engine seized. Electing to stay with the aircraft, he jettisoned the hood and made a successful ditching near the South Goodwins. Unlike Beake of 92 Squadron, he then had considerable trouble in opening the gas cylinder to inflate the dinghy, and it promptly exploded. Hughes-Rees was finally picked up, wounded and unconscious with fatigue, by a passing boat.

The intensity with which the enemy was now meeting the constant threat posed by RAF operations in the Channel area was clearly evident, and the fighting on 8 July made lasting impressions. Kingaby had arrived over the French coast nervously calculating the vulnerable exit route from the target:

We took off at first light to take Stirlings to Lens. When we arrived over the French coast the sun was still just above the horizon on our port bow. I realised that when we had reached the target and turned for home we would be in a very sticky position as the 109s would be able to come in straight and level behind us and we would not be able to see them on account of the sun. We crossed the coast and had got about ten miles in when a 109 came in at me out of the sun and almost head-on. I only saw him at the last moment and didn't have time to fire at him. He flashed past me and fired off a Verey cartridge. From that time on until we crossed out again all Hell seemed to let loose. The 109s poured in from all directions and we were so busy dealing with them that it wasn't possible to see what happened to anything we fired at. Then the Hun flak joined in with great gusto and winged one of the Stirlings. A thin stream of smoke began to pour from his outboard port engine, but he carried on and at last we reached the target. Down went the bombs and the target was obliterated in clouds of smoke and dust. The bombers turned for home and then we had the sun right up our tails and things got even hotter than before, as the 109s steamed in, out of the sun, whilst we were blinded looking into it for them.

The Stirling that had been hit before received another nasty knock from the flak over the target and a fire now began in the outboard engine. Gradually the fire spread along the wing towards the cockpit and then she heeled over like a stricken ship and went plunging to her doom. Only three of the crew baled out and, like a flaming torch, she screamed down into the middle of a factory in a small town about ten miles from the target. We forced on and eventually reached the coast without losing the other bombers.

I had fired off all my ammunition but couldn't even claim a damaged because I had been too busy to see what happened when I fired. After crossing the coast the attacks faded out and I throttled back to conserve my petrol which was getting pretty low. I landed at a forward airfield to refuel and just after two more Spitties taxied in. Now the show that morning had been laid on at very short notice and no-one had had time to eat anything – a very bad thing to fly on an empty stomach. I wasn't feeling too good myself, but when the occupants of the other two Spitties got out of their cockpits I couldn't restrain a grin. They were as green as the sea they had just flown over and both hurriedly disappeared from sight behind the nearest building! (Flight Sergeant Don Kingaby, unpublished memoirs)

The major operation of the 9th was Circus 41 to the power station at Mazingarbe. The constant pressure not only to be on the offensive but also to be showing strength meant that many crews had worked through the night. Ninety-two squadron and their comrades at 609 had each had one Cat.E write-off, but this aside the Wing had been relatively fortunate during the previous day's encounters with the Luftwaffe.

Circus 41 was planned for the early afternoon, allowing crews to do much of the routine preparatory work in the morning, and enabling some of those longer jobs that had started in the night to be completed. In the armament section of 92 Squadron, late evening had consisted of some overhauls on a number of cannon and .303s, and with most of the squadron having fired on the 8th there was the need to check them over very thoroughly.

While the squadron armourers had set to this routine preparation, Chiefy Stewart was now using some of the growing expertise of his Group Five Armourers to concentrate on supporting particular aspects of this work. Davies, Campbell, Woods and Healey found their time at dispersal focusing more and more on handling of the 20mm cannons, now working alongside the regular and new squadron armourers to make sure that their specialised knowledge was being cascaded to others.

From the pilots' perspective, on the one hand they expected that the airmen working on their 'kite' all did what was required, but at the same time were enthused by the dedication that these men had for their work. Furthermore, this essential partnership forged close professional understandings of each other's role and idiosyncrasies. Kingaby, for instance, tended to like a higher percentage of tracer shells in his ammunition as he considered this gave him a better sighting once 'on target'.

So in the afternoon, having managed breakfast and a bit of lunch, Don climbed up into his cockpit, shuffling about to get a little more comfortable perched on his dinghy pack. A fitter stood alongside with one knee resting against the door frame, holding the straps of Don's parachute and his Sutton harness over his shoulders as he buckled in. Davies did a quick check of the ejectors once more before giving the thumbs-up to Don. Kingaby acknowledged with a nod and a characteristic grin. The fitter gave Don a reassuring pat on the arm and latched the side door in the half-cocked position. 'Boy, it was hot today,' thought Davies, wiping the beads of perspiration from his forehead and glancing skywards. He even heard rumour that 609's CO had become one of the non-effective sick the previous day from burning his hand whilst swinging on a rather hot pitot head.

There was the usual silence as they all waited for the start-up signal, delaying as much as possible to avoid idling the engine for too long in these conditions. The Merlin was prone to overheating quickly on the ground as the radiators were partially masked by the undercarriage oleos. Even with the radiator flaps fully open, in this heat it was advisable to keep the taxiing and the time between start-up and take-off to a practical minimum. Biggin's winding taxi-way did not do them any favours either.

The signal must have been given, as slowly the props began to turn, and then there was the crack of the Merlin as it burst into life. Kingaby leaned a little to one side of the windshield, finding some relief in the bluster of the prop-wash. The ground crews too seemed to edge that little bit closer to the buffeting slipstream. But it was all too brief, and the heat soon returned as the aircraft were swung round and picked their ways carefully along the peri-track. Then they were gone.

It was high cover duties today and the pilots cooled as the altitude increased. In these moist air conditions the drop in temperature was between one-and-a-half and three degrees centigrade per thousand feet. So while the ground crews might still be working in thirty-degree heat, the aircrews were now enduring freezing temperatures at altitude. During the climb both 609 and 92 managed to gain a little time and arrived over Mazingarbe three minutes before the Stirlings were sighted.

For once it seemed like the enemy had got wind of their intentions and soon there were a number of Me109s probing the defensive screen of fighters, attempting a way through into the bomber formation. As the lead squadron, 92 bore the brunt of these attacks and soon the usual mêlée prevailed. Rankin turned W3312 on a number of Me109Fs managing to send one spiralling into the sea below and severely damaging another. Further claims from the squadron put 92's tally at five destroyed, one probable and a further two damaged.

Up at 30,000 feet 609 Squadron met little opposition but fought a holding-off action. Later, blue section of 609 were engaged while on the way home, Flight Lieutenant Bisdee firing a number of short bursts into an Me109F until it finally trailed an inky black smoke into the sands at Le Touquet Plage.

Escorts & Capital Ships:

Practically every day was hectic – routine in the sense that it had happened before and it was likely to continue in much the same way. Yet all memorable for one thing or another. The 11th could have been like any number of the days during that heady summer of 1941, but for the Biggin Hill Wing the official statistics dryly and unemotionally summed up a hard day's work.

Circus 44 was intended as a large fighter sweep, operating as a decoy for a raid in the vicinity of Lille. At the end of the day, the Wing had claimed six destroyed, four probably destroyed and four damaged. 609 Squadron recorded the greatest proportions of these successes. As their operational record book detailed:

Circus 44 ensued in the afternoon, and was about 609's most successful day since May 8th. Special feature was the electrical machinations of an IFF Blenheim to deceive the enemy prior to the entry of the bombers, and connected with a diversionary sweep in which Biggin took part. 609, in the lead at 27,000 feet crossed the coast 7 miles east of Dunkirk, and turning towards Cassel, sighted 30–40 Me109Fs climbing up through cumulus cloud, perhaps in answer to the Blenheim's ethereal vibrations. Convinced that their plan was to gain height and catch our formation from up-sun as it exited via Gravelines, S/Ldr Robinson turned the Wing right and flew parallel with the coast about 15 miles inland, gradually converging on the enemy with a height advantage of 1,000 feet, and 2,000 feet higher than schedule. E/A were in three squadrons line astern. The first was allowed to go by unmolested, then Yellow section (led by Flight Lieutenant Richey) attacked the second squadron, and Red section (S/Ldr Robinson) the last. The CO soon shot one down from dead astern, and the pilot baled out. He followed another into a steep dive from 27,000 feet to 10,000 feet, firing with m.g.'s all the way. Just as he was ... running out of ammunition, his No.2 (the Station Commander G/C Barwell) who had stuck with him all the way, leapt into the breach, and firing cannon and m/g 'turned the 109 into a ball of fire', this pilot also baled out. Previous to this the Group Captain, without losing touch with S/Ldr Robinson, had fired at what must have been the third of the same formation of three and caused it to emit black smoke

Meanwhile Red 3 (Pilot Officer Seghers) had followed another e/a which broke right and dived on a Spitfire. Pilot Officer Seghers attacked and the e/a rolled on its back, smoking. He was then surprised to see a parachute open. Meanwhile Yellow section had been doing some fine team work, leader using his R/t to give orders and warnings with such good effect that the section stuck together during three consecutive engagements. During the first Flight Lieutenant Richey used all his cannon shells at close range on an e/a which went down pouring smoke after attempting to climb, and is claimed as probably destroyed. The section then dived on another e/a only to find these were already being pursued by other Spitfires (probably Blue section). They therefore broke off this attack, and using the speed of their dive, climbed up to 4 other 109s. Leaving the nearer pair to his section, Flight Lieutenant Richey attacked and damaged both the others with frontal and rear quarter attacks respectively. During these and other attacks Yellow 2 (Sergeant Boyd) destroyed one and damaged another e/a (shattering the top of the cockpit and killing the pilot of the first); Yellow 3 (Pilot Officer du Monceau) probably destroyed another which turned on its back and fell sideways out of control: Yellow 4 (Sergeant Bramble) damaged another. During the whole engagement, there was only one pilot of 609 squadron who did not fire his guns. It was a proper bounce.
(609 Squadron Operational Record Book, 11 July 1941)

Kingaby's day had started with confirmation of the award of his second DFM. Word soon got around and down at dispersal his ground crew was over the moon at the recognition of 'Kingo's' bravery and success. Having completed preparations for Circus 44, Davies too offered his congratulations.

> *I was just finishing the prep on Kingo's cannons, really just making sure everything was in order as it was pretty much something we knew off pat by then. I was sitting on the leading edge with the cannon bay cover off when Don came up and asked 'Everything OK, Taff?' I shuffled round and I said 'Certainly, Flight, I just thought I'd make extra sure that these guns would be up to your next DFM!' He laughed and I shook his hand, congratulating him on the bar [to his DFM]. He said then that it was really as much ours [the ground crew] as his and that when we were all next in the Bell [The Royal Bell Hotel] in Bromley he'd have to buy us a round.* (LAC Raymond Davies, interview, 2002)

As Kingaby recounted, there was to be no respite from operations and Circus 44, and the bravery of one of 92's pilots in particular stood as a clear example of the intensity of their experiences.

> *The Wing went off on a diversionary sweep to the St Omer area to draw the enemy's attention from the main raid further to the west. Soon after we crossed in high over the French coast David Lloyd came up past the CO waggling his wings and banging at his microphone to indicate that his radio had failed and that he was returning to base. He peeled off in a diving turn for home and his number two, Pilot Officer Dougal, the young Canadian, followed him, as was the custom. We carried on to St Omer and pitched straight into a dogfight in which Tommy Lund, now our Flight Commander, and Pietrasiak each destroyed a 109. Twice I got behind huns during this battle, firing at both of them, but failed to hit them, and we emerged from the combat apparently unscathed.*
>
> *When we returned to Biggin Dave Lloyd, white of face and full of remorse, told us that Dougal had been shot down, and related the story of that officer's great gallantry. Soon after they had left the formation they were jumped by four 109s. Dougal had not had time to draw abreast of Lloyd and was still some fifty yards behind him. The 109s dived down, attacked Dougal, setting his aircraft on fire, and pulled up again for an attack on Lloyd. Whilst they were doing this Dougal was unable to give any warning over the R/t, as Lloyd's radio was completely unserviceable, and he was flying on completely unaware of the 109s' presence. The first he knew of it was the sight of Dougal's blazing Spitfire overhauling him and turning in to him to make him break, before it plunged away … below. Dougal had*

deliberately delayed bailing out, despite the state of his aircraft, until he could warn Lloyd. Lloyd managed to escape the four 109s and news came through weeks later that Dougal was a PoW, but severely wounded. In the end his gallant action cost him an arm and a leg. (Flight Sergeant Don Kingaby, unpublished memoirs)

On 13 July the seemingly unending heat finally broke into thunderstorms, giving a welcome relief to 72 and 609 Squadrons who were stood down for most of the day. It also gave Biggin an opportunity to toast the station's 750th victory and, as if in recognition of this, the sun returned in the early evening so that the continuing celebrations could be played out on the terrace of the officers' mess overlooking the valley. The following day saw the loss of two Spitfires – probably of 72 Squadron – in a mid-air collision while on a circus to Hazebrouck. Flying as Target Support to six Blenheims, the Wing was harassed by two large formations of Me109s that had been first spotted high about 609's height of 27,000 feet. Using their superior performance at this altitude, the Me109s dived in pairs through the formations – a tactic that was very effective in unnerving even the most experienced of Biggin's pilots. As Alec 'Joe' Atkinson commented:

On sweeps they (the 109s) would dive through our formation and this, to me at any rate, was very shaking, very shaking. (Pilot Officer Alec 'Joe' Atkinson, interview 28/03/2004)

Ably supported by Goldy Palmer, Mike Robinson managed to shoot down one of the many assailants, fifty-plus of which continued to position themselves up sun waiting to pick off stragglers.

Warning the Wing of the e/a up sun, S/L Robinson proceeded to attack a pair, missing one with a deflection shot, and firing a long-range burst at the second. Following as it took evasive action, he fired from 300 yards range in a dive that lasted from 26,000 to 2,000 feet. E/A went down shedding pieces and black smoke, and at 2,000 feet its dive exceeded the vertical. At the last moment he had to break away to avoid the attack of another E/A. He speaks highly of Red 2 (Sergeant Palmer) who stuck to him so closely that his aircraft was actually struck by a piece of the E/A destroyed. The speed of the dive carried them all (including the attacking E/A) back to 17,000 feet, but though Sergeant Palmer fired at this, they were beaten on the climb. Sergeant Palmer also fired at one or two other E/A as did Pilot Officer Malengreau, but they were unable to see any definite results. Pilot Officer Malengreau also made the mistake of joining up with a formation of 109s, but realised his error in time. Pilot Officer de Hemptine attacked a trawler off Boulogne and the rare event of 2 Spitfires colliding is reported. (609 Squadron Operational Record Book, 14 July 1941)

On the 24th Davies was woken from a heavy sleep by Harry Woods tugging at his arm. 'Come on, Taff, there's some flap on, early ops by the looks,' urged Harry. In the dim light of the barracks Davies could make out the others all in various states of awakening, some – like himself – only having bedded down some three hours before. It was 4.00 am. Some unsociably keen type turned the lights on, meeting a chorus of expletives. Irritably, Davies pulled on his uniform, shouting a stream of questions at Harry: what's the gen, what time down the flight, any breakfast, seen Chiefy? It was 4.30 am when they got down to dispersal, Davies immediately calling in on the armoury to check in with Chiefy Stewart. 'What's the gen, Chiefy?' he asked, surprising himself a little with his early morning informality. 'Anyone's guess,' replied Stewart. 'You and Campbell on the CO's aircraft. Get Healey and Broomhead away on Kingcome's. When you've finished, take one of those new postings and help anyone else. Wing's off at first light.' 'Right you are, Flight Sergeant,' he acknowledged, spotting Cammie and Broomhead already with some 60-round drums. Grabbing them both, he reiterated the Flight's orders and made for Rankin's 'Moonraker' (QJ-J). They hadn't been long at work when Harry Woods came over with new instructions from Flight Sergeant Stewart. Ops had called down, looked like things had been put on hold. Being put on hold was probably the worst, especially at such an early hour. It was pointless trying to snatch some sleep, though in and around dispersal many a head nodded involuntarily, and many eyelids closed momentarily. Remembering Chiefy's other request, Davies sought out one of the new postings to 92's armament section, and took the 19-year-old Londoner over to one of the aircraft. It was 7.00 am.

By 7.45 am, whatever the flap had been was now back on, and word from 'Spy' Weise said that take-off was probably going to be around 0900 hours. With most of the work completed, it was just a case of checking over the 'prepped' aircraft. Davies walked back over to QJ-J, taking the new recruit with him. Campbell was up on the port wing, making one last check on the alignment of the cannon feed. They had encountered some stoppages with Rankin's cannon when doing a test firing on the butts a few days ago. 'Couldn't have anything happening to 'Jammy'', thought Davies, smiling to himself at his own feigned favouritism – all pilots he tended received equal care and attention. The early start meant that the next hour dragged on a bit and the excitement of the morning rush to dispersal wore a little thin. The arrival of 72 Squadron from Gravesend for briefing lifted their spirits and their sense of purpose. Yet at 0910 hours the ops telephone rang conveying the message that the show was now indefinitely postponed. Rankin sent word for the crews to grab some breakfast, knowing that they had been up since 0400 hours.

In the absence of Circus 61, Group decided that it would be a good idea to send the Wing off on a roadstead, targeting some enemy shipping off Fécamp. A flight of Beaufort torpedo bombers sped towards the large merchantman as 609 and 92 Squadrons engaged the five flak ships that made up its escort. A few Me109s also ventured into the boiling cauldron of waterspouts, fire, cannon shells and shrapnel, attempting to get through to the Beauforts. Though the torpedoes did not find their target, Tommy Rigler of 609 managed to make a mess of one of the flak ships and Brian Kingcome sent one of the Me109Fs tumbling into the churning seas. It was with some relief that the squadrons turned for home, not being too keen on the combination of flak, fighters and the uninviting Channel at such close quarters. The return to Biggin was, however, of little welcome as Group had now rescheduled Circus 61. The purpose: a diversionary raid on Hazebrouck, planned to draw Luftwaffe attention away from a massed bomber force of Halifaxes, Hampdens and Wellingtons sent against three of Germany's capital ships – *Scharnhorst*, *Gneisenau* and *Prinz Eugen* – taking refuge in the deep harbours at Brest and La Pallice. It was not a popular rescheduling amongst ground and aircrew of the Wing.

Group meanwhile had decided that Circus 61 should now take place at 13.40, ignoring the fact that pilots would only land about 13.10, and that machines must be refuelled and rearmed. Pilots who to no avail had risen early and hurried over their breakfast were hardly pleased, immediately on landing, to be directed straight to the Intell. Office, there to submit to a hasty briefing accompanied by dry sandwiches, the beer arriving too late. They actually took off again at 14.01, as High Cover Wing to 9 Blenheims raiding Hazebrouck, the Blenheims, not for the first time, crossing slap over Dunkirk, instead of five miles to the east. Long before the French coast was reached large formations of 109s were observed, and after crossing the coast W/C Malan ordered the squadrons to separate and attack, 609 being awarded the main formation. A number of dogfights followed, but most of these were abortive because the 109s were not eager to remain. S/L Robinson however scored a damaged when he attacked an odd pair on the left of the formation. He then went after another formation, and after using all his ammunition from 100 yards on one of them saw it shed large and small pieces and go down 'spinning like a top'. Meanwhile Sergeant Rigler had been doing his stuff with another. A burst from 200 yards had no apparent effect, so 'rather unsteadily' he fired another. 'I suddenly became aware of a part detached which immediately opened out into a parachute' (to his surprise). (609 Squadron Operational Record Book, 24 July 1941)

Over at 92 Squadron, log book entries and combat reports such as those of Johnnie Johnston, recorded the ferocity of the Luftwaffe's response and the frantic fights for survival that all pilots endured.

> *24th July: In at Dunkirk then got engaged. Attacked by 2, then 3 – Chased by 7. Landed Hornchurch with 2 gallons! Claimed 2 probables.* (Sergeant Walter 'Johnnie' Johnston, 92 Squadron, log book entry)

> *I was flying at 23,000ft, 5 miles south of Dunkirk alone and saw two 109s about 2000ft above me and off to the left. They circled behind me and came in to attack, one from each quarter. I turned left and was fired on by one 109. I immediately half rolled to the right and on pulling out found that one of the 109s had followed me down but pulled out too soon and dived straight over me. I fired about a three second burst and immediately observed the E/A to start spouting black smoke. He dropped his port wing and went into a spiral dive, still belching clouds of smoke. He appeared to be out of control and I then lost sight of him. I then circled round and after about five or ten minutes I saw three other 109s about 3000ft above me. They went into line astern. The end machine peeled off and dived to attack me. He commenced firing well out of range. I throttled right back and he passed straight across my path at a range of about 150 yards. I opened fire allowing a great deal of deflection and continued firing until he passed right through my burst. His wings wobbled violently, dropped his port wing and he also went into a tight spiral. About 1–2,000ft lower, smoke began to pour from his machine. I lost him when he was about 1,500ft, smoke still being emitted.* (Sergeant Walter 'Johnnie' Johnston, 92 Squadron, Combat Report, 24 July 1941)

In the now familiar rotation, it was 609 Squadron's turn to move out to Gravesend, with 72 Squadron taking its place on south camp at Biggin. So on 26 July the pilots of 609 made ready for their move into the opulent surroundings of Cobham Hall, the estate of Lord Darnley. In comparison with Biggin's purpose-built accommodation, Cobham was unusual – antique oak furniture and panelling, beds in which Queen Elizabeth had slept, decorative wash-hand basins and hallways bedecked with portraits of past and present earls. Equally, the ground crews found themselves in the decidedly different Laughing Waters Hotel. Seventy-two Squadron took their place at the Bump. For 609 Squadron the last days of July heralded further change with the posting of Mike Robinson as Wing Commander Flying Biggin Hill.

In spite of his protests, the 'Sailor' was to be rested, having been on operations continuously since the outbreak of war. Dunkirk, the Battle of Britain, and a solid seven months on sweeps over France, Malan was beginning to show signs of fatigue and the Wing was more frequently being led by Squadron Leader Michael Robinson. Though it was unsurprising then that Michael was promoted to Wing Leader at Biggin, 609 were not all that happy to be losing their CO, but at least he was not moving far. The last few days of the month saw continued operations, although the weather now was beginning to break. Another month of successes and losses, some weighing more heavily than others. Amongst the NCO pilots in 92 Squadron the loss of Bowen-Morris was one that had been particularly felt. He was not inexperienced, having been with the squadron for some time. He was lost coming to the aid of a fellow pilot. Others such as Sergeant Waldern had also been shot down, presumed killed. While a modicum of experience seemed to significantly improve the chances of survival, many considered that luck stood you equally in good stead. In the following months the fortunes of the Biggin Hill Wing would show that luck – good or bad – often had the upper hand over experience.

Chapter Ten

August Storms, Prangs and Time Off

Fog, Fighters and Abortive Ops:

The long, balmy days of June and July, with their clear, cloudless blue skies, had served as a great ally to the RAF's fighter offensive of summer 1941. Not only had they provided generally good flying conditions, the excellent visibility had made rendezvous with bomber forces and other elements of the fighter cover largely trouble-free. However, for both air and ground crews they were long, long days. For the pilots of the Biggin Hill Wing – and other Wings alike – the good weather meant that they flew an average of three sweeps over enemy territory per day. Almost every evening they returned fatigued, often cold from the reduced temperatures at height, and exhausted from combat. A few hours' sleep, then wakened perhaps at 4 am ready for the coming of first light. Under these protracted operational conditions, there were disadvantages for ground maintenance as well. Dawn till dusk readiness and three ops a day presented many challenges when keeping the squadrons on top line. Routine major inspections were conducted in rotation so as not to draw too many aircraft off the 'operational' list at any one time. Any 'extra' development work – as Davies found working on Chiefy Stewart's 20mm cannon team – seemed to take place late in the evening and often into the early hours. It was with some relief that the crews welcomed the changeable weather conditions of August.

During the first week a number of operations were detailed then postponed. Sometimes the Wing risked take-off in rain and low cloud, only to have the operation aborted due to the adverse conditions. On 5 August the Wing was ordered up in 10/10ths cloud to escort some Blenheims for an attack on St Omer airfield. Miraculously, rendezvous was made with the bombers but only then to see them turning back mid-Channel! Flying largely on instruments, 609 and 92 turned for home, cursing the office-bound tacticians that had decided that someone somewhere should be trying something! The first major encounter with the enemy occurred two days later when the Wing and the Blenheims were ordered to St Omer in the morning and to Lille in the late afternoon.

In the second of these operations (Circus 67) the Luftwaffe reacted in force. First to be engaged were 92 and 609 Squadrons in their capacity as high cover to the Blenheims. The Me109s adopted now characteristic tactics, diving unnervingly through the formation and attempting to pick off stragglers. However, as Rankin and 609's new CO 'Sheep' Gilroy directed elements of their squadrons at the larger threats, eventually the coherence of the sections was lost. The Blenheims somehow 'lost' the target and retired early, while the Spitfires tried to cover their retreat. With the Luftwaffe being somewhat already alerted by the morning's incursions a huge dogfight developed in the region of St Omer and Gravelines. By his own admission Flight Lieutenant Paul Richey of 609 had a lapse of concentration and was flying rather 'sloppily', trying to clear the icing that had developed on his hood and windscreen.

He was then shot up by a gaily coloured 109, and all his glycol was lost. He got into a spin, could see nothing for smoke and glycol, decided to bale out, but could not unfasten his harness pin. He then with great skill and difficulty recovered from his spin, evaded the attack of another 109, and somehow nursed his plane (and engine) all the way back to Manston, where he made a fast belly landing with a still smoking aircraft. W/C Robinson stated that the weather was unsuitable in every way for the operation. (609 Squadron Operational Record Book, 7 August 1941)

Rankin, with elements of 92 Squadron, encountered numerous gaggles of Me109s over Gravelines and Dunkirk and with his usual skill and determination managed to severely damage two, while claiming a third Me109F as definitely destroyed. Kingaby too, flying W3320, was able to claim an Me109F as a probable and another as damaged while in the St Omer area. Hampered by the marginal visibility – particularly at lower levels – it proved almost impossible to see any definite results, even though nearly all pilots fired their guns. Somewhere one of 92's sergeant pilots, 'Kiwi' Howard, was shot down, though none of the Squadron or the Wing were able to shed any light on the circumstances of his loss. He was later reported as a PoW.

Similar cloud conditions prevailed the following day but again, with poor visibility both en route and over the target, the Wing was sent off to escort six Blenheims to a power station at Gosnay (Circus 68). Significant difficulties were encountered in gathering the fighter cover together into their positions and though the Biggin Hill, North Weald and Tangmere Wings eventually were able to proceed as planned, rendezvous with Kenley's squadrons was not forthcoming. Flying as Biggin Hill Wing Leader, Rankin saw what he thought was the Kenley Wing, albeit out of position.

Rendezvous was made with 609 Squadron over Gravesend at 1735 hours and Wing climbed through 10/10ths cloud over Kent. I flew south to establish position and managed to identify Dungeness through small gap in cloud. Height was then gained inland and wing arrived over Rye at 1759 hours, with squadrons at 24, 25 and 30,000 feet. Kenley Wing could not be seen, so one orbit was made and I set off at 1803 hours without them. Another wing was seen ahead over the Channel at 24,000 feet, which I assumed to be Kenley at greater height than they should have been. It transpired that it was not the Kenley Wing. Crossed between Boulogne and Hardelot at 1812 hours. One squadron of the Wing in front dived down almost immediately and at this time I saw 8–12 '109s coming from inland and turning round behind us from Le Touquet. I tried to get Knockout Squadron to attack them, then my Yellow Section, but neither could spot [the enemy]. Therefore, attacked with Red Section.

The squadron split up into fours and was continually engaged…. Enemy aircraft were very numerous above, below and at same height and there was no difficulty in finding targets. Two formations of seven, which I chased with Red Section, were caught, and in both cases, I hit Me109Fs with cannon, high explosive strikes being visible. Later, at Griz Nez, when dogfighting with three '109s, I saw 10–12 more coming up and ordered section to dive out and squadron to return to base. One '109F followed us down at more than 450 mph from 20,000 feet to 1,000 feet, where he opened fire. I swung hard right and he overshot. Turning back onto him, I fired with ten degrees deflection with my machine-guns only (cannon finished) and this enemy aircraft, now at 500 feet, tried to turn right while pulling out and crashed into the sea, sending up a splash about 100 feet high. I then returned to base. Me109s were much more inclined to stay and fight, and the engagement in the area Boulogne – St Omer was one large dogfight. We could out-turn the '109Fs easily, but had not enough speed to close range when in a good position. R/t interference was experienced all the time over France and prevented my bringing Knockout Squadron, who were not engaged, into the mêlée. (Squadron Leader James Rankin, Combat Report, 9 August 1941)

The adverse conditions of the 9th had made the coordination of the Wings very difficult and communication between them less effective. Combined with the strong reaction of the enemy, Circus 68 had been a hard-fought and costly affair. Over at Tangmere, pilots and ground crew of the Wing were shocked by the loss of their Wing Leader, the irrepressible Douglas Bader. As one of those pilots later wrote:

We, too, were silent when we drove to the mess, for we knew that even if our wing leader was alive he would have little chance of evading capture with his tin legs. Before this we rarely thought of his artificial limbs…. At Tangmere we had simply judged him on his ability as a leader and a fighter pilot, and for us the sky would never be the same. Gone was the confident, eager, often scornful voice. Exhorting us, sometimes cursing us, but always holding us together in the fight. (Johnson, *Wing Leader*, 1956, p. 117)

Yet despite these difficulties, operations of this kind continued into the second week of August – a constant battle with both the enemy and the weather. There were even more daring and extensive raids mounted such as the use of a force of Hampdens from No.4 Group Bomber Command on a return trip to Gosnay. Again, on the 14th the Biggin Hill Wing flew a fighter sweep, escorting twelve Blenheims to bomb 'E' boats at Boulogne. Such incursions, while generating some response from the Luftwaffe, brought home the dangers of the increasing flak over these targets.

Low-level with 'Dickie' Milne:
It was flak that gave Dickie Milne an exciting operational debut with 92 Squadron on 19 August. Flight Lieutenant Richard Milne had gained considerable experience since the outbreak of war. Flying Hurricanes with 151 Squadron he had fought his way out of France and had achieved a number of successes during the subsequent summer battles of 1940. After earning a DFC in August of that year he had then been posted to the Central Flying School (CFS) at Upavon, first becoming an 'A' Category instructor and, later, a staff instructor and flight commander. At the beginning of August 1941 he resumed his operational career with 92 Squadron, posted in as 'A' Flight Commander. While his experience was unquestionable, Milne was shrewd enough to know that he had been some time off 'ops' and certainly did not know the form regarding the fighter sweeps and escorts that were now the mainstay of the RAF's daylight offensive. For his first operation then, Dickie decided that it might be better to see what it looked like from the 'back seat' and approached the now much-experienced Sergeant Johnnie Johnston with the view of flying as number two. However, as Johnston recalled, Dickie's eagerness rather altered what he had originally intended.

Dickie Milne did the dirty on us! The first trip he did with 92, he came in, here's this handsome young fella and I was supposed to be flying as his number two. And we walked out and we happened to be parked together and he stopped me and he said, 'When we get airborne, I'm your number two.' So I said, 'what for, Sir?' And he said, 'Because I haven't done any sweeps, you have. I just want you to treat me just like your number two so I can see what's going on.' But lo and behold, damn it, we had hardly crossed over into France, nought feet, and suddenly this voice said '109s!' and away goes Dickie! And I'm peering out and I can see this dot in the distance! Now Dickie already had a Battle of Britain DFC, he was no new boy on the block. So I slammed the throttle open and eventually got near to him and was waggling my wings and gesturing to him you see but he took no damn notice, none at all! And he lines himself up behind these two 109s, down at nought feet – they were at hedge level, using the hedges as camouflage. So there's Dickie and me and suddenly this hedge took fire! There was a battery of two multiple 20mms underneath! Gosh, what a barrage they put up! I actually had rounds bouncing off my wings. We were right over Calais-Marck airfield!

Dickie got hit and he says, 'I'm hit, I'm hit,' and so I said, 'OK, come on, OK, I'm with you, I'll stay with you.' I gave him a rough course to steer, he led and I went round him as we were going along and I couldn't see any trouble [with his aircraft]. I thought it might have been at one point – there seemed to be a bit of paint off. Anyway we got back – landed in at Manston – and he came in very, very carefully and I came in beside him. After we'd landed I said, 'Where were you hit, sir?' He said 'you saw me hit didn't you?' I said 'yes, but where on your wagon, did you get it? I saw what was firing at you.' And I added, 'After you very carefully broke away from me!' 'Ah well,' he said, 'err, it was too great a chance. Don't tell anyone.' So we then tried to find where he'd been hit and we searched and searched, and then just in front of his tailplane there was one tiny entry hole from a machine gun bullet – one entry hole and none coming out! He said, 'That can't be it can it?' I said, 'Well there isn't another one'. He said, 'Well, what about that 20mm?' So I showed him the bounce marks on my aircraft from that lot and he said 'mm, well better luck next time!' There was one hole in his aircraft and thirty-six in mine! That was Dickie, a grand lad. He was one of those that wanted to find out and didn't just stick himself up at the front. I liked Dickie, he was good.
(Sergeant Walter 'Johnnie' Johnston, interview 2003)

It was a sudden introduction to the life of the Biggin Hill Wing, and Milne was quick to catch on. When Rankin was promoted from CO of 92 to Wing Leader at Biggin, it would be Dickie that would be given the squadron.

Rotten Luck and Coming of Age:
On the morning of the 21st a small package and letter arrived for Davies – a small box carefully wrapped in brown paper and marked 'fragile'. He recognised the postmark and the handwritten address, and decided it was probably one of 'Mam's treats', as he called them. It was his father who was the letter writer, often writing more than five pages in his gloriously descriptive and emotive style. Charlie Davies had always enjoyed writing and oration, reflecting on his time in France

and Belgium during the First War, and on everyday things that drew his attention. His letters to Raymond were rich, short stories of continuing life in the Valleys, as well as the usual advice to take care. Letters from Jinny were more practical and report-like – news of Howard, Eric and Glynn – and there were sometimes a few lines from Leighton. Wanting time to savour the connection with home that this post brought, Davies slipped the letter into his breast pocket and left the package in his locker before going down to dispersal.

There was some confusion prior to the afternoon's Circus. With an expected visit from the C in C, the crews were all asked to smarten up. To the sound of 609 Squadron taking off for Gravesend to retrieve their ties, Davies volunteered to go back to the billets for Campbell, Woods, Broomhead and Pete Long so as to do the same. Borrowing 'Dad' Best's bicycle, he was there in no time and took a few minutes to open the package from home. Teasing open the brown paper and cardboard wrapping, he grinned, catching sight of two packets of twenty Players cigarettes. There was also a photo from his mate Steve who had just joined up. He fumbled around in his pockets to find the accompanying letter. It began 'My dearest Raymond, We all hope that you get this before the journey back to Nelson for your birthday. We're all looking forward to seeing you, and hope that your leave is agreed – seven days! Marvellous!' 'Yes, a whole seven days leave,' thought Davies as he put the letter in his locker for a later, second read at close of day. Gathering his mates' ties together he hurried back to the Flight, cycling past some of 72 Squadron's 'erks' who seemed to have had the same idea.

Ninety-two Squadron's Sergeant Johnston shared the same birthday as Davies. On 28 August they would both turn 21 and as an early present, Johnnie had received a new wristwatch. Coming out of the briefing, Sergeant Stan Harrison caught hold of Johnnie's arm. He had left his own wristwatch back at the farmhouse down Brasted Hill where all 92's NCO pilots were billeted together, and he would need one for the 'op'. 'No problem, Stan. You can borrow my old one, as long as I get it back,' said Johnnie, giving Harrison a reassuring pat on the back. He and Stan went back a long way – in fighter pilots' terms – having been on 152 Squadron at Warmwell together and posted together, along with 'Noisy Hunk' Humphries, to 92 Squadron in June 1941. However, as Johnnie recalled, the circumstances of the watch's return were to be tragic.

When we took off on this trip, Stan was flying as my number two which he had been on 152 [Squadron], and he was taxiing round the perimeter track behind me and there was a notorious bend, this big bend in the perimeter track at Biggin. Now 72 Squadron were the second one off and they were taking off just as we [92 Squadron] came to the bend and I had taxied round it and 72 were coming *up on the port side – thirty or forty feet away. Stan came round behind me in the right position and he got hit by the outside aircraft of this flight of 72 Squadron. Chewed him to pieces, absolutely to pieces! The prop of the 72 Squadron aircraft had chewed right up the wing root area and into the cockpit and so Stan was in a bad way. There was nothing we could do and so had to take off. When I got back I went to see what had happened to him and someone had retrieved what they thought was his watch from his arm. It had been on the arm when handed in. We lost Sergeant Aherne on that one as well.* (Sergeant Walter 'Johnnie' Johnston, interview 2003)*

Both Johnnie and Davies had been granted leave for the end of the month. While Johnnie had only a 48-hour pass – and a journey to Newcastle to make – Davies had managed to secure seven days. With barely a week to go they were both looking forward to some time off. For Davies, this was the first real leave that he had managed, working hard and putting in the extra hours on the cannon development team. Chiefy Stewart had made a point of this and had a quiet word about Davies' diligence to Rankin. So Davies' application for seven days' leave was approved and he had arranged to catch the train from Paddington on the 27th. For Johnston, the events of 27 August almost cancelled his leave indefinitely.

Narrow Escapes:
At 4.00 am on the 27th Davies was stirred out of his sleep by a gentle voice. 'Taff,' it whispered, and Davies tried to resist its persistence, feeling that it was still early. 'Raymond,' it came again, this time accompanied by a gentle shaking of his shoulder by the unseen hand. In the half-light he tried to focus, bleary-eyed on the outline of someone bending over the bed. 'What is it Cam,' said Davies, his friend's face now coming into focus? 'It's 4 o'clock,' said Campbell, 'but you don't need to get up with us today 'cos you're off on leave, remember!' 'Oh God, Cam, you're a bastard,' exclaimed Davies, still not fully awake! There was a peal of laughter from around the room and the lights came on to reveal the usual gaggle of 'erks' that he had the misfortune to consider his mates! 'Now don't be like that, Raymond mi lad. We've all congregated especially to wish you a good leave and a jolly twenty-first,' piped up Harry Woods in a mock fatherly tone. Davies got to his feet and play-sparred with the assembled crowd as they gathered round to offer congratulations and talked of how they were going to help him celebrate on his return to Biggin.

Over at the Brasted Hill farmhouse, the ringing telephone brought Johnnie Johnston out of his usual light sleep. He too had planned to get away from Biggin at a good hour, as the journey to and from his home in Newcastle-upon-Tyne would take up a sizeable chunk of his allotted forty-eight hours leave. However, as Johnston recalled, 'ops' seemed to have made different plans for him.

The 28th August was my 21st birthday and I had managed to have a 48 hour pass to get home for the occasion. My mother was a nurse, having joined the Civil Nursing Reserve pre-war when I joined the RAFVR. My father had died in 1940. She had fixed time off for me being home. I was to leave Biggin around noon on the 27th and be back at noon on the 29th, not leaving much time to get to Newcastle-upon-Tyne!! The NCO pilots of 92 used to sleep out in a farm house down Brasted Hill – couldn't risk the night raids on Biggin – and I had the phone in my room, being the lightest sleeper. I was awakened at around 4.00 am on the 27th by the C.O. giving me the names of those required for a show. Transport was already on the way to pick up for briefing at 5.00 am 'ish'. And I was one of them!! I mentioned to him [Rankin] about my 21st and the answer was 'Don't worry, with this early take-off you'll be back on time!' The detail of my log book shows that I nearly didn't! I returned [from Newcastle] as expected, having spent less than a day at home! (Sergeant Walter 'Johnnie' Johnston, letter 2003)

Just after 5.00 am, Johnston, Kingaby and the other NCO pilots of 92 Squadron joined the rest of the assembled aircrew in the briefing room. The target for today was a familiar one – the marshalling yards at Hazebrouck. As part of Circus 85, the Biggin Hill Wing would fly as target support wing and would thus have a free rein around the St Omer area. At 25,000/30,000 feet, the Wing would patrol north and west of the target, where six Blenheims were being sent in to stir up the usual trouble.

Davies walked round to the mess for an early breakfast, feeling rather detached as some of the crew wagons rumbled by on their way to dispersal. Looking across the airfield, he could hear the throb of the Merlins as the pilots guided their aircraft round the taxiway and then lined up for take-off. He paused for a while, looking down towards the Leaves Green end of Biggin, and then instinctively checked his sidecap as the first section of 72 Squadron roared over the boundary fence, with the WingCo, Michael Robinson, leading. He waited just long enough to see the last Spittie of 92 climb into the morning sky, before continuing his way down to South Camp. To himself, he silently wished them all the greatest luck.

Luck was, however, not with the Blenheims that day. None managed to make the rendezvous point and the operation as planned was aborted. Instead, Circus 85 continued as a fighter sweep and prompted a considerable response from the enemy. Many Me109s threatened the Wing from up sun and from height, using their better performance at altitude to their advantage. Robinson, accompanied by his number two (Sous-Lieutenant Maurice Choron of 609 Squadron), dived on four black Me109s, sending two down trailing smoke in quick succession. Over with 92 Squadron, Sergeant Johnston was 'nibbled at by 109s', but managed to avoid serious damage. Not only did the squadrons report the ferocity of the Luftwaffe's attacks on their formation, but noted that the flak was particularly heavy on this day. One of 92's new NCO pilots, Sergeant Roff, was hit badly by ground fire, causing his engine to seize. Still with some height in hand, Sergeant Johnston formed up on him to escort him as far back across the Channel as could be achieved.

We had a comparatively new sergeant who was very keen, very good, very nice. We'd been in [over France] and we got bounced, we got bounced very badly. We got split up and separated. It wasn't far inland that this happened because we'd actually been having a belt at some barges. They had a lot of outward-pointing guns and so we tried to come in head-on, this being a little better than letting them fire up your bum! We would break off inland and fanfare out. But this young fella … I saw this aircraft going in and I thought, kept thinking 'break, break, break' and I started to shout 'break, break.' From where I was I couldn't see who it was and so couldn't give any signal. Then I saw a flak burst fairly near. I was higher than he was and so tried to keep my eyes on him, him being way down there. And I turned back in where there were some 109s and I sparred with them for a while but set off [back home].

Later, I came across him and he was going on slightly down. As soon as I saw that I thought 'Oh God, he's trimmed down so he won't stall, he's been hit.' So I came alongside him and was looking up right round him, and he had a lot of hits around the back of the cockpit. I came alongside and he looked at me and he was a bit slumped. I thought 'Oh God,' so I moved off to give him room and not to attract attention, and it was quite obvious that he wasn't going to make it. So I climbed up and gave a M'aidez and then dropped down again to take care of him and I managed to get him back to somewhere round about mid-Channel, not quite mid-Channel. I tried like mad to get him to understand when I came alongside that he should hop out, and he just sort of looked at me and carried on. I could not get him to do it. Then eventually I got him to understand and he nodded his head so I gave him a sign and stayed tucked right in underneath him so to get him to climb a bit … and he managed 300 or 400 feet higher and nodded his head and I backed off. At first he didn't do anything and so I got closer in and kept gesturing to him and he then jettisoned his hood and dropped. He'd left it late but the 'chute opened in time but he was very, very close to the water.

His dinghy was way out, away from him – he hadn't got it fastened – and he just floated. I tried to get my own dinghy pack out to drop but could I, Hell? Could I, damn it? I couldn't get mine off, no way. So I had to leave it and so stayed there

[circling] until I was just about showing nothing [on the fuel gauge] and I went
down and went round him, pulled the hood back and waved to him. And he looked
up and gave a weak wave, he must have been hellish badly hit, but I had to go.
I went off and climbed as much as I could, bearing in mind the lack of juice, and
gave M'aidez continuously all the way through. I lobbed down at Manston and
they literally filled the tank – I was flying on air. He wasn't picked up. (Sergeant
Walter 'Johnnie' Johnston, interview 2003)

It had been a difficult day and as the aircraft returned the squadron intelligence
officers picked their way around the pilots. Some of them chattered excitedly
about action, of encounters with many Me109s, of the intense and unnervingly
accurate flak, and there were queries all round about what had happened to others
that had not returned. Pilot Officer Vicki Ortmans of 609 Squadron had tried to
help out a Spitfire that was being chased by a number of Me109s, but was too far
away and sadly, and angrily, watched its demise. One of 72 Squadron's pilots was
missing – was it him? Other returning pilots sat quietly with their own thoughts,
though their comrades tried to involve them – it seemed no good to dwell, to play
things round in the solitude of one's mind. In public and with their comrades they
tried not to let it show, to put a brave face on it. Yet in private, in the confines of
their room or somewhere else where they found themselves in a quiet moment
alone, it was difficult not to reflect on their day-in–day-out experiences. It was the
loss of their friends that hit hard, perhaps those formed in the peacetime RAF
more than any – such friendships had been given the time to develop without any
real, constant fear of loss.

Ground crews had seemingly some level of detachment but it would be wrong
to suggest that the organisational demarcations between air and ground personnel
meant that the latter were unaffected. Affected, deeply affected they were. In the
closely knit, social and professional microcosm that the squadron represented
it was impossible to remain untouched by the losses, the badly mauled returns,
and the prangs. Of course as things wore on many attempted to be somewhat
distant, telling themselves that they would not make close friendships. Yet in
reality this often proved a thin veil of defence and one could not help but warm
to certain individuals and be privately affected by their passing. The relationships
that ground and aircrew formed were thus, unsurprisingly, characterised by the
individuals involved. Some, like Don Kingaby and Johnnie Johnston, formed
close professional relations with their ground crews that sometimes spilled into
communal social lives. Others chose not to, while still being appreciative of each
other's contribution. As the end of the second year of war approached, the physical
and emotional strain continued to take its toll.

Chapter Eleven

Good Ol' Ninety-Two

Inclement September:

Under a clouded, rain-threatening sky Davies returned to Biggin Hill on 8 September savouring the last few days at home. It had been a much-welcomed rest, though he had found himself talking about Biggin and the squadron more than he expected. All things considered, perhaps it wasn't surprising. The RAF, Biggin and the squadron was his life now and, although catching up on village and family life seemed the proper concerns of his time off, they seemed a little abstract at times. Leighton was particularly inquisitive about his elder brother's experiences and had taken to looking out for him in the newsreel footage that their mother took them to see at the local picture house. The BBC always seemed to be on an aerodrome somewhere south of London. For Leighton, it was invariably the one where 'our Raymond' was, and those Spitfires taking off were always ones of his brother's squadron. Oddly enough, the film crews often visited Biggin – not that the censors let on. His father's gentle inquiries were more considered and Raymond found that in some of the quiet moments late at night, sitting up with Charlie, he would talk a little more about watching the aircraft coming back, some badly shot up. He talked about the sickened, nervous feeling he had when watching some young pilot struggling to get an undercarriage locked down, then going nose-over at the end of the landing. And there were other accidents. Most who had been at dispersal on 21 August had seen the collision in which Stan Harrison had been fatally injured and many had helped retrieve the bits of wreckage of the three aircraft from the landing field. It was the worst that Raymond had seen that summer. It was difficult not to be affected by these experiences. Charlie had listened quietly, understanding fully of such feelings. The First War was fresh as ever in his own memory.

Of course the trip home had not been without some jollity. Celebrating one's coming of age was something to be taken seriously and he had managed to get down to Treharris and Pontypridd for a number of nights out. He had even convinced his elder brother Glynn to come out to a local dance. Not known for his dancing, Glynn had helped Raymond celebrate by getting himself rather drunk and together the two of them had staggered the four or so miles back to Glynn's and Rene's house in Ystred. On the way, Raymond spotted an English Red Setter.

It was one of Offney Thomas's show dogs, and, knowing this, he had tied his tie to the dog's collar with the intention of returning it. However, as always mischief got the better of Raymond and, standing in the doorway of Glynn's house, he attempted to convince Rene that they had got the dog as a present for her! As he walked away down the garden path he could still hear Rene chastising her inebriated husband that she would not have that beast of a dog in her house and that Raymond should know better than to get him drunk!

Aside from these reinvigorating memories of his seven days away from the squadron, his twenty-first birthday had been marked with a quite exceptional present from the family. Like Sergeant Johnnie Johnston, Davies received a wristwatch to mark this important anniversary. He knew it represented a not insignificant investment of family funds, particularly in such belt-tightening times. To his mild protests of 'Mam, you shouldn't have,' he was cajoled into accepting this grand gesture by his mother's talk of taking on a little more baking for the street and for Leighton to run a few more errands for Mrs Beddoes. So now, reporting in to the main gate at Biggin, Davies instinctively checked his wrist for the time. It was 0800 hours and he was back on the RAF's time.

Drinks All Round:
Having changed into his overalls Davies caught some transport that was heading down to 92 Squadron's dispersal but found the armoury strangely deserted. A few of 'B' Flight stood around and he made enquiries about everyone's whereabouts. 'What's the gen?' he asked a chatting corporal. 'Nothing much doing, Taff,' came the reply. 'Ops cancelled again this morning. Bloody weather!' 'Seen anything of 'A' Flight?' Davies quizzed, quietly hoping that they had been stood down? 'All gone up to breakfast, I think,' said the corporal, 'either that or gone preening themselves ready for tonight's celebrations.' 'Celebrations?' asked Davies. 'Yeah, Squadron's been on the Bump a whole year,' came the reply. With a smart about face, Davies started back in the direction of the main camp, with the good idea of getting some breakfast – after all he had been travelling since the early hours to reach Biggin by 0900 hours as expected. He stopped by his billets to lose his working clothes and then to the Mess. As he got into the hall and was looking for his favourite devilled kidneys, a familiar voice called out, 'don't give 'im any, he's been on a seven-day feeding back in the Valleys!' It was Campbell, grinning from ear to ear, looking distinctly pleased to have his partner in mischief back in the fold.

Sitting there with Campbell and Healey, Davies got the gen on the last few days. Mainly the weather had been absolutely bloody, resulting in a number of cancelled operations. To everyone's frustration, such cancellations often seemed to occur after being called to readiness at some ungodly hour. Down to dispersal before sunrise, then stood down, postponed indefinitely, and off to breakfast. Other ops, rather like those of August, had got as far as mid-Channel only to be recalled in 10/10ths cloud. There had been some promotions, most notably Rankin's promotion to Wing Leader with the departure of Mike Robinson. Dickie Milne had taken on command of 92 Squadron. There had been a few prangs, mainly due to the dicey weather and poor visibility, the most spectacular being that of Sergeant Muller's from 609 Squadron who managed to touch down half way along the runway and go straight through a hangar. Fortunately, the hangar was empty and Muller escaped serious injury. His aircraft, however, was a bit of a mess!

With little to do, the rest of the day seemed rather slow but Davies was thankful for the easy start to his time back. He reported in to Chiefy Stewart and Sergeant Rains, chatting with them about the 20mm cannon work. 'Claude' had spent the last few days carrying out a number of major inspections on 609's cannons and had seen the squadron off for some practice firing in the afternoon. They returned with schoolboyish grins as their cannon firing into the sea had managed to set off a mine – what an explosion! There was still work to be done and perhaps the let up from operations might enable the team to do some concerted test firings this month. In the late afternoon attention turned to the celebration of 92 Squadron's twelve months at Biggin and Davies noted a lot of DFCs around. Returning commanding officers, former squadron pilots, and a celebrity crowd from London all were in attendance. Biggin was used to such visits. Alongside those dignitaries directly associated with the RAF – for example MRAF Sir Hugh Trenchard and Sir Archibald Sinclair – actors such as Noel Coward and Leslie Howard were not infrequent visitors. Howard, in particular, had visited Biggin a number of times with his film crews, collecting footage and research for his film of R.J. Mitchell's life. *The First of the Few* premiered at London's Leicester Square Theatre in August 1942 and two notable characters from 92 Squadron managed to get their faces on the silver screen: Brian Kingcome and Tony Bartley.

With the squadron stood down, Campbell, Healey and the others of the team managed to twist Davies' arm into going down to the King's Arms for the more personal celebration of his twenty-first birthday. Though now more than a week into his twenty-second year, it had been the first opportunity for them to mark this momentous anniversary together. So as good old 92 was toasted elsewhere – no doubt with champagne – Davies received his fair share of oaths and allegiances from the assembled crowd. Not being much of a drinker, Davies soon found that he had begun to lose count of the usual few half-pints. He could vaguely remember Titch Thornton mentioning whisky, and made some weak protest that he'd never had any before. Yet before he realised it, Davies became aware of the sharpness of taste followed by a wonderful warmth as it slipped down his throat. Now this was how to celebrate.

There was one thing that repeatedly jarred his senses: a cackle of laughter from a woman sitting over in the opposite corner. This shrill, cutting sound served to punctuate the comforting hum of normal conversation, and her rather overstated befeathered hat acted like a signpost of her whereabouts to those hard-of-hearing patrons that had failed to notice her from her laughter alone! It was irritating, and though usually able to confine his mischief to barely audible comment, Davies found that the whisky seemed to make his voice carry a little more and that the feather had become some sort of homing beacon, drawing him ever closer. Before he knew it – and before Cammie could stop him – he was across the room, standing right in front of her and his now strident voice was offering some uncompromising advice as to where best to stick the feather, and in doing so how it would facilitate her flying home! Before she could recover her ability to speak, Harry Woods and Healey had bustled him out of the door, spilling into the road outside. It was Campbell who now lost the power of speech and his sides ached from laughing as he rolled around on the tarmac. Momentarily Davies regained his composure to say, 'well, she was asking for it for Boyo,' before his shoulders began to shake in fits of hysterics.

Delicate Work:
The following day Flight Sergeant Stewart called his team together to brief them on what he saw as the progress they had been making with the operation of the 20mm cannons. Reporting on the maintenance and test-firing opportunities from all the squadrons of the Wing, he assessed that a number of the difficulties they had encountered over the last seven months were becoming less frequent. Most of the improvements were largely attributable to ammunition handling. Stewart had a feeling that they were getting less extractor failures now and the quality of the ammunition seemed to be settling down – they had fewer incidents of stoppages caused by collapsed shoulders, or over and undersized cartridges. Davies and Campbell had also put their minds to handling procedures and it seemed to make a significant difference to the successful and complete firing of a magazine. Laboriously they had checked every round before they had loaded them into the magazine and had experimented with different dilutions and types of oil. Taking measurements of the magazines' spring tensioners had also alerted the team to the possibility that as these became worn they became less efficient in feeding the rounds into the breech. Attention to these details was, in the teams' estimations, making some difference.

The main problem remained that in a system that relied partially on gas-assisted recoil, often they were on the limits of possible adjustment using the spring recoil section of the gun alone. They had no problems with measuring the recoil accurately, but often their experience told them that being able to increase the recoil a fraction more would probably allow just enough extra clearance for the next round to enter the breech successfully, irrespective of minor aberrations in quality, alignment and play through wear and tear. The foul weather between 9 and 16 September pretty much ruled out extensive operations. Yet it gave Stewart's team some useful time to think through the problem.

It was Corporal Jones that had the flash of inspiration. As they stood packing up after a rather long night in the workshop, Jones took a step back from the workbench, holding the gas cylinder of a cannon he and Davies had been working on. 'Taff,' quizzed Jones, 'the amount of recoil is our biggest bind isn't it?' 'Yes, I reckon so,' replied Davies, 'we've pretty much played around with everything else on these damn guns!' 'And we've played around with probably every moving part on it, haven't we?' 'What if,' continued Jones, 'we were able to tinker with the only bit we've so far left alone – the gas assistance?' 'Well, yes,' said Davies, throwing a wad of cleaning cloth into the bin. 'We've all wondered that Jonesy but how …' Davies stopped without finishing the sentence. Jones was already gone, not even stopping to collect his overcoat and forage cap that hung off a makeshift hook on the side of a rack of shelving. As Davies recalled in later years:

Sometime the next day Corporal Jones appeared at our workshop, a bit late he was but he'd come via Chiefy's office and they were deep in excited conversation. He got me and Campbell to bring in one of the cannons we'd been working on – one that was already stripped down. Then Jones produced this small drill bit, the smallest one I'd ever seen. It was like a hair, it was so fine. He'd been in the machine shop and had got one of the fitters to make up this drill. We all watched as Jonesy then took out a small sliver of metal from the gas vent hole, just this small curl of metal. But the effect of this was to slightly increase the amount of gas that came back in to assist the rearward movement of the breech. We cleaned it up [the hole] and then Chiefy got me and Campbell to reassemble the gun and then take it down to the butts. We fitted it to a Spit that was already in the bay – we'd been working on it earlier and the cannon we'd got was off this aircraft. We got the cannon in the wing and connected it all up. Corporal Jones and Chiefy came down and had collected 'Claude' [Rains] from 609. We then went through our usual procedures and checks before firing. (LAC Raymond Davies, interview 2003)

Over the next few days the team spent as much time as they could on the firing butts with this one aircraft, getting special permission from Dickie Milne to keep this one kite off the line – at least while the weather was still restricting operations. Feeling like they were on the verge of a breakthrough, Davies and his comrades stayed late into the evening, test firing and making various adjustments. It was very late one evening when Davies became aware of a hand on his shoulder as he stood by a steadying trestle waiting as Jones fired off the last rounds from a full drum of 20mm. Davies turned and was just about to remind the owner of the hand about distracting him during a firing when he noticed it was the WingCo! Blurting out some surprised recognition of his commanding officer, Davies attempted to bring himself to attention and look around to alert the rest of the team to the WingCo's presence. 'Ok Davies, no need for that,' said Rankin, giving him a friendly pat on the back. That was one thing that Davies noticed about Jamie: one knew that even as a lowly 'erk', Rankin saw you as another link in the chain – everyone as important as the next. Overall things were good at Biggin, and much of this was due to the way that it and its squadrons had been commanded. Back in June, Davies had seen how, for Rankin, it was his men that were important and if things were not right for them, then he made sure that any problems were sorted out. As Davies recalled:

Generally the food at Biggin was good but there was this one time when we went down to the mess and for about a month the food was awful. We couldn't make out what it was at first but it was as if something was off. Anyway, we had this corporal who was quite friendly with Jamie. You know, he was usually able to chat with Rankin directly. Now Rankin was the sort that, he'd get to know you, at least he'd take the time to know your name, where you were from, enough to have a chat and make you feel part of the team. So we couldn't stand this food any longer and so this corporal went to see Jamie. Later that same day, the next time we sat down for food, Jamie appeared in our mess. He walked up to the end of the hall where they were serving up and he took a ladle of the stuff we were being fed. He took one mouthful, then passed the rest to the chief cook and ordered him to taste it as well. The cooks started with some excuses but Jamie was having none of it and shouted, 'I don't expect any of my men to eat this!' He ordered us to scrape the food we had on our plates back into the pots and then ordered the cookhouse staff to pour it all away. From then on the food was back to its usual good standard – and Jamie came back the next week to make sure for himself. Things always got done with Jamie and quick. (LAC Raymond Davies, interview 2002)

Johnnie Johnston too remembered the brief lapse in Biggin's cookhouse fare, noting that the experience also extended to the sergeant's mess.

Yes, [Ray] is right. It was only for a brief period but the food was diabolical! Usually it was very good, we had no complaints. But there was this time when – and I think it was the meat – we had some stuff in the [sergeant's] mess and me and Don looked up at each other and we both had the same look of disgust. We thought it was a one-off but this continued for a few weeks. Something must have been said because not very long after it was back to normal. We heard rumours that it was one of the cooks who was in charge of buying in the meat. He had been buying in cheap stuff and had some scam going with the good meat that he was being supplied with. Someone said they thought it was goat's meat. (Sergeant Walter 'Johnnie' Johnston, interview 2003)

Leaning against the team's workbench, Rankin picked up on their excitement at once and took time to let them talk through what they had been doing over the last few days. Davies got the feeling that Jamie had some sense that they thought a breakthrough had been made, and that more than likely Dickie Milne or perhaps Kingaby had kept the WingCo informed. After some twenty minutes or so Rankin once more praised them all for their diligence and hard work. Turning to go, he looked back towards Stewart and said, 'Now Jimmy, get your boys off to bed. I think you've all done enough for tonight.'

In amongst the progress that was being made, for Davies there was one personal loss that he would remember clearly in the years to come. Seemingly the fine-tuning of the cannon operations was not conducive to the delicate workings of his 21st birthday wristwatch!

Now, my mother had managed to get the jeweller in Nelson … His name was Mr Edwards, but everybody called him 'Ted Watch'. And Ted Watch had built this wristwatch for me and it was the first watch I had ever owned of my own, and Oh gosh, I thought it was wonderful. Anyhow, I got back off leave and Sergeant Rains said we still haven't got the cannons going Davies so you'll have to come back on your usual job. So, of course we were back on the butts. So I was working on the port side, testing the port cannon. We couldn't get the starboard going, so we thought we'd have a go at the port one. Now the one day Sergeant Rains fired off a round and after this one shot we had a stoppage. The breach [block] had come back only half-way 'cos the recoil wasn't correct. Then 'Claude' shouted to me 'OK Davies, I've cleared the guns. Take a full turn off the recoil reducer.' So I had my wristwatch on and I turned one turn and I could hear everything falling to pieces inside, it was so distinct! I took the wristwatch off, opened it and every part fell out! And Oh gosh I was so disappointed because when my mother asked Mr Edwards to make a watch up for me because they were so scarce, well to me it was the best 21st present that I had. Anyhow, I wouldn't dare tell my mother so I had to tell a white lie, and I told her that it was stolen. (LAC Raymond Davies, interview 2001)

For a few more days, while the weather still limited operations, Campbell, Davies, Jones and Sergeant Rains were continually back down on the butts for some final adjustments. The opening of the gas vent made all the difference. With those cannons they had modified, it was now rare that the breech block would not travel far enough rearwards for the locking piece to engage, thus holding the breech open for the next shell to enter. They were pretty certain that they had got it 'taped' and that it was just a case of checking that the operations of the last few days could be replicated and the new routines set in their minds. 'Claude' had been taking careful note of the procedures they had been using as eventually these working practices would have to be cascaded to others. Corporal Jones's ingenuity proved to be the turning point and once again the team's skill and hard work had enabled them to turn the idea into a reality. To an extent, luck had also smiled on them as there really was no way of knowing the degree to which the gas vent needed to be enlarged. As Davies summarised:

The 20mm system was a combination of recoil spring and gas-assistance. When the gun fired, some of the exhaust gases were channelled through a small hole into the chamber, assisting the return of the breech-block to its starting position. Well, we couldn't get enough gas and so all of the adjustment in recoil had to be done with the recoil reducer at the front of the gun. And we were on the limits with this adjustment. Then one evening Corporal Jones had an idea to enlarge the hole – and made up a special drill, smaller than anything available – and the next day he took out a sliver of metal from this hole for the exhaust gases. Then we tried it out and it was just what it needed. It was a bit of luck as well – if he'd made the drill any larger, the hole would have let too much gas through, speeding up the action and maybe damaging the cannon and the aircraft! (LAC Raymond Davies, interview, 2001)

With that fine adjustment, and that combination of skill and luck, the Biggin Hill Wing and Fighter Command gained a formidable weapon that would serve with distinction for the duration of the war and beyond. The experience and know-how that Davies and his comrades had gained during these first eight months at Biggin made them 20mm specialists and would stand them in good stead in the years to come.

Close Calls and a VIP:
17 September saw a return to the full-scale operations of the Wing. The weather had changed and 'Ops' had detailed no less than three shows. The second of these, Circus 95 to Mazingarbe, saw the Wing's first encounters with the Luftwaffe's new fighter, the formidable Focke Wulf 190. The twenty-four Blenheims that the Wing was detailed to escort were early and 609 and 92 put their noses down in order to catch them up. In the haste, the squadrons passed off the invitation to intercept a gaggle of some twenty-plus Me109s. However, two pilots of 609 Squadron – Goldy Palmer and Vicki Ortmans – were caught. It was in this heavy engagement that Flying Officer Ortmans witnessed the performance of an unfamiliar opponent and was lucky to survive. As the Squadron diary recorded:

> *Flying Officer V. Ortmans and Sergeant Palmer … are mightily assailed, Flying Officer Ortman's aircraft is hit, and Sergeant Palmer has to lose altitude owing to trouble with his oxygen equipment. One of Flying Officer Ortmans' assailants is what he describes as a '109 with a radial engine', and this later turns out to be one of the first times the new German fighter, the Fw190, has been encountered. Chief impression of Vicki: its ability to change from the horizontal to the vertical without engine cutting.* (609 Squadron Operational Record Book, 17 October 1941)

By the third operation of the day (Circus 96 to the Marquise armament factory) many of the pilots were starting to feel the strain. For Alec 'Joe' Atkinson, it was fatigue that perhaps contributed to his 'getting caught'.

> *[Flying three operations a day] you got tired and I'm sure that when I was shot down, I'm sure it was because I was tired. I could see somebody shooting at me but I was convinced it was a Spitfire – I'm not absolutely sure now that it wasn't – but I thought 'well he's never going to hit me, 'cos he's not got enough deflection.' But at that moment when I was feeling a bit smug about it a bullet came in through the hood. Whether it was that machine that I'd seen firing or whether it was a quite different machine, I have no idea. The bullet went into the gauge that showed you what the Glycol temperature was and so I had no idea what the engine temperature was but I began to see flames coming from under the cowling. So I thought I'd better bale out. I didn't really think of the consequences of this 'cos I was very near the coast. So I baled out and landed in the drink and there was a little bit of*

*a breeze and it blew my parachute along and blew me along with it 'cos I couldn't
get my foot out of the harness. Well I did manage to do that and you could blow up
the dinghy with an automatic thing at the top. So I sat in the dinghy and it was
late in the day, beginning to get dusk, so I wasn't very keen on this. Fortunately
a number of Hurricanes came along and spotted me and dropped flares, and after
about half-an-hour a Naval launch arrived and picked me up. They said could
they have my wings [as a memento], I said they could have anything they liked!*
(Pilot Officer Alec 'Joe' Atkinson, interview 28/03/2004)

Hearing that 'Joe' was safe, some of his comrades, including some of the Belgian
pilots on the squadron, decided to drive down from Gravesend to pick him up.
However, the combination of flying kit, 'foreign' accents and the cover of darkness
made for Joe's second 'rescue' of the day being nearly as dramatic as the first.

*So they took me back to Dover and by that time it was dark. They gave me some
old clothes to put on and took me to the Lord Warden Hotel which was the Naval
headquarters. When [the squadron] heard that I had been picked up they said 'Oh
let's go down and fetch him.' We had a car which we called the 'Belgian Barouche',
given to us by the Belgian government, and some of the pilots piled into this and
they had their Irvin jackets on. They drove down to Dover and when they got
there, there was an air raid on, and one of them poked his head out of the window
and said [heavily accented] 'Lord Warden Hotel?' It was a Salvation Army chap
that was walking along the pavement and after a bit of hesitation he told them how
to get there and then, apparently, immediately rang up the Police and said there
is a car full of parachutists going to take the Lord Warden Hotel. So there I was
sitting and drinking in the bar and my friends came in, but behind them were men
with guns!* (Pilot Officer Alec 'Joe' Atkinson, interview 28/03/2004)

The break in the weather proved short-lived and for seven out of the next ten
days operations were hampered by thick and continuous fog. During this time
92 Squadron exchanged places with 609 at Gravesend, with the latter returning
to Biggin to take up 92's old dispersal on North Camp. The 27th brought fairer
weather and one of the most intense battles with some very close calls. Circus
103B took the squadrons of the Wing back to Mazingarbe, flying as high cover to
eleven Blenheims. Although a familiar target, this trip was perhaps not routine. As
Sergeant Johnston of 92 Squadron recalled:

*We went over to [Biggin] to be briefed and did not particularly like what we got.
We were told that the trip was to be a sweep to try and raise a lot of 109s as a*

VVVVVIP was to be in the Ops room. We assumed this to mean our King. The show was to be at the 'suitable time' and we would carry it out despite the time of day. It should be appreciated that the sun played a great part in deciding, not the target, but which way we went in and came out. We did not like the sun behind us when coming out for home, and this decided whether the job was AM or PM – if we had a choice! (Sergeant Walter 'Johnnie' Johnston, letter, 1997)

In the first instance, it seemed that the enemy was not going to take the bait and the squadrons had been briefed to maintain strict R/t discipline, especially as they had such an important audience. As Dickie Milne and the rest of 92 scanned the sky, some pilots began to get restless.

We had been told: 'Good R/t procedure!!! OR ELSE!' We raised nothing, and began to take the mickey. Affected voices on the R/t such as 'I say old boy, have you seen anything?' Answer: 'Not a thing old bean, not a sausage!' Then we were told 'Quiet!' I had a good pair of eyes in those days and often was put in as Red 4 with instructions to report at once if anything suspicious, and then it was me who would call the break generally. I was sitting there, minding my own business when I saw a gaggle of black dots dropping on us from out of the sun. I forgot the VVVIP and yelled out 'Jesus Christ look at those bastards coming out of the sun. BREAK, BREAK!!' (Sergeant Walter 'Johnnie' Johnston, letter, 1997)

When the attack came in, Percy Beake had been maintaining formation, flying with his cockpit hood latched wide open to allay his primary fear of being trapped in the aircraft should it be set on fire. Now, more on this day than any others, the ferocious reaction from the Luftwaffe was something he was hoping to avoid.

During this period one op stands out in my mind. That was on Sept. 27th when our role was top cover in a circus operation attacking Mazingarbe. My main reason for remembering this op is that I was due to marry on October 1st. I had become engaged during Easter 41 and my fiancée and I planned then to marry in six months' time. Soon after joining 92 in late June, I asked if I could book some leave at the end of September. My request was hardly taken seriously for our Adjutant said 'we don't plan anything this far ahead Beakey – a lot can happen here in a short time!' However, as the date drew nearer he said, 'Beakey, I'd like to arrange for you to go on a parachute packing course just prior to your nuptials.' I jauntily replied, 'Thank you Adj., but I would prefer to remain with the squadron.' It transpired that on Sept. 27th … we all had a hectic time getting back. I managed at least to damage one 109 but was myself attacked by others who scored several hits but happily not in any particularly vulnerable parts of my aircraft. One bullet whistling through my cockpit passed through the right leg of my flying suit just grazing and scorching the back of my calf. As all this was happening I thought my fiancée might well be deprived of her wedding day and regretted having dissuaded our Adj. from arranging that parachute packing course! (Flying Officer Percy Beake, letter, 2003)

As Beake and the rest of the section wheeled round, it was Johnnie Johnston who came to his comrade's aid, fully aware of Beakey's impending marriage. It was with some degree of luck that Johnnie shot an Me109 off Beake's tail.

I cannot recall exactly the make up of our section but it did have the C.O. (No.1), I think 'Chips' Carpenter (Sergeant No.2), Pilot Officer Beake (No.3) and me at No.4. Beakey was leaving the next day to be married!! We broke into the 109s to starboard and climbing, at the top we turned port and I was lagging a bit. A very prettily marked 109 came across my front from starboard and fastened onto Beakey. I hauled round, pulled through the 109 & fired a burst. It took off his rudder and a few more pieces, finally showing strikes aft of the cockpit. And then I realised I'd done this without a gunsight! I had forgotten to switch it on! Later I fired at another but with only a few strikes. We reformed into a squadron, of course just mixed sections. When nearly out we were caught again by the 109s who had also regrouped. I claimed one probable. (Sergeant Walter 'Johnnie' Johnston, letter, 1997)

Frustratingly for Johnston, both his cannons jammed very early in the engagement, after firing only nineteen rounds. Still the effect of the cannon strikes was significant enough for him to report the damage they inflicted on submitting his report to 'Spy' Weise.

When flying in Red 4 position I was attacked from behind by two Me109s. Warning the section I took evasive action and thus lost the rest of the section. The two 109s mixed in with me and we finished up as 109, Spit and a 109 turning in a circle. I opened fire with my cannon at about 250 yards and then they jammed. I closed in to 150 yards using m.g. My first burst of cannon had torn two huge holes just on and behind the cockpit. He turned away with a flick and dived. The second 109 was then on my tail. I shook him off and observed a parachute floating down at about 6–8,000ft. I believe it was from the first 109. The rest of the section came up then and we started on our way out. One yellow-tailed 109 attacked, followed by two more. The first attacked me and the other two went onto the rest of the section. I evaded the first and then went on to help the others. I closed in on his tail and opened up with m.g. at about 300 yards and observed pieces fall off his tail. Another then tagged onto me and I promptly disappeared into cloud. (Sergeant Walter 'Johnnie' Johnston, 92 Squadron, Combat Report, 27 September 1941)

The rest of the Wing was assailed as incessantly. Leading with 609 Squadron, Rankin had taken the Wing in at 27,000 feet over Mardyck. Some 5,000 feet below, a huge formation of Me109s were spotted and, leaving some sections of 92 as top cover, Rankin had led the Wing to intercept. It was only then that the size of the enemy response became apparent and quickly the squadrons became split into sections and lone individuals. On their return, 609's intelligence officer, Frank Ziegler, managed to capture the intensity from the Squadron's perspective:

Sergeant van Schaick is attacked 4 times. Flying Officer Dieu becomes involved in a turning competition with a 109 until the latter makes the mistake of turning in the opposite direction, thus presenting Flying Officer Dieu with a nice beam shot (m/g only) at 40 yards – E/A dives vertically streaming white, then black smoke. Flying Officer V. Ortmans follows W/C Rankin to target area, and on the way back informs him of 2 109s about to attack; but the latter does not hear clearly, and Flying Officer Ortmans is engaged alone, his a/c being hit in the fuselage. Two other Spits relieve him, but by the time he leaves the French coast at Le Touquet, he has only 7 gallons of petrol. Informing Controller, he bales out, having reached a point 5 miles off Dover by gliding, and within 15 minutes is picked up by a fishing boat, whence he is transferred to the same rescue boat which rescued him a few weeks ago. Meanwhile Yellow section, led by S/L Gilroy, has also been engaged and has followed the beehive to the target. Off Le Touquet it becomes engaged again with 2 Fw190s, and off Dungeness meet two 109Es. As for Blue section, Flight Lieutenant Offenberg, after damaging a 109, blacks out and afterwards joins up again with Blue 2, Pilot Officer du Monceau. Approaching the coast they are attacked by two more 109s, and 5 miles off the coast Pilot Officer du Monceau succeeds in bringing one plunging down toward the sea, a pilot of 72 being instrumental in getting this confirmed. (609 Squadron Operational Record Book, 27 October 1941)

Fighting their way out, the pilots of the Wing were relieved to see the French coast disappearing behind them, though the enemy continued to snap at their heels for some way across the Channel. Most squadrons, including those from Hornchurch and Northolt Wings, had been engaged and on return both 72 Squadron from

Biggin and Hornchurch's 603 Squadron had lost two pilots each. There had been some successes, most notably for Jamie Rankin.

Davies had eagerly awaited the WingCo's return and, as he saw QJ-J coming into land, it was hard to contain his excitement. The cannons on Jamie's aircraft had been some of the first to be modified in line with the work of Stewart's team and so Davies had been over the moon when Stewart had given him the nod to 'look after' the WingCo on this day. Rankin had led with 609 Squadron and 'Claude' Rains and Davies had delivered the 20mm magazines to his aircraft themselves, prepared with the utmost care – so much so that they had managed to resist the offers of help from a number of armourers' assistants and had 'plumbed' them in personally. As Rankin taxied in, Davies could see that the patches on the Brownings and the covers for the 20mms had been shot away. The tension was excruciating! With the propeller still milling to a stop, Rankin threw back the hood and dropped the side door.

Well this day, the aircraft were coming back in ones and twos, perhaps threes and we were anxiously waiting. So Rankin came back and I was standing by the aircraft and out he jumped and shouted 'I've shot down three!' By Christ, he was excited and I was for him! Now to shoot three down in the same sortie, whether it was a scramble or any other operation, was unheard of. Of course the riggers were ready to get out their paint and up three Swastikas on his aircraft. Now I think this brought his score up to thirty-two. Before it had only been singles. From what I can remember, I believe that this 'kite' was QJ-J. (LAC Raymond Davies, memoir 30/12/2001)

Dickie Milne and other pilots of 92 Squadron were ordered to land back at Biggin for the benefit of the mysterious VIP who had been 'entertained' by 'Ops', listening in to the action and the R/t chatter of the pilots. As Sergeant Johnston recalled:

We had orders to land back at Biggin, which we duly did, and I think we were the last to land from the Wing. Because the CO (Milne) was with us we were ushered up to the front of a very ragged parade. We were in our usual flying dress, by the way. Battledress was out by this time, and we were all in shirt sleeves, no ties, Mae Wests and the same trousers – so no difference shown really between ranks. We had been lined up waiting – Milne, Beake, Carpenter, Johnston. Then the VIPs were late. We had been perspiring a lot in the cockpits and not all due to sunshine! So we were beginning to feel chilly and wanted a smoke. But the main party arrived, and it was not the King, but the Prime Minister – plus Sir Archibald Sinclair, who proceeded to give us a pep talk about the Hurris [Hurricanes] which had first gone to Russia. Finally the P.M. came along to speak to us. Apparently he had been impressed by the way the engagement unfolded via the R/t and had expressed a wish to speak to some of those who had been involved. He started with the end [of the line] and the CO. Introduced [he] then said 'and so you are Dickie then?' [Then he] went to Beake, wished him a good wedding day to come and wagged his finger and said 'You're a lucky fellow.' Then to Carpenter, to whom he said 'and obviously, you are "Chips" are you not?' Then to me on the end, introduced as 'Johnston' but at the same time he said [having heard the R/t chatter and expletives], 'Ah! And you must be Johnnie, the Geordie with the fine flow of language!' I claimed one probable and one severely damaged. A very intense and fraught trip indeed. (Sergeant Walter 'Johnnie' Johnston, letter, 1997)

So ended September. The last few days saw little more than a couple of aborted 'ops' for 92 Squadron and the Biggin Wing. A few pilots managed air tests and, on the ground, crews used the time to catch up on maintenance and repairs. In all, it had been a disjointed, unsettled month – that was if you really ever could settle into such an existence. Yes, there were aspects that could be considered routine: the daily inspections, readiness, briefing, preparation. Then there was the 'familiar': Finding a dance or a pub, settling down in the mess, a game of snooker, reading the odd book or letter from home. Perhaps these were the routines that you relied upon to get you through the day, the ones you could lose yourself in and lose time in? Perhaps even death could become routine? It certainly seemed commonplace. But without being sometimes 'matter of fact' about it, the gravity of the situation and the experience of loss started to work its way back into the forefront of one's mind. Damaging, sometimes paralysing. Always saddening. The 27th had also heralded a change in fortunes for the RAF – if you could call any of this fortunate. For 92 Squadron the following week would prove shattering. As 1941's glorious summer drew to a close, it was clear that the balance was shifting.

Chapter Twelve

Bloody October

Gravesend Satellite:
With 92 Squadron's move to Gravesend, Davies sensed a change in the pattern of his work. He had started at Biggin very much like numerous other airmen, assigned to the role of armourers' assistant. Yet his association with 92 Squadron at such a critical time in the development of the Spitfire's main armament had meant that his duties were perhaps not characteristic of his trade. Being part of Chiefy Stewart's team had not only put him at the forefront of the development of the 20mm cannon as an effective weapon, but it had meant that his deployment with 92 Squadron had been specialised rather than general. Furthermore, his assignment to particular pilots was perhaps indicative of the realities of operational conditions where the personal preferences of pilots required a familiarity amongst their ground crews. In armament terms, for some pilots this might mean the harmonisation settings that one felt gave the best results. For others, such as Kingaby, it was also about the ratio of high explosive, armour piercing and tracer rounds that one liked. Knowing a pilot's idiosyncrasies meant that in practice some armourers found themselves assigned to specific pilots, rather than being organised more generally to attend any aircraft.

During those first eight months of his service he had spent time assigned to Kingcome, Rankin and Kingaby, though at other times he had worked generally on 'A' Flight's aircraft, including 'Boy' Wellum's and now Dickie Milne's. Having 92 Squadron out at Gravesend, Chiefy Stewart now decided to send Davies, Campbell and Woods over from Biggin, considering it useful to have some of the team to be at hand for reporting on and hopefully managing any cannon problems that occurred. Davies' other comrades, Broomhead and Healey, remained at Biggin with 3034 Echelon. Yet Davies' and the squadron's stay at Gravesend was to be short-lived and marked the final period of 92 Squadron's time in the sector.

After a number of countermanding orders on the 1st, the Wing was finally sent off on a fighter sweep of the Channel. A layer of altostratus extended for much of the course of the sweep – or 'rodeo' as they were now officially known – and so Rankin set 609 Squadron to stay above cloud, with 92 and 72 Squadrons operating below. As a result of this deployment, the majority of the former squadron failed to make contact with a force of Me109s that were encountered at the lower level. In the region of Gris Nez, Dickie Milne caught sight of a formation of approximately thirty-plus bandits and took 92 Squadron to intercept their climb. Don Kingaby latched onto an Me109F in the turn and gave it a burst of 20mm that proved fatal. Later, Don sent another Me109F spiralling earthwards, though this time was unable to confirm its destruction. Landing back at Biggin, Flight Lieutenant Kasinsky had claimed a further Me109, making 92's total two destroyed and one probable.

Though 92 Squadron was still clearly an effective fighting unit, it seemed a different squadron to some. Certainly, many of the characters that had made the squadron what it was were gone – posted out, rested, missing or killed. Others had been shot down and now found themselves 'in the bag', enduring life as prisoners of war. Of those that had been with the squadron during 1940, only Don Kingaby and Tommy Lund remained into October. While there seemed little outward sign of any loss of morale, in private many were feeling the effects of combat fatigue. The loss of Tommy Lund on 2 October perhaps stood as the embodiment of how the senior squadron of the Wing was in need of rest.

Tommy Lund:
John Lund was born on 6 May 1919 in Norton, North Yorkshire. Tom, as he was universally known, was educated at Kingswood School near Bath. Kingswood was a Wesleyan school and both Tom and another pupil joining at this time, John Alec Atkinson, were sons of Methodist ministers. With this common background they soon got to know each other well.

> *We were both sons of Methodist ministers, that's why we went to the School which had been founded by John Wesley. So I knew Tom throughout his school-days. Of course his name wasn't really 'Tom', why he was called Tom I don't know but he always was. He was John Wilfred. Ultimately, he was the head prefect and I was a house prefect so we shared a study together. Sharing a room with him was very agreeable, he was a very interesting chap, very keen on playing cricket and he was keen on his studies which related to mediaeval history. These were unlike mine which were a mixture of history and science but we always got on well together.* (Pilot Officer Alec 'Joe' Atkinson, interview 2005)

At Kingswood, Tom excelled academically and on leaving in the summer of 1938 went up to Oriel College, Oxford to read history. Atkinson too received a scholarship for Queens College at Oxford, reading politics, philosophy and economics. So their association continued. While life pretty much followed a usual pattern for any university undergraduates, there was a real sense of war looming on the darkened horizon. Thus, both Lund and Atkinson decided to join the University Air Squadron.

There was very much so a feeling that war was coming. It was perfectly obvious that there was going to be a war and everybody was really living under that cloud but were determined to have a good time while they still could. So there was a lot of jollification! I met my later wife, she was an undergraduate at St Anne's and we were very happy together but we didn't marry until after the war. Tom and I both joined the Air Squadron. My primary motivation was that I didn't want to go into the infantry – that seemed very hum-drum and I thought it would be very interesting to fly. I didn't have any fascination for flying before I joined. Tom and I talked about joining the Air Squadron together and though we joined at the same time, he got a bit ahead of me because we had a summer camp at Lympne and he did more flying there which qualified him to be taken through to final training – earlier than I was and the consequence was that he joined a squadron before I did. (Pilot Officer Alec 'Joe' Atkinson, interview 2005)

It was at RAF Abingdon in Oxfordshire that their flying training began.

We were taught to fly at Abingdon and later (though we didn't get to that stage) people were taught night flying at Brize Norton. We would drive out to Abingdon, perhaps once or twice a week – not necessarily at weekends – and we would have instruction but I didn't manage to go solo until the summer camp, I don't think Tom did either. I remember my first solo, how light the plane felt when I was by myself – otherwise of course you'd got someone else with their feet on the pedals in the other cockpit. The aircraft was an Avro Tutor. (Pilot Officer Alec 'Joe' Atkinson, interview 2005)

Tom, perhaps, was a little more excited by the experience than Alec for whom, though exhilarated, never really described himself as having the 'flying bug'. There were more serious undertakings, as the University Air Squadrons were part of the Royal Air Force Volunteer Reserve.

Of course we were automatically in the Volunteer Reserve and a day or two before the beginning of the war I remember travelling to Oxford by train and travelling up to the Centre. I happened to go up in the same taxi as Leonard Cheshire, so in the light of after events that was rather auspicious! He was a very wild young man and he was very agreeable. I met his brother at the initial training wing at Cambridge and their father was a very eminent lawyer, an academic lawyer – it was 'Cheshire on Torts'. They were very memorable chaps. (Pilot Officer Alec 'Joe' Atkinson, interview 2005)

So in November 1939 Tom left his studies at Oxford to continue his training at RAF Cranwell. On graduation he then spent a brief spell with No.1 School of Army Co-operation before being posted to 5 OTU at Aston Down. After converting to Spitfires Tom's first operational posting was to 611 Squadron at Digby, flying in support of the evacuation of the BEF at Dunkirk and then in defence of the east coast as part of 12 Group Fighter Command. While 611 Squadron remained in the North, Lund was posted to 92 Squadron in the later stages of the Battle of Britain, arriving at Biggin Hill on 2 October 1940.

Sometime very soon after Tom's posting to 92 Squadron he wrote to Alec Atkinson, clearly pleased to be with such a squadron and characteristically up-beat.

I remember him writing to me at the beginning of the war when he was in 92 Squadron and saying that I might like to try and join a squadron of that sort 'cos he said 'it's not really Death around the corner, it's all very good fun'. He obviously was enjoying himself and I think he was a very popular member of the Squadron. (Pilot Officer Alec 'Joe' Atkinson, interview 2005)

'Mac' McGowan, the Squadron Adjutant, brought Tom down to dispersal on his first day with 92 Squadron and introduced him to the assembled crowd. One of the first to be introduced, and destined to become a great friend of Tom's, was Geoffrey Wellum.

My first impression of him [Tom] was a delightful man. I mean he was obviously intelligent, in fact he'd got a degree at Oxford. He was well spoken and extremely polite. He was a very very agreeable character. I felt an immediate friendship with him and it continued that we got on well together as he did with the rest of the squadron, mind you. But I mean we went to the theatre in London when we were released, I can remember. We used to night fly together. We were night flying one night and we were released in the morning so we went up to a matinee in London. And we used to drink our beer together. He was friendly with everybody, particularly 'Joe' Atkinson.

He had some experience [when he came to 92 Squadron] and this was a very very great help to him. If you went with no experience to a squadron, if you could survive the first three weeks you were, well you weren't home and dry but you had a bloody good chance. Tommy seemed to know his way around a bit. I wouldn't say

he was a very aggressive fighter pilot, but he was a steady, utterly reliable chap.
(Flight Lieutenant Geoffrey Wellum, interview 2006)

Little known to his fellow pilots, Tommy also took it upon himself to be somewhat of an exclusive diarist for the ground crew. Most probably fuelled by his sense of history and the importance of it being recorded, he began writing short 'newsletters' under a pseudonym. Almost daily, at least when 92 Squadron had been in action, one of these single page accounts of the day's operations would appear. As Davies remembered:

We were never really told, officially, about what the squadron had been doing. We would get some information from our pilots in general chat when they got down. But there was one pilot with 92 who would, every time the Squadron had been action, write like a news report, a bulletin that told us of the day's events. It started to appear on the ground crew notice board at dispersal – I'll never forget them because they were a fantastic source of information that gave us a real boost, knowing what we had contributed to. They were called 'Nobby Lund's Dispatches', so we presumed that it was Tommy Lund. I always wondered what happened to them because they were a fantastic record. (LAC Raymond Davies, memoir 2003)[2]

So whether Tommy knew it or not, his act of recording these moments in history made a tremendous contribution to the morale of the ground crew. For Davies and his comrades it made them feel even closer to the ultimate results. When they watched the kites go off every day, it gave them a sense of pride to send them up and they worked day and night – whatever hours it took – to get their squadron on top line. Already, when the squadron took off on operations, they felt as if they were flying with them to go do battle with the enemy. Tommy had brought them even closer. Sadly, the second day of October brought an abrupt end to the daily dispatches.

After briefing at Biggin on 2 October, Tommy and the rest of 92's pilots settled into their cockpits waiting for the signal from Des Sheen, acting as WingCo. At 1241 hours, Sheen led 72 Squadron off, passing out towards the West in a gentle climb, with 609 and 92 Squadrons following in their wake. Acting as a diversionary sweep

---

2. Unfortunately I was not able to track down the diary either. At one point Brian Kingcome had it, as it was mentioned in Graham Wallace's acknowledgements for his book about Biggin Hill, written in 1956. Having checked with Geoffrey Wellum and Kingcome's widow, Lesley, it seems to have been lost over the years.

for Circus 104, the Wing planned to approach from Berck, with 609 Squadron positioned as top cover. Drifting some distance to the south, landfall was actually made near Le Crotoy. Some of 92's pilots, operating at a lower altitude than 609 Squadron, could make out the distinctive tributaries and dunes that characterised the Baie de Somme, with Le Crotoy and St Valery-sur-Somme at the jaws of the estuary. It had been the Wing's intention to keep a lid on the Abbeville boys, but from their lofty perch 609 Squadron spotted formations of Me109s already in the distance with altitude at hand. Perhaps by way of offering protection to one of his charges that had developed a glycol leak, Tommy Lund's Blue section of 92 Squadron had dropped lower than the rest of the formation. The enemy was quick to take advantage. Flying in red section, Johnnie Johnston described how the Luftwaffe attack broke through the upper elements of the squadron and exploited Blue section's vulnerable position:

October 2nd: To Biggin for a briefing, then on a patrol to be a diversionary sweep to Abbeville – and its yellow-nosed lads! For some reason, Blue section were well below the other section, much too low for us to help. There were many 109Fs around and what later on we understood to be Fw190s. A mixed bunch were above us and dived into the attack, which we evaded. They continued the dive and caught Blue section. We all saw it happen but even a shout was too late. Flight Lieutenant Tommy Lund, Sergeant Norman Edge, and Sergeant Port went down immediately, while Tony Bruce, though hit, managed to get home and to hospital. I think a cannon shell hit the top of his armour plate and sprayed fine splinters up into his neck and scalp. So all four were gone. (Sergeant Walter 'Johnnie' Johnston, interview 2004)

Landing back in at Gravesend, pilots and ground crew took stock. Four lost in a day – most on the squadron had not experienced this before, not since the desperate times of 1940. The loss of Tommy weighed heavily for all. No more would his laughter and wry humour lighten the spirit, nor defuse the blackest of moments. His long-time school and university friend Alec 'Joe' Atkinson had flown the same operation with 609 Squadron and, on landing, heard that Tom had been shot down. The loss of such a close friend he found very shaking.

As a character he was a good-looking chap and well-built, and very personable. He got on well with people. He didn't take himself too seriously. I don't think he was a great teller of funny stories, but he had a quizzical sort of attitude to life which imported a good sense of humour – he was always prepared to have a laugh about something. He was capable of doing most things but he wasn't by any means

92 (East India) Squadron displaying its tally board in early 1941. L-R are: unknown; Weise (IO); Mottram; Havercroft; Kingcome; Kent (CO); Sherington; Saunders; Holland; Wright; Bowen-Morris; Lund. (*Courtesy of IWM*)

'Sailor' Malan, Biggin Hill's Wing Leader at the start of 1941, when the Wing comprised of 92, 609 and 74 squadrons. (*Courtesy of IWM*)

'Sailor' Malan and 609 Squadron's CO Michael Lister Robinson down at 609's dispersal. (*Courtesy of Jim Earnshaw and 609 Squadron Association*)

Jamie Rankin, photographed later in the war as a Group Captain. Davies worked closely with Rankin, first when CO of 92 Squadron and then as Wing Leader after Malan was rested. (*Courtesy of IWM*)

Allan Wright flying Spitfire Vb R6923. This Spitfire was one of the first batch of Mark I Spitfires converted to Vb status by Rolls Royce at Hucknall. As Wright's personal aircraft for most of his time with 92 in 1941, he nicknamed it 'Satan'. (*Courtesy of IWM*)

Armourers practice arming a Spitfire Vb whilst wearing protective clothing during a simulated poisoned gas attack. The bulk of the 60-round drum for the 20mm Hispano cannon is clearly evident here, as the armourer on the wing drops it into position. The armourer under the wing is loading .303 ammunition for the outboard Browning machine guns. (*Courtesy of IWM*)

Ronald 'Claude' Rains of 609 Squadron. 'Claude' was one of the senior NCOs on the specialist armourers' team to which Davies was assigned. (*Courtesy of Jim Earnshaw and 609 Squadron Association*)

A studio portrait of Don Kingaby. Kingaby was the first pilot with whom Davies worked when Don was a sergeant with 92 Squadron. He was the only pilot ever to be awarded three Distinguished Flying Medals (DFM). (*Courtesy of IWM*)

Some of 609 Squadron's ground crew congregate around Spitfire Vb 'City of Leeds'. When 92 Squadron left Biggin Hill, Jamie Rankin's personal aircraft was looked after by 609 Squadron. As one of Jamie's armourers, Davies spent time at 609's dispersal and mistook the name of this aircraft for the name of the Squadron. (*Courtesy of Jim Earnshaw and 609 Squadron Association*)

Sergeant Walter 'Johnnie' Johnston in his 92 Squadron Spitfire, QJ-H. (*Courtesy of 'Johnnie' Johnston*)

Sergeant Hugh Bowen-Morris. 'Bowie' was a long-serving NCO with 92 Squadron but was shot down in July 1941. Seriously wounded, he lost an arm and was eventually repatriated in 1943, just in time to attend Don and Helen Kingaby's wedding. (*Courtesy of 'Johnnie' Johnston*)

Sergeant 'Johnnie' Johnston with one of his ground crew with 92 Squadron. 'Johnnie' and Davies shared the same birthday, 28th August 1920. (*Courtesy of 'Johnnie' Johnston*)

Bowen-Morris in the cockpit of his 92 Squadron aircraft at Biggin Hill in 1941. (*Courtesy of 'Johnnie' Johnston*)

Sergeant David Lloyd with 92 Squadron in 1941. Lloyd survived the intensity of operations with the Wing and was posted out to 61 OTU at Heston in August 1941. Tragically he was killed in an air accident in March 1942. (*Courtesy of 'Johnnie' Johnston*)

Sergeant Ralph 'Tich' Havercroft. Another of 92 Squadron's long-serving and experienced NCOs, Havercroft flew with the Squadron throughout Dunkirk, The Battle of Britain and the fighter offensive of 1941. He was eventually posted away in June 1941, having flown 173 operations and been on 'ops' continuously for twenty-one months. (*Courtesy of 'Johnnie' Johnston*)

Xavier De Montbron accepted a commission whilst flying with 92 Squadron in 1941. On 'ops' throughout 1940 and 41, 'Monty' was posted missing in action in July 1941 and later reported as a POW. Post-war he rose to rank of Commandant in the French Air Force but was killed flying a De Havilland Vampire in May 1955. (*Courtesy of 'Johnnie' Johnston*)

92 Squadron line up their Spitfire Vbs at Biggin, 1941. The CO, Jamie Rankin's aircraft (R7161) is nearest the camera. Working closely with Rankin, Davies would regularly tend to this aircraft's cannons. (*Courtesy of IWM*)

Above: Pilots of 92 Squadron in 1941 after Jamie Rankin took over as CO. L-R are: Brettell; De Montbron; Kingcome; Le Cheminant; Kingaby; unknown; Bowen-Morris; Mottram; Rankin; Archer; unknown; unknown; Wright; Duke; unknown; McGowan (Adj); Gaskell (*Courtesy of IWM*)

Right: Flight Lieutenant Brian Kingcome and Flying Officer Geoffrey 'Boy' Wellum at Biggin Hill in 1941. (*Courtesy of IWM*)

11 July 1941. Kingcome's Spitfire Vb (QJ-F) gets an inspection from the Prime Minister of New Zealand, Rt Hon Peter Frazer. This photo was taken in the evening after a particularly challenging operation, Circus 44, in which Pilot Officer Dougal had been lost, coming to the aid of David Lloyd. Rankin's aircraft can be seen in the distance with its attendant ground crew. (*Courtesy of IWM*)

Pilot Officer Neville Duke. It was a fresh-faced and inexperienced Duke that joined 92 Squadron at Biggin in April 1941. He would rise to become a successful Squadron Leader in the Western Desert and Italy campaigns. Post-war he was well-known as a test pilot with Hawker Aviation Company and holder of the world air speed record in 1953. (*Courtesy of IWM*)

Sergeant Mercer, 609 Squadron. Mercer was one of 609's experienced NCO pilots, having been with them throughout the Battle of Britain. On 9th May 1941 when attempting a forced landing in Spitfire P7305 at St Margaret's Bay, Kent, his aircraft struck and exploded a mine, killing Mercer. (*Courtesy of Jim Earnshaw and 609 Squadron Association*)

609 Squadron's Commanding Officer, Michael Lister Robinson. Portrait by the artist Cuthbert Orde. Captain Orde had been a pilot in World War One and would often travel the 11 miles from his home at Edenbridge to Biggin Hill to sketch its pilots. (*Courtesy of Jim Earnshaw and 609 Squadron Association*)

Flying Officer Alec 'Joe' Atkinson, portrait by Cuthbert Orde, 1941. (*Courtesy of Jim Earnshaw and 609 Squadron Association*)

Another of 609 Squadron's long-serving NCO pilots, Sergeant 'Goldy' Palmer. Palmer was killed in action on 21st October 1941. (*Courtesy of Jim Earnshaw and 609 Squadron Association*)

Flying Officer John Alexander Atkinson. 609 Squadron's 'Joe' Atkinson flew with them at Biggin Hill throughout 1941. He served with the squadron into 1943, becoming their longest serving pilot. (*Courtesy of Jim Earnshaw and 609 Squadron Association*)

609 Squadron's pennant flying above their dispersal at Biggin Hill. The CO, Mike Robinson awaits the call to readiness. (*Courtesy of Jim Earnshaw and 609 Squadron Association*)

Sergeant Tommy Rigler, 609 Squadron, inspects damage to his Spitfire Vb on return to Biggin. (*Courtesy of Jim Earnshaw and 609 Squadron Association*)

(*Right*) A modern photograph of the King's Arms at Leaves Green. This public house was a frequent rendezvous for Davies and his comrades. When they didn't have a pass out of camp, it could be reached via a hole in the fence not far from 92 Squadron's dispersal. (*Author's collection*)

The Old Jail public house. This was a favourite watering hole for the NCOs and ground crews at Biggin. Close to the airfield, this was one of the regular off-duty places for Davies, Don Kingaby and Johnnie Johnston. Popular with 609 Squadron, it was its Belgian landlady, 'Biddy', that gave the squadron its feisty mascot, William de Goat. (*Courtesy of Jim Earnshaw and 609 Squadron Association*)

OC Biggin Hill, Group Captain 'Dickie' Barwell, and Wing Commander Jamie Rankin enjoying a beer on the steps of the Officers' Mess at Biggin. It was Barwell and Rankin that were instrumental in keeping the specialist armourers team together under Warrant Officer Stewart throughout 1941–42. (*Courtesy of John Barwell*)

Wing Commander Jamie Rankin in a later role at the Fighter Leaders School. Rankin sits centre front row. Flight Lieutenant Percy Beake, formerly of 92 Squadron, stands at the far right, third row. Beake would become Davies' commanding officer later in the war, when they were both posted to 164 Squadron. (*Courtesy of Percy Beake*)

Biggin Hill's briefing room, showing details of Circus 62, flown at the end of July 1941. (*Courtesy of Jim Earnshaw and 609 Squadron Association*)

Rankin (left) chats to one of 609 Squadron's Belgian pilots, Jean Offenberg at dispersal. (*Courtesy of Jim Earnshaw and 609 Squadron Association*)

Newly appointed as CO 92 Squadron, Squadron Leader 'Dickie' Milne sits in his Spitfire Vb 'New Yorklin'. Milne was to be 92's last commanding officer before they left the sector for RAF Digby, Lincolnshire. (*Courtesy of IWM*)

Ground crews attend to Spitfire P7881, 609 Squadron. With the loss of permanent hangarage during the Battle of Britain, most servicing at Biggin in 1941–42 was conducted either in the open or in these hastily-erected 'blister' hangars. This specific aircraft was often flown by the OC Biggin Hill, as it coincidentally bore his initials – Philip Reginald Barwell. (*Courtesy of Jim Earnshaw and 609 Squadron Association*)

Squadron Leader Bobbie Oxspring flew with 91 Squadron, being one of the first pilots to spot the German capital ships in the Channel during Operation Fuller. Later Oxspring took over from Kingcome as CO of 72 Squadron as part of the Biggin Hill Wing in 1942. (*Courtesy of IWM*)

Group Captain Philip Barwell, Officer Commanding Biggin Hill (left), seen here with Lord Trenchard (MRAF) and Squadron Leader Michael Lister Robinson. 'Dickie' Barwell was held in high regard by all and his loss in July 1942 deeply affected everyone that had served under him at Biggin. (*Courtesy of Jim Earnshaw and 609 Squadron Association*)

Spitfire Vb (W3365) of 72 Squadron lies with its back broken at Layham's Farm, West Wickham. Electing to air test this aircraft in order to identify some recurring problems, Group Captain Barwell was forced to land the aircraft when the engine cut, shortly after take off at 15.25 hours, 9th August 1941. (*Courtesy of John Barwell*)

Ground crew arrive to recover the wreckage of Spitfire Vb (W3365) following Barwell's forced landing. Barwell fractured his 2nd and 4th lumbar vertebrae in the accident. He was admitted to Orpington Hospital and discharged on 22nd August 1941. In significant pain, Barwell resumed his duties as Station Commander but had to be re-admitted to hospital on 11th September 1941. With a plaster 'waistcoat' fitted, the doctors reluctantly discharged him to the care of Biggin Hill on the 15th September 1941. He was back to work immediately. (*Courtesy of John Barwell*)

Cockpit of Barwell's crashed Spitfire Vb (W3365). Careful inspection reveals the main fracture point of the fuselage, in line with the pilot's seat. (*Courtesy of John Barwell*)

72 Squadron lined up at Biggin Hill's satellite airfield at Gravesend. During Davies' time at Biggin, 72 flew with the Wing, first led by Desmond Sheen, then Brian Kingcome and lastly by Bobbie Oxspring. (*Courtesy of IWM*)

Ground crews attend to a Spitfire Vb of 222 Squadron. This photograph clearly shows the typical range of duties carried out in preparation for 'ops'. Just in front of the port wing lies one of the large 60-round ammunition drums for the 20mm Hispano cannon. (*Courtesy of IWM*)

Pictured here against his 71 (Eagle) Squadron aircraft, Carroll McColpin became 133 (Eagle) Squadron's commander towards the end of their time with the Biggin Hill Wing. (*Courtesy of IWM*)

Study of a Fighter Leader: Formerly Davies' CO with 92 Squadron in September and October 1941, here Wing Commander Richard Maxwell Milne poses for the camera on his return to Biggin Hill as Wing Leader in 1943. It was his fourth tour of duty. (*Courtesy of IWM*)

An aircraft of 64 Squadron is run up with ground crew sitting on the tail to stop it lifting during high power engine runs. Although assigned specific trades, ground crews assisted with a general range of tasks on front-line airfields and squadrons. (*Courtesy of IWM*)

A harmonisation board, set up at Biggin Hill. Armourer used these structures in order to set the degrees of spread and point of convergence for an aircraft's guns. The four small, outer placards mark the focusing points for the Spitfire's four .303 machine guns. The larger outboard placards are for the 20mm cannon. The two other large discs (near to the centre line) mark the line of sight and the camera gun positions. (*Courtesy of IWM*)

A familiar yet unforgettable sight. Spitfire Vbs of the Biggin Hill Wing take off over their attendant ground crews at dispersal, summer 1941. Now all there was to do was wait and hope for their safe return. (*Courtesy of Jim Earnshaw and 609 Squadron Association*)

a self-advertiser. I remember him as a good, sterling chap. (Pilot Officer Alec 'Joe' Atkinson, interview 2005)

His close friend Geoffrey Wellum, now posted on rest, was also deeply affected by the news:

I heard about it on the grapevine. I can't remember who it was but somebody phoned me. It could have been Bill Igoe who was a controller. It upset me very very much. Tom and I ... he was friendly with everybody ... but I would like to think that he and I were as close as it was possible to get.

He was a very pleasant, gentle man. In pubs in the evening after we had been released, drinking pints with him and being in his company. I don't know, it was always a nice feeling to be in the company of such a bloke. All pilots were, those of us that survived the Battle [of Britain] had a very great affinity, I mean we were survivors and Tommy was one of those. I found him a very gentle, quiet, always smiling – a very very charming man. He had a terrific sense of humour, absolutely terrific: a little bit dry at times but he seemed always to have a twinkle in his eye. Ladies liked him, you know, my God did they! You could see when he was being a little bit flippant ... but very charming. Mischief was written all over him, particular after a couple of pints! (Flight Lieutenant Geoffrey Wellum, interview 2006)

For Davies and other ground crew, Tommy, in his guise as Nobby Lund, had been their diarist, their insight into the squadron's contribution to this war. Tommy had brought closer the outcome and purpose of their labours, had made more personal and real the meaning of '*doing your bit*'.

Kingo's Tenacity:
As 92 Squadron's pilots dragged themselves back to their billets, many of the ground crews faced a long night attempting to bring enough Spitfires up to readiness for the next morning. The losses of the 2nd meant that a number that had been in for inspections were feverishly worked upon in the effort to bring the squadron up to strength. When there was not too much in the way of armament work to be carried out, Davies and Campbell would help out some of the fitters – mainly fetching and carrying, de-panelling, but picking up some 'gen' along the way. Some of the aircrew stayed around to do the same when they knew their ground crews would be putting in maximum effort to get their aircraft on line for the morning – both Johnnie Johnston and Don Kingaby were known to hand a spanner, pass a screwdriver here and there. By morning light on 3 October, the

Tilley lamps were slowly extinguished and the tarpaulins of the blister hangars were rolled back. Eight aircraft for today.

Circus 105, at least at briefing, seemed pretty much a standard affair – escort to a number of Blenheims bombing Ostend. Yet perhaps a mixture of fatigue and the heavy casualties of the previous day made it seem a little more unpleasant as a way of passing the time! For Kingaby, and 92 Squadron, it was to be one of the toughest days.

While Don was not known to be superstitious, the crackling of his R/t on the route out perhaps should have signalled to him that worse was to come. Keeping formation in his No.3 position, he tried to put out of his mind the popping and spitting coming through his headset, hoping that it was just bad static and that the interference would eventually pass. It was not to be. All of a sudden there was nothing – not even the static. Don thought about making his predicament known, and looked over at Johnston to make the usual hand signals to indicate that his R/t was now u/s. It was a perfectly justifiable reason to return to base, he might only be a hindrance to the rest of the squadron. He might not hear a warning if they were bounced. Decidedly dicey! But leaving the formation would leave the Squadron very short – they were only eight as it stood. Doing it by the book would require Don and an escorting wingman to head for home, leaving a mere six to do the work normally expected of the full squadron. So Don tucked in a little closer, kept his eyes fixed on Johnston and decided to stay. Johnnie, flying as No.4 in the outside section of the formation, had noticed his pal's attentiveness.

There had been reports of landing craft seen in the harbours and docks area at Ostend, and [we had] 6 Blenheims as the bombers. We flew along the Channel coast, Blenheims on our landward (starboard) side. So we were looking over them, over the land where e/a would have come. To our left, and above, were 609 Squadron, who were covering us, the close escort, and the Blenheims. After the first run, we turned to return for a second and remained on the seaward side of the Blenheims. Once again I was No.4, and one of the outside section. Don was No.3 in the other, and I had been conscious all the time that he had been looking at me rather a lot. (Sergeant Walter 'Johnnie' Johnston, letter, 2002)

There was possibly some misunderstanding as far as 609 Squadron were concerned and as they approached the target. Contrary to what had been briefed, the bombers seemed to be further inland than expected, by some fifteen miles.

... with the result that 609, some 8000ft above 92 as top cover, loses sight of the formation, only sighting the bombers again over Ostend thanks to intensive flak. (609 Squadron Operational Record Book, 3 October 1941)

Kingaby continued to keep a close watch on the keen-sighted Johnston who was scanning the sky for any sight of trouble while still wondering why Don was continuing to look over. It was at this point that the Luftwaffe made its move, to devastating effect.

No doubt about it, we really did get hammered.... We'd been flying eastwards up the Channel watching [the] Blenheims ... and 609 Squadron were supposed to be sitting up on us and doing the top cover but when we turned to come back down again, they should have done a cross-over turn. I looked up and I saw a gaggle of aircraft up on my starboard side, just where I expected 609 to have been – I was quite happy. Don was still spending a lot of time looking over actually at me but I didn't think anything of it. I reported these aircraft and then, like a bolt out of the blue, just as I was finishing the transmission, they suddenly just winged over and dropped down and I realised that there were a gaggle of about 30+ 109s – they had taken up the position that 609 should have had. We were in terrible trouble. I called up, reported them and shouted 'break' and while I was saying that I was actually breaking. (Sergeant Walter 'Johnnie' Johnston, interview 2002)

As Johnston called the break, Kingaby – still without any radio – interpreted his pal's urgent and violent actions and followed suit in a desperate manoeuvre to avoid the diving Messerschmitts. Keeping watch on Johnston paid off, as Kingaby knew full well – he and Johnnie seemed to share the same luck and sense of self-preservation! He considered that if he broke when Johnnie broke, then there was a good chance that he'd be all right.

We broke out to starboard but they [the 109s] had anticipated our move only too well. As I hauled round I saw Don doing the same, but almost at the same time the 109s came into his section. Sergeant Cox (No.4) had his tail broken off and an explosion up front. No.3 – Don – was out of the way so they went straight into No.2 Sergeant Wood-Scawen. [He] received a terrible lot of firepower. He just rolled over and went straight down. (Sergeant Walter 'Johnnie' Johnston, letter, 2002)

The ferocity of the initial attack had managed to split 92 Squadron – now numbering only six pilots. Kingaby, feeling helpless without any means of communication, frustratedly made one more attempt to find the source of the problem, trying to look round in the cockpit for any signs of a fault – a loose connector perhaps? Yet the problem, as Don knew, was more deep-rooted and the R/t failure was only one facet of the general failure of the aircraft's electrical system. Another symptom was that he now had no cross-hairs showing on the glass of the reflector gunsight: it had shorted out as they had approached the target. With his head in the cockpit rather than 'on the swivel' looking out, he became detached from the squadron, lagging some way behind. Johnston too, after what seemed like a lifetime of evasive action, found himself alone in a clear part of the sky.

> *I felt I'd been hit, but couldn't find anything wrong with old 'H' to account for the clang and sort of twitch it had given. But I didn't want to be too violent with it. I was quite suddenly in a large empty space of sky and set course gently and merrily for England.* (Sergeant Walter 'Johnnie' Johnston, letter 2002)

However, Johnston's respite from enemy attacks was to be short-lived and soon he became the focus of three Me109s – characteristically preying on lone aircraft that were on their way home and probably low on fuel.

> *I stuffed the nose down to get some more speed, but they caught me up and went into line abreast so that whichever way I turned, I was covered. Five more joined them and it was like a lot of cats after one mouse! I got the impression that they were indeed playing with me. The leader kept having a squirt, but was generally out of range and a lousy shot. I wondered if he was the leader who had to make his name safely. I had no place to go except downwards, and began to think that I'd be safer if I jumped hoping they would then not attack me in the drink.* (Sergeant Walter 'Johnnie' Johnston, letter 2002)

Kingaby pushed the throttle through the gate in an attempt to intercept, coaxing every ounce of power out of the Merlin. Without R/t and gunsight, it was perhaps a desperate act but he had to do something to break up the snapping Me109s. Just as Johnston thought it was all over, he caught sight of this lone Spitfire.

> *I saw this aircraft coming in from the starboard and he was flying right at me – it was a Spit so I knew it was all right…. it was coming down and lined up on the 109s. They had got careless and were engrossed with me. It [the Spitfire] came down, more or less along the line and fired like hell all the way. [It went] over the top in a flash, climbed and cut away in front and came back, flying alongside. I realised, of course, it was Don by his [identification] letter and he made signs that*

his R/t was u/s. He then was waving his hand and pointing with his finger – he wanted me to get cracking and try to get back to the coast (we weren't a long way away from the coast). Now, I know that out of the aircraft that were behind me, when I got away and I looked back, they were two short. I can't remember whether he claimed two on that trip or not but I know that I put it down when I came back that I was sure that he had collected two on that trip. I believe he got them in his first run. (Sergeant Walter 'Johnnie' Johnston – compiled from letter and interview 2002)

As Johnnie made for the coast, Don was now faced with the remaining Me109s, bearing bright, yellow nose markings.

For a couple of minutes I twisted and turned and evaded their attacks, but then I found them coming in on me from each quarter. If I broke away to the left or right I knew that one of them would have a sitting shot at me, so I rammed the stick forward and went down in a spiral dive from 22,000 to 4,000 feet. As I went down I looked over my shoulder and saw [two] of them firing at me and thought for a moment that they would collide. Then a shower of coolant mixture flew up over the instrument panel and over my face, and I thought they had got me. My only chance now was to get the hell out of it as fast as I could and hope that I would shake them off in the dive. As I came out at the bottom of the dive I looked around but couldn't see anything of them. I heaved a sigh of relief which quickly abated when I remembered the leaking coolant! The engine still seemed to be running OK and [so] I had a look round the cockpit to find out where the stuff had come from. [The Glycol] was from a small tank in the bottom of the cockpit … intended for clearing the windscreen in icy conditions! The cork had come out and hence the deluge! (Flight Sergeant Don Kingaby, unpublished memoirs)

Kingaby's elation at the discovery that his engine had suffered no damage was rudely interrupted by a lone Luftwaffe pilot – a press-on type of the group from which he had managed to escape only moments before.

A stream of tracer whizzed past my starboard wing tip and I broke violently round to port to find a 109 sitting about 200 yards away pumping lead at me as hard as he could go. He was all alone and must have been following me all the time. I wondered if he would stay and fight it out now that he had missed his golden opportunity or whether he would make use of his superior speed and buzz off home. He decided that he would try to get me though. We were fighting just above the sea and when I began to throw him off my tail he climbed above me and tried to half-roll down on to me again. At the last moment he realised that he was too low down to do this, and to avoid going straight into the drink he had to roll out again in the same direction as myself. I saw this happening and yanked the throttle back to slow down as quickly as possible. The 109 came out about 150 yards ahead of me and I let him have it from dead astern. Bits flew off him, there was a great cloud of smoke and he went straight in. (Flight Sergeant Don Kingaby, unpublished memoirs)

It was clear to the attendant ground crews that the squadron had, for the second day running, been badly mauled. Davies watched nervously as QJ-H, Johnston's aircraft, dropped onto the grass and weaved its exhausted way to the dispersal. The other three aircraft that had arrived back were in much the same condition, with their pilots fatigued and edgy – all trying to piece together what had happened. Their conversations seemed breathless and fragmented, and now and again Davies would catch a few phrases, disjointed, searching, confirmatory, then once again questioning. He was then conscious of his own voice asking 'any news on Don … err … what about Kingaby?' He looked around for Johnnie who was now chatting with his ground crew and explaining the many started rivets on his wings. He was just about to ask Johnnie about Kingaby when another aircraft struggled into view – it was Sergeant Carpenter.

I got back to Gravesend to find three out of our eight down before me. All of them were quite shaken. Then, while they and my ground crew and Spy, of course, were sorting the action out we heard an awful clattering, and over the hedge came 'Chips' Carpenter. I think he had a bullet in his calf. (Sergeant Walter 'Johnnie' Johnston, letter 2002)

There were now five of them accounted for, yet even a phone call to Manston by the intelligence officer brought no news of Kingaby. Control had been calling, but with Don's R/t out of action they had been unable to raise a response. Meanwhile, Don had put down on the coast as a precaution.

I steamed off home and landed at a forward base to check up on my kite in case it had been damaged during the combat. It frequently happens that in the heat of a scrap one can be badly damaged and not know it. I got out of the cockpit and did a quick check but the faithful 'Spittie' wasn't even scratched. So I set off again. (Flight Sergeant Don Kingaby, unpublished memoirs)

The sound of Don's engine as he approached Gravesend brought much celebration amongst the awaiting crowd of pilots, ground crew and squadron staff. Davies felt overjoyed at the sight of Don as he clambered out and was one of the first to greet him, running to the aircraft along with a few others of Don's ground crew. Don looked tired as he climbed down, mopping his face with his scarf and rubbing his hands through his hair. The others were here now, and after their genuine relief at Don's safe return had been expressed with some usual ribald, affectionate remarks, the piecing together of the day's events continued. Davies, listened for a while before starting his usual post-flight inspection of the Spitfire's cannons. Don came back to the aircraft a little while after and Davies caught his arm and attempted a casual 'glad to have you back, really thought you'd had it' sort of thing. With such phrases he, like others, conveyed a real sense of affection for 'his' pilot. In that moment, Davies saw that twinkling return to Don's eyes and his face opened into wide smile. 'Nearly,' he said, his eyebrows turning upwards in an expression of relief. He paused for a while then patted Davies on the shoulder and said 'and instead, Taff, you can put another one up for definite,' pointing to the row of black crosses under '3320's cockpit glazing.

Bromley & the 'Bomb':
It was while at Gravesend that one night Flight Sergeant Stewart had the idea of going into Bromley, to one of their favourite haunts, The Bell. It was a large pub and hotel that stood at the top of Bromley High Street, a towering building with a large central staircase and bars either side of the main door. There were other watering holes in Bromley. Davies remembered the odd custom that was observed in one:

> *There was one place in Bromley that would only allow you to have a drink after a certain time if you also had something to eat. On the bar they had these awful, dry ham rolls, hard as bullets they were and you couldn't eat them! So because of this rule, we would order a drink and one of these ham rolls. Campbell would sometimes whack the bloody things against the table and laugh how hard and stale they were. We'd sit there with our beer and these rolls and then when we left, we'd put them back on the bar! I think they were the same ones every time we went in – just passed around!* (LAC Raymond Davies, memoir 2002)

The Bell, however, had some added attractions that Stewart, Kingaby, Johnston, Davies and Campbell were well aware of. The landlord was particularly welcoming to them and had on many occasions given the lads a few 'after-hours' pints. He had even been known to reopen and stand a pint for this particularly boisterous and persuasive group when he had already taken to bed and they were reluctant to start weaving back to Biggin!

Stewart collected Davies and Campbell, meeting them at the Armoury where he had signed out a wagon for the journey into Bromley. With Stewart driving, Davies and Cammie jumped into the back and gave Kingaby and Johnston a lift in when they reached their rendezvous point for the night's operation. Reaching The Bell, Chiefy Stewart parked up a little way along the High Street and the five scrambled out into the hotel and its awaiting hospitality. With the events of recent days, they felt in need of a good letting off steam and alongside this it was actually the first time they'd all had to get together – air and ground crew – to celebrate Don's further bar to his DFM. If they needed any excuse, it was as good as they came. Although bound together by uniform and service, they tried to talk little of shop. Sometimes they drifted into conversations about the Squadron and Biggin before one of the others would tell them to wrap up. Being great modern music lovers – Jazz and the likes – Davies and Kingaby spent some time chatting about the latest they'd heard. So the night wore on, and it was rather late when the five of them tumbled out on to the pavement and perhaps some of the road as well! But the gathering of such mischievous souls meant that there was great reluctance to calm the revelry as they attempted to clamber back into the wagon. Something lying in the back caught their eyes and imagination. As Johnston recalled the night:

There was this one incident – I guess us pre-war VRs were a bit wild, a bit rowdy and the young pilots joining us used to take the lead from us. So we were up in Bromley, had gotten up there in a 1500 weight truck from the armaments section. A few of us had decided to get out and let off some steam, I think there was some event we were celebrating, perhaps Don's bar to his DFM, not really sure. Anyway there was me and Don, a couple of armourers – one being your grandfather [Davies] – and Jimmy Stewart the chief armaments officer for 92. We had been in the Bell Hotel at the top of the high street, one of our favourite places and we'd had rather a lot. We found this practice bomb – a small one filled with sand – in the back of the wagon. It had probably been used for some practice or something and had been accidentally left in the back. So we got this bomb out of the back and started to throw it to each other, passing it like a rugby ball! Rolling it down the High Street … And the locals were running all over the place! I think there had been a raid a few nights before or maybe earlier, so I guess they could have been a bit twitchy, so it was a daft thing to do. (Sergeant Walter 'Johnnie' Johnston, interview 2004)

Before long, with civilians giving them a wide berth, the service police arrived on the scene and they were being quietly escorted back to Gravesend. It was with sheepish faces and suppressed giggles that they stood in front of the Wing Commander the next day.

The SPs [Service Police] reported it and so we got pulled up in front of Jamie (Rankin) on a charge – under the influence! But it was a sort of tongue in cheek telling off. Jamie would give you a right rocketing, but the SPs would report you for all sorts of things, so he would rarely have it appear on your records. But we did get it. (Sergeant Walter 'Johnnie' Johnston, interview 2004)

So Don's DFM had been rightly celebrated in fine, unforgettable style. It could have easily been the last toast for the 92nd Foot and Mouth in the Biggin Hill sector, for they were to leave in a matter of days. It was up to the CO, Dickie Milne, to make sure that the other aspect of the Squadron's reputation – that of one of 11 Group's top squadrons – was maintained.

Milne's Three in a Day:
Circus 108b gave 92 Squadron their final claims with the Biggin Hill Wing and it was only fitting that these should be made by the commanding officer, Squadron Leader Dickie Milne. As per usual, the Squadron flew over to Biggin for a morning briefing for the operation, a familiar escort run to Mazingarbe in the company of eighteen Blenheims. It was 1230 hours when the Wing took off, heading for the rendezvous point and climbing into the crisp autumn air. With 92 detailed to be high cover, Milne gained altitude but was suddenly faced with a serious oxygen leak. Signalling to the rest of the boys, Dickie indicated that he was going to lose height but that the squadron should continue to keep position. Without oxygen he would be unable to operate above 10,000 feet or so, and it would have been correct procedure for him to return to base. Dickie, however, elected to continue the sortie, although having to leave his position as leader of the high cover squadron. The events that followed were ably detailed in the combat report that he submitted on his return.

We were acting as High Cover to a bombing raid on Mazingarbe. I developed a very bad oxygen leak and it was obvious I would be unable to remain at my height for long, so I signalled to my 'A' Flight Commander that I was going down. Breaking away, I joined another squadron lower down in the Beehive and continued into France. I saw the odd '109 making an occasional dart at our Spitfires, but no large formations appeared. We were just southeast of St. Omer and I decided to get down even lower, as I still had a long trip ahead without oxygen.

It was as I turned slightly and dived that a single Me109 came in at me and forced me to take evasive action. I turned hard to port and watched him as I went. I expected him to break off as soon as he saw me turn, but he didn't and so forced me to turn completely round in defence. The pilot of this enemy aircraft was quite determined, but broke away hard down with his throttle wide open when he saw I was getting round onto his tail. I was not going to try catching him, as he was in a '109F and in a hurry!

After this short episode I found myself completely alone and couldn't see a single aeroplane anywhere. I suddenly realised the seriousness of this position and set off hard for home. I was now at 9,000 feet and had been flying a cautious zig-zag course to keep my tail vision clear when I sighted two '109s, well above and behind me. These, I thought, had sighted me but, as they came lower, I saw I was in the blind spot beneath their noses, so still undetected.

They passed over me and I, below and slightly behind, closed on the No.2 and opened fire. I hit him very hard and he rolled slowly over, emitting a lot of smoke and then burst into flames as he went down. I turned onto the leader, who had now seen me, and I just had time to fire a short burst at him before he accelerated away with his nose stuffed well down. I saw I had hit his radiator, for a lot of glycol came out. Beneath me, I saw the first aircraft hit the ground. Both of these were Me109Fs.

It was very relieving to find I was still getting near the coast and I hadn't run into any large formations of enemy aircraft.

I continued to work my way home and was beginning to feel quite safe, when two '109s appeared from nowhere in my mirror. I hadn't seen them approach, so possibly they may have climbed up. I just had time to skid wildly to the left and slam my throttle shut. The leading '109 went past me and his No.2 pulled slightly up to the right, overshooting also. They obviously expected to take me by surprise, for they were certainly not ready for my action. I swung in quickly behind the leader, just as he was about to make off by accelerating and diving, and I opened fire at about 70 yards, my shells hitting him all the way up the fuselage. A lot of grey smoke puffed out and he pulled sharply up and to the right immediately, into the position his No.2 had got into by overshooting. The leader crashed into the bottom of the other aircraft and pieces flew everywhere. I have never seen such a scene. They fell together and I saw the pilot of the uppermost aircraft bale out. I didn't hang about to see him land, but headed on to the north, losing my last 1,500 feet just before reaching the coast. I crossed west of Gravelines without receiving any flak and flew on at nought feet, landing, re-arming and refuelling at Manston.

(R.M. Milne, Squadron Leader, Combat Report, 13 October 1941)

Thus with this combination of skill and some degree of luck, Milne managed to claim one Me109E destroyed, two Me109Fs destroyed and one Me109E damaged – the total claimed by his squadron on the day. The rest of the Wing were also engaged and over at 609 Squadron's dispersal the pilots and ground crews celebrated a further one '109 destroyed and one damaged for no loss.

Farewell to 92 Squadron:

A few days after the CO's exemplary performance, 92 Squadron were readying for another move. Few 'ops' were flown after the trip to Mazingarbe on the 13th. On the 15th the Squadron flew what was to be their last Channel patrol as part of the Biggin Hill Wing. In keeping with his 'speciality', Kingaby flew a rhubarb on the 16th and fired at an Me109 head-on but with no visible effect. When he got back, Davies was waiting for him – as excited as ever to see the gun-port patches ragged and frayed. Rumours abounded and as they walked back along the peri-track he and Don chatted about what looked like 92's final days in 11 Group. Davies and Campbell first heard that the Squadron was moving away – out of the sector – and that they had been detailed to move with them. Although leaving Biggin rested uneasily with them both, they couldn't think of a better squadron with which to stay. On the 18th Jimmy Stewart gave them the gen. They were to pack their kit and move back to Biggin. He had been promoted to Warrant Officer in charge of Biggin's armament section and had requested that 'his team' of six armourers be kept together. The request had been granted – both Barwell, as Station Commander, and Rankin, as Wing Commander Flying, had given it their full support.

So on 20 October 1941, Davies saw 92 Squadron off for the last time. He sensed their disappointment at leaving the sector, bound for Digby, Lincolnshire for a rest and remuster. Already new personnel had started to arrive. Yet while it was a changed squadron, with many of the personalities that had made it so special now gone, Davies felt a pang of regret that he would not be going with them. Neither Kingaby nor Johnston would stay with the Squadron very long. In fact many of those that had 'cut their teeth' on 92 during those heady days of 1941 would find postings elsewhere. Kingaby finally accepted a commission and was posted to 58 OTU at Grangemouth as an instructor. Neville Duke and 'Noisy Hunk' Humphries both volunteered for operational tours in the Middle East, both in time becoming successful squadron commanders. Percy Beake, after a brief spell as 'B' Flight Commander, also got a posting to a squadron in later December '41. His time with 601 Squadron at Duxford and later Acaster Malbis was far cry from his experiences with 92 Squadron as 601 were at the time trying out a new aircraft, the Bell Airacobra, and having very little luck. And what of Johnston? Johnnie was posted to 61 OTU at Heston, fast becoming something of an ex-Biggin Hill flying club. He was amongst good, familiar company:

> *61 OTU was like an off-shoot of Biggin Hill, especially 92 Squadron. On the staff were S/L 'Pancho' Villa, Flight Lieutenant Brian Kingcome, Flying Officer R.H. (Bobby) Holland, Sergeant Lloyd and myself, all ex-92. The C.O. was Sailor Malan. While at OTU I did a C.F.S. course at Upavon, then C.G.S (Fighter Gunnery) course at Sutton Bridge under Malan, who then asked me back later to go on the staff.* (Sergeant Walter 'Johnnie' Johnston, letter 1997)

With his own kit packed and ready to go, Davies watched Don's aircraft and Johnston's as they tucked up their undercarts and climbed away, north. Coming to attention, Davies gave them one last salute.

> *There was good old Ninety-two up in the sky, shoot 'em down*
> *There was good old Ninety-two up in the sky, shoot 'em down*
> *There was good old Ninety-two, good old Ninety-two –ooh*
> *Good old Ninety-two up in the sky*
>
> (Squadron song, anon)

Chapter Thirteen

Winter's Return

Back to Biggin:

In the return to Biggin, Davies was immediately busied by the daily tasks of keeping the squadrons of 'the Bump' in fighting trim. It seemed that as soon as the wheels of the transport from Gravesend had slowed, he was back in familiar surroundings with not much time to think. As Chiefy Stewart informed him, there were new squadrons coming into Biggin. That meant new personnel, and more specifically armourers who, in spite of their training, would not be up to speed with the realities of keeping the 20mm cannon on top line. This had been Stewart's reasoning behind keeping his team of armourers together. If you could in any way be seen to 'understand' such a piece of inanimate machinery such as the Hispano, then Stewart had considered that in operational terms, meeting the challenges of this often temperamental device, the team were the best he could hope for. The way to best make use of their skills and experience was now forming in his mind.

The gap left by 92 Squadron's departure was immediately filled by 401 Squadron. It was the first Canadian squadron that Davies had encountered and he was mightily impressed by their flying skills. What would be important now was their ability to get to know 'the form' in their first sweeps as part of the Wing. Though they were not complete novices – having had a creditable performance during the Battle of Britain – even the veterans of the Wing were keen to point out the distinct operational challenges that came with their leaning toward France. The title of senior squadron at Biggin was now afforded to 609 Squadron and with his old 92 Squadron gone, Wing Commander Rankin decided to have his aircraft looked after by its ground crew. Whether it was on Rankin's insistence cannot be known, but Davies was also loaned to 609 at this time and, with others from Stewart's team, tended to be assigned to Jamie. It was not an official posting, nor was his movement to 609 Squadron, but with familiar faces such as 'Claude' Rains and Corporal Jones around it was an easy transition. Yet it was not without some mild confusion. Noting that one of the aircraft had 'City of Leeds' emblazoned on its cowling, Davies convinced himself that this must be the name of the Squadron – just as 'East India' had been 92's. However, it was far too busy for it to be important and so as winter came, Davies settled into the routine of this Yorkshire squadron.

'Killer' Rankin:

In just under nine months Jamie Rankin had acquired an awe-inspiring reputation. He had started out feeling his way with 92 Squadron, careful to earn his position of command and seemingly have it bestowed upon him by the Squadron itself. He had learned fast that 92 Squadron was an able and proud unit, protective of its own and somewhat wary of inexperienced 'outsiders'. When they left the sector, with Jamie remaining as Biggin's Wing Leader, it was a separation marked with mutual respect and affection. His leadership throughout his months at Biggin had been exemplary, and as a tactician both at squadron and now Wing level, he was unrivalled. In the air, his flying was precise, his commands clear and decisive. He seemed cool-headed in battle and was fearless beyond measure. He had picked up a couple of nicknames along the way: Some knew him as 'one-a-day Rankin', with reference to the frequency with which he seemed to dispatch enemy aircraft. Others, such as Davies, called him 'Jammy', an affectionate accreditation of his mounting combat claims and his largely unscathed dicing with the Hun as being down to luck! However, there were times when his fearlessness coincided with his sheer contempt for the enemy with dramatic consequence. Thus he acquired the lesser-known name of 'Killer Rankin'.

It was a few days before 92 Squadron left Biggin when fearlessness, prowess, fortune and an irrepressible need to bloody the enemy's nose were aligned. There had been a sweep planned for the morning of 16 October but, as frustrating as ever, it had been scrubbed. For Rankin the wait was unbearable. He had come over to chat to Chiefy Stewart earlier in the morning, eager to do a test firing after the team had carried out some modifications during the previous evening. Davies talked through the work they had done, Rankin listening intently as he leaned forward on the mainplane. The WingCo's impatience was further heightened by the sight of Flight Lieutenant François de Spirlet and Flying Officer Dieu being scrambled to intercept an unknown raider over Mayfield. Davies turned back to Rankin to continue talking but Jamie was already up in the cockpit and was strapping himself in. In a moment Rankin had left his attendant crew standing, the wheels of his aircraft bouncing across the grass as QJ-J quickly gained flying speed. So began one of Jamie's infamous air-tests!

Apart from the trade that de Spirlet and Dieu had gone after, a quick call to Biggin's 'ops' drew a blank as far as other possible targets were concerned. Not one to disappoint the enemy or to fail in his purpose of testing those guns for Chiefy and the team, Rankin pointed the nose of the aircraft towards France. Perhaps some target of opportunity may rear its head? There was one strategy that he favoured in approaching the enemy's hostile coast – going in low, hugging the contours of the land and flying just above the waves. This way, Rankin rightly surmised, he would avoid the enemy's radar and only make his presence known at the last moment.

The ploy paid off and Rankin approached the French coast unopposed, then setting about looking for something worthy of his attention. Alternately switching his scan between the sea, land and sky, his keen eyes suddenly caught sight of some intriguing-looking grey shapes sitting just off the coast, in the estuary of one of the many outlets that characterised this northern French coastline. Ships perhaps? Yes! Quickly the outline of two, clearly military vessels came into view and he could pick out what seemed like turreted enclosures and the unmistakable protrusions of multiple gun barrels. Flak ships! 'What a result,' thought Rankin as he thumbed the rocker switch that allowed selection of .303s and 20mm. It was only at the last second before he himself opened fire that a gunner saw the approaching fighter and let off a quick burst in defiance. Rankin's aim was accurate and the first ship disappeared amongst a tumult of waterspouts, steam and black smoke. Keeping his Spitfire low to avoid return fire, Jamie was just about to position to attack a second vessel when he instinctively checked the sky above and behind. Sure enough there were a couple of Me109s bearing down on him. Whether the pilots considered him to be a 'sitter', or whether they were put off by the sheer audacity of a lone Spitfire that had the gumption to go after as formidable targets as flak ships is not known, but after a twisting tail-chase Rankin had done enough to discourage them. He was once again on his own, and then decided to attack the other flak ship before heading for home:

W/C Rankin, who keeps his aircraft with 609's … attacks some ships, is attacked by 2 109s, then attacks another ship out of pique! (609 Squadron Operational Record Book, 16 October 1941)

Sixty-four years later the astonishment and admiration was still fresh in the memory of one of his compatriots – Alec 'Joe' Atkinson:

Rankin, I think he must have had nerves of steel! I remember him once coming back when we were going on a sweep in the afternoon and he said 'Oh I flew over to have a practice in firing my guns, to see if they were all right, and so I saw a flak ship and went and attacked the flak ship.' Well I mean, what a mad thing to do! He was on his own.

He was a very nice man and I remember him explaining how he took 92 at very low-level over to France and, I think it was Abbeville where the German fighters were based at, and the moment they got over the coast they climbed like mad until they were above the airfield while the Abbeville chaps were taking off. They then attacked them of course and made mincemeat of them. This was a very brave thing to do and he [Rankin] wouldn't think twice about it. (Pilot Officer Alec 'Joe' Atkinson, interview 2004)

Goldy & Vicki:
With 92 Squadron away to Lincolnshire, 609 now found itself as the senior squadron of the Wing, a title that they took within their stride and led by example. Quite fortunately, the Squadron had been lucky with its operational losses throughout the summer of '41, particularly as regards the senior pilots. Like 92, they had maintained a strong, proud identity. October, however, was proving to be a difficult, hard-fought month and the increasing numbers of Fw190s were making their presence felt. The day after 92 Squadron's departure, 21 October, 609 and the rest of the Wing were hard-pressed and were to lose two of their longstanding and well-respected pilots – Flying Officer Vicki Ortmans and Sergeant 'Goldy' Palmer.

Just after 1100 hours Rankin led 609 and the Wing on a large 'Rodeo' fighter sweep of the Boulogne area. With no bombers in attendance, it was largely thought that the Luftwaffe would not bite. Yet on this occasion they needed no such encouragement. Flying as Blue leader, 609's CO 'Sheep' Gilroy had taken the inexperienced Christian Ortmans as his number two. It was Christian's first operational flight with the Squadron. In the same section were Vicki – Christian's older and experienced brother – and 'Goldy' Palmer, flying as Blue Three and Four respectively. Catching sight of twenty or so Me109s, Gilroy made the call that he was going to engage. Yet, as the Squadron diary recorded, the order was either not heard or misunderstood.

Suddenly, the CO sees 15–20 109s coming down and calls that he is going down too, as there are too many to deal with. The order is either not heard or misunderstood, for the rest of the section does not follow, and by the time the CO has climbed back to rejoin them, Blue 3 and 4 are already in the thick of it. Sergeant Palmer, hit with a deflection shot, is seen to spin down, recover, then make a good landing on the water. But he does not get out, and his aircraft sinks upside down. No one sees at all what happens to Vicki. (609 Squadron Operational Record Book, 21 October 1941)

With a quick turn around on the ground, 609 were back in the air and, together with Rankin leading an extra section and 91 Squadron's ASR Spitfires, they scoured the Channel for any signs of life. But there was nothing, just empty water. It was at times like this that you questioned whose side nature was on. The Channel, fickle in its allegiances: sometimes a mighty, protective barrier to those that would bear arms against this fair isle. Now, as deceitful and treacherous as the enemy, as threatening as any bomber or hunting fighter. It was with heavy hearts that they turned for home, saddened all the more because of Christian's presence.

So great was their effort in searching for Ortmans and Palmer, that a number of the squadron were caught out and very nearly 'bought it'. As the diary continued:

The search is fruitless, but leads to a number of tragi-comedies which helps dispel the gloom. Flying Officer Malengreau, instead of taking Ops' vector home, flies off on a reciprocal, leading his section straight to France. After much anxious R/t conversation, his followers decide to desert. The flight has, however, led to petrol shortage, and mist makes ground visibility practically nil. All pilots need a homing, and the R/t contains priceless examples of excited French. Lt Choron force lands in a field near Rye, Flying Officer Malengreau lands with 7 other pilots at Hawkinge (smugly referring to the amount of flak he experienced over Boulogne), Sergeant Rigler lands at Lympne, others at Manston, and only 4 at Biggin, these include Sergeant Evans with 6 gallons of petrol after 2 hours and 20 minutes in the air. (609 Squadron Operational Record Book, 21 October 1941)

Early Lessons for the Canadians:
For any new squadron, being posted to Biggin brought with it both honour and apprehension. The Bump had maintained the reputation it had gained in 1940 as being the RAF's equivalent to the front line. Its record against the enemy was unprecedented and so to be posted in from one of the operational backwaters to Biggin Hill was almost a mark of esteem. From a fighter squadron's viewpoint, it was from here that you could have a real crack at the enemy. Other airfields could boast that they were closer to France – Hawkinge, Manston, Lympne – but Biggin had the spirit of an elite. Yet such a posting for replacement squadrons also brought with it a sense of stepping into dead men's shoes. Biggin was not somewhere you practiced operationally, this *was* it and your squadron's posting-in meant that another had been posted out for a much-needed rest and remuster. So it was with honour and apprehension that 401 Canadian Squadron took up residence on 20 October 1941.

Formerly known as No.1 Squadron, Royal Canadian Air Force, 401 had been the first Canadian squadron to arrive in Britain. Based at Croydon, it spent the early stages of the Battle of Britain gaining experience from 111 Squadron with whom it shared the airfield. On becoming operational later in the Battle, the Squadron operated out of RAF Northolt situated on the western outskirts of London. From here it had been thrown into the thick of the desperate struggles for survival and, though successful, it was withdrawn to Scotland in October of 1940, its numbers severely depleted. It was March of 1941 when 401 moved further south to take up residence at Digby, Lincolnshire, having been renumbered (like all Canadian squadrons) with a 400 prefix to avoid confusion with No.1 Squadron RAF. At this time it was still operating Hurricane IIas and did not receive its Spitfire IIs until September. Thus, it was with little operational experience of the Spitfire that the Squadron arrived at Biggin in October, quickly being re-equipped with Mark Vbs.

A pattern of operations from Biggin throughout 1941 had shown that usually the Luftwaffe needed something more than an incursion by fighters alone to draw them to battle. When a few bombers – Blenheims and now and again some Stirlings – were thrown into the equation, then it seemed that they were more likely to react. Encounters with the enemy fighter force were a rarity when the RAF elected to send fighter-only sweeps into northern France. For the benefit of 401 Squadron, one such 'rodeo' was organised on 27 October, the idea being that because of the limited enemy reaction that it was likely to prompt, it would be an easier introduction to Wing operations. They could gain some useful organisational experience, listen into how the Wing Leader and squadron leaders worked together, and also get to know the geography of this area of operations. As 401 took up position in the formation, neither they nor the more experienced pilots of the Wing were aware of how uncooperative the Luftwaffe could be.

As 609 Squadron's 'Sheep' Gilroy brought the Wing round in an orbit behind Gravelines, it became clear that the enemy were keen to engage – perhaps encouraged by the arrival in the sector of greater numbers of their new fighter, the Fw190. In a matter of minutes, the Wing was hit hard. As 609 Squadron's diary recorded:

S/L Gilroy is leading the wing, and as it is orbiting behind Gravelines to allow stragglers to catch up, he reports up to 50 e/a building up behind them – suggested reason: that the wing is on the route of Circus operations against Lille. Though 401 bears the brunt of the attack, 609's Red section does well to get back intact, two of them being hit, Sergeant Galloway (Canadian) by a cannon shell that puts his compressor out of action. Half-rolling, he sees a 109 and 2 Fw190, gets on the tail of one of the latter, only to find his guns will not work. He eludes them and lands at Manston without brakes or flaps. Pilot Officer Smith also suffers a damaged compressor, and his guns won't work either. S/L Gilroy is engaged with 3 109s in mid-Channel, comes down to sea level and up again in a series of head-on attacks. The remaining member of Red section, Lt Choron, sees 2 Fw190s proceeding towards Manston at 5000ft. He dives on one, and after his attack it drops a wheel and dives from 15000 to 2000ft, at which point Choron's attention is directed to 4 more Fw190s, one of which is firing at him, with m/g only apparently. He causes this one to overshoot, and firing at it from the quarter, produces a stream of white smoke. The others are not shaken off until 5 miles off Manston after an engagement lasting 10 minutes, and Choron lands at Southend.... The other squadrons lose 6 pilots, 5 of them from 401, and only get a destroyed, a probable and a damaged. (609 Squadron Operational Record Book, 27 October 1941)

The 'damaged' enemy aircraft claimed by one of the squadrons other than 609 was 401's and in the combat report submitted by the pilot, Pilot Officer Harley, it is evident that the squadron had been caught largely unawares.

I was Blue 3, leading the section. When seven miles north of Poperinghe, I noticed Spitfires on my starboard and port sides apparently hit, and they went down out of control. Several Me109s then dove past me and continued downward in steep dives. I followed them down and fired a three-second burst at about 300 yards range and another four-second burst at about 350 yards. I saw black smoke coming from the enemy aircraft and I broke away at 12,000 feet. I then returned to base at 1250 hours. (Pilot Officer A.E. Harley, 401 Squadron, Combat Report, 27 October 1941)

In all, the Canadian's suffered fifty per cent losses in this, their first operation with the Wing. As the aircraft returned to Biggin the ground crews hastened to get them turned round as quickly as possible – rearmed and refuelled. Those members of 401 who had managed to fight their way back now stood waiting for any sight or sound of any late returns while their intelligence officer picked his way amongst them, trying to piece together what had happened. Their mood was lifted slightly by the sight of 609 Squadron scrambling to assist the rescue launches that were scouring the Channel for any downed pilots from the morning's operation. Though 152 and 611 Squadrons were also detailed to the search, 609 found itself dangerously alone, intercepted by yet more mixed formations of Me109s and Fw190s. Yet the signal acts of bravery committed by Jamie Rankin made possible the squadron's return. Back at Biggin, their intelligence officer Frank Ziegler penned the following account:

... 609 are ordered off again to protect two rescue boats searching the Channel for the missing pilots. This proves to be almost as exciting an affair as the other [earlier operation], and Intelligence has its worst day for months as battles accumulate, Group agitates for reports, and these become hours overdue. It might, in fact, easily have been the end of 609 West Riding squadron, Ops plotting no less than 3 lots

of 15 plus, 2 of 12 plus, a 9 plus and a 3 plus, with 609 and W/C Rankin as the only defence, S/L Gilroy's appeal for help going apparently unheeded until too late. Effective assistance is however given by the Wing Commander, who appoints himself 'high cover' to 609 and chases 15 109s back to France single-handed, probably destroying one. He then draws off 5 Fw190s and chases them back as well. Meanwhile 609, down below near Dover, have been attacked by another lot of 15 109s. S/L Gilroy manages to get within range of the last pair, and fires at both, one being seen to turn on its back and go vertically down. The effect of this is to bring the rest of the enemy formation round into the sun to attack, and an exciting time is had by all till the enemy eventually decides to go home. (Newspapers report a hostile sweep over England has been intercepted). German newspapers report a German ace, back from the Russian front, today obtained his 100th victory, and the unwonted boldness of the Jerries in approaching our shores suggests this is due to pilots returning to the Pas de Calais, and not knowing that this is no longer the 'form'). Big surprise is the report of Flight Lieutenant Demozay (French) of 91 Squadron, aloft at the time, that no less than 3 a/c have dived into the 'drink'. As none of our a/c are missing, and no others are up, 2 of these are eventually awarded to S/L Gilroy, one to W/C Rankin, in addition to his 'probable'. (609 Squadron Operational Record Book, 27 October 1941)

As ever there were always lessons to be learned. From the experiences of the Wing during this engagement, Rankin suggested that a pair of aircraft should always remain as high cover when air/sea rescue operations were in progress. The suggestion was tabled for consideration at Group and adopted with immediate effect.

November Goodbyes:

There were few operations in November of '41. As winter set in, fog, rain and the occasional sleet hampered Fighter Command's winter offensive. At Biggin, many operations were planned and prepared for, then scrubbed when the weather grounded either the Wing or its partner airfields. Those operations that did materialise were generally in support of a few Hurricane squadrons whose aircraft had been recently modified to carry bombs. Experimenting with low-level insurgency, the Wing flew in its usual cover role over the targets – alcohol distilleries it seemed were favourite. It was questionable whether such operations made any real contribution aside from nuisance. Some may have even questioned whether the risks involved (including often intense flak) outweighed the outcomes. But there was a place for experimentation. Perhaps, taking some chances now would pay dividends in the future. 'Who knows,' thought Davies to himself, 'we might even win the war!' As operations had shown, sometimes taking chances and being innovative often made a real difference. Rankin ahead of three squadrons, driving low and fast across the Channel, then climbing hard to catch 'Jerry' napping – that was innovative and effective!

Jamie was long overdue a rest. One day after getting back, Davies had seen him lighting a cigarette – his hands shaking. 'Everything OK, Sir?' he had inquired. He found that sometimes making conversation brought them round, back to the present, perhaps back to a realisation that they were safe again – at least for another day. Rankin had looked up and then paused, as if trying to collect his thoughts. It was only for a moment. Then it was back to 'no problems, Taff. Cannon's fine, better check the … ' The I.O. and a few pilots had then arrived and Jamie seemed himself once again.

Davies' spell of duty with 609 Squadron lasted until the 19th when – like 92 Squadron before them – the Squadron flew north to Digby. It seemed the end of an era. The last of the original squadrons of the Wing had now gone and what a time it had been! How those names would sing out in his memories of these days for years to come. He would tell his grandchildren about Rankin, Kingaby, Milne, Tommy Lund, Robinson, Gilroy and Rigler, Malan, Mungo-Park. The end of an era it may have been, but Davies' position as part of Chiefy Stewart's team at Biggin meant that there were new squadrons to tend. There was no let up.

Retiring to Digby, 609 too were still 'operational', though the pace of life in Lincolnshire was wholly different to Biggin. Their old blood brothers at 92 Squadron were quick to update them as to the 'form' at their new station. Overall, there seemed a lot of 'bull', 'red tape' and 'duff gen' – often considered the anathema of military units that knew the realities of war and 'getting on with it'. Percy Beake contrasted the feeling of relief at being away from the intensity of the front line with those of being answerable to a vigorous authority.

When posted to Digby, I was newly married; had taken part in 50 offensive operations with 92 Squadron, as well as umpteen scrambles and protective patrols; had damaged two Me109s; had been shot up and shot down and I can't say that I had any real regrets at leaving the 11 Group theatre of operations. Our discipline in the war zone had tended to be somewhat lax. Tired from operational flying, we often wore flying boots in the Mess during the day and probably looked a little scruffy. Digby was different: It was more like the peace-time RAF and the discipline was quite strict. The change was not welcomed by many members of the Squadron and we had a very rough time settling in. Discipline was also different. We had an Authorisation Book in which each flight and its purpose had to be detailed, authorised by the Flight Commander and signed by the pilot concerned before taking off. This took close monitoring and must have taken its toll on me. A little anecdote might help illustrate this.

As soon as we arrived at Digby, I started looking for accommodation. There was little to be found close to the station but, from the air, I spotted a building not far away. After landing I set about trying to find this dwelling which turned out to be a Lodge solely inhabited by a lady. She listened to my overtures and agreed to rent us two rooms. The bedroom tended to be relatively long but somewhat narrow and two single beds were positioned diagonally opposed to each other. Though this was less than ideal for a newly married couple, the Lodge was quite close to the airfield and, as I was being required to be on the Station from dawn until dusk, this was an important consideration.

After I had collected Eve from Gravesend, we both used to sleep in one bed. Even so, after a day's flying, I was often quite tired and one night as I was slipping into the arms of Morpheus, Eve said 'Darling, I'm right on the edge of the bed,' to which I am reputed to have said 'Don't forget to sign the Authorisation Book before you drop off!' (Flying Officer Percy Beake, letter 2006)

Patrols too, generated no excitement. In comparison to Biggin, they were largely 'stooges', with nothing or very little to report. For new arrivals, it was a gentler introduction to operational life – one that you had a better chance of surviving (unless you were one of those unfortunate clots that managed to write yourself off in an accident). For the older, more experienced hands it was rather lacklustre – you sometimes really did not know what to do with yourself and there was a limit to how many times you could chase a target drogue around the sky and then sit viewing camera-gun footage. Yet, it was a much-needed rest and relief came in many ways, often progressively more daring. As Johnnie Johnston of 92 Squadron recalled:

We had many good times at Digby – it was really a rest we needed and they had stopped individual postings out of Biggin, so we were all up there. 609 came up a few months after to join us. We had some interesting ways to relieve the boredom. There was this section of railway line that was dead straight, as a die. It went on for miles and there was plenty of space either side and it was all very flat around there. So we all used to go up there and get low on these rails – and you could get very low, ten feet off them. If you got it right you could wait until there was a train coming and fly straight at it along these rails! Don't know what the poor drivers thought coming towards us – sometimes you could catch sight of their startled white faces as you pulled up! And you could do it in a way they didn't see your code letters. Fat, bald Tommy Rigler was the best. He used to say that he did it upside-down so that they couldn't see his codes! (Sergeant Walter 'Johnnie' Johnston, interview 2005)

Chapter Fourteen

New Encounters

A New WingCo:

With the departure of Jamie Rankin there was some uncertainty as to who would take over the Wing. Whoever it was that could take up the auspicious post of Wing Commander, Flying, Biggin Hill, it would have to be someone of significant reputation and operational prowess. Up until now, the squadrons of the Wing had been very experienced and for the duration of '41 it had been possible to pick a wing leader from the experienced squadron commanders that had been in residence. Malan had risen from 74 Squadron, Rankin from 92, Robinson from 609. At other times, when there was a requirement for a squadron commander to act up into the role of WingCo, the senior squadron of the Wing could also put forward significantly experienced people to fill the post – Des Sheen from 72 and 'Sheep' Gilroy from 609.

Yet the situation at Biggin at the end of November was somewhat different. With 609's departure, Biggin was left with two relatively inexperienced squadrons. The Canadians of 401 Squadron had been barely a month with the wing and in that time had suffered badly. The replacement for 609, 124 Squadron, arrived towards the end of November. They had come down from Castletown, Scotland and also lacked the experience of a 'front line' operational posting that Biggin presented. At Fighter Command headquarters, however, there was perhaps very little decision to be made about who should take the lead at Biggin Hill. There was an ideal candidate for the job. Almost by way of continuing 92 Squadron's link with Biggin, it was another 'Foot and Mouth' man that arrived to take up the reins as Wing Commander Flying – Bob Stanford-Tuck.

Tuck was well known. Since Dunkirk, he had proved himself to be one of the great fighter leaders of the war, first as a flight commander with 92 Squadron – a contemporary of Kingcome and Wright – then, in the later stages of the Battle of Britain, as OC 257 'Burma' Squadron. Posted into 257 Squadron alongside Tuck was Pete Brothers who remembered clearly his keenness and leadership qualities:

I first met Bob when he and I joined 257 Squadron at Martlesham Heath. That would have been about 7th or 8th September 1940. He was a great chap and became a great friend. We both arrived as flight commanders but the morale of the squadron was right down in the cellar! Both flight commanders had been killed the same day and so you can imagine the young lads looking at each other and saying, 'what chance have I got?' So our first job was to build up the morale. We had a useless squadron commander, I'm afraid, and for example when we were told to patrol over the Maidstone line at 20,000 feet, we proceeded to do this and when we saw this great phalanx of enemy aircraft approaching and said 'there they are', his reply was that we had been told to patrol the Maidstone line and that we will do until we're told otherwise. So we all pushed off and left him and got stuck in. By the time this had happened three times in succession we came to the conclusion that he [the CO] didn't wish to be involved in any risky air fighting. So having primed ourselves with a lot of booze we rang up the AOC and complained bitterly about the chap and he was posted within 24 hours and Bob was six months senior to me in the Air Force so he became the squadron commander. (Air Commodore Pete Brothers, interview August 2006)

Taking the reins at 257 Squadron allowed Tuck to further develop his leadership style and given the rough time that the squadron had experienced, he and Brothers set about getting them to think and work as a team. Such team-building extended to their social as well as operational activities. As Brothers recalled their approach:

[Bob and I], *we were friends and we tried to make the young lads friends. There was no pomposity about it … we were able to raise the morale of the chaps by making sure they knew what it was all about and how they should be operating and that sort of thing, and we took them out for lots of Squadron parties! It was his enthusiasm and background knowledge that made him successful and popular. In 1941, I formed an all Aussie squadron, 457 funnily enough – must be my lucky number 57 – and Bob by then was Wing Commander Flying at Biggin and he came up and had lunch with me one day which gave a great boost to my Aussies who weren't operational as yet. That was the last time I saw Bob until he came back from the PoW camp and joined us at Tangmere where I was the station commander for the Central Fighter Establishment. Bob came in as Wing Commander, Tactics.* (Air Commodore Pete Brothers, interview August 2006)

In October 1941, Tuck had been rested and sent off to the United States on a liaison and familiarisation trip. From Fighter Command, two other senior, experienced commanders had accompanied him – Harry Broadhurst and 'Sailor' Malan. Whilst in America, they had been far from sightseers and had spent time familiarising themselves with the range of American fighter aircraft and passing on their experience and expertise to the young US pilots. The United States were not yet in the war, but it was something of an inevitability that they would be very soon. So trips such as Tuck's had an important part to play in enabling the United States air forces to gain some appreciation of the challenges ahead.

In the first few days, Tuck made time to get round the squadrons of the Wing and to reacquaint himself with Biggin Hill. He was on old territory, and even when he had been up at Coltishall with 257 Squadron, he had managed to drop in at 'the Bump'. On a few occasions he had borrowed an aircraft and flown with his old 92 Squadron on operations and in October 1940 had the audacity to claim an Me109E over Dover. It had been 92 Squadron's only claim that day and there had been much banter as Bob and the Squadron argued whether it was technically 92's or 257's, as Tuck was a serving officer with the latter squadron. Although 92 Squadron were no longer at Biggin their ex-Chief Armament's Officer – Jimmy Stewart – remained. Well known to Bob from his days with the Squadron, it was on a cold morning in the second week of December that Jimmy received a visit.

I had seen Bob [Tuck] at Biggin before, because he sometimes came to visit 92. In early December, I think it was, me and Jimmy Stewart were in the armoury going through some paperwork on modifications. Stewart hated paperwork and was trying to get me, as one of the team, to do it. So while we were both trying to get out of it, the door opened and in walked Tuck. He was one of those who looked every inch an officer – the other two I remember who were like this were 'Batchy' Atcherley and Dickie Barwell. He had a bit of a sort of rah rah accent, I thought, but I found him really easy to get on with later. Now he and Stewart already knew each other from 92 so there was a bit of a reunion of sorts. Chiefy had a reputation for being one of those that would get things done, a professional in every sense and so I think that the pilots had great respect for him. Anyhow, I was introduced to Tuck and of course Chiefy was telling him about the work we had been doing on the 20mm. After a bit, Tuck said 'well, I hope you're going to put one of your lads on my kite, Jimmy?' When Tuck had left, Chiefy then told me that he was going to assign me to Bob's aircraft which of course was a great honour to be looking after the Wing leader's guns. (LAC Raymond Davies, memoir, 2002)

So it was that in December 1941, Davies began what was to be a short-lived but memorable time working alongside one of the greatest names of Fighter Command. It was indeed an auspicious assignment, and when he first set eyes on Tuck's newly arrived aircraft, it was clear to him that here was a pilot who knew the form inside out. Spitfire Vb (BL336), like Tuck, was newly arrived on the Wing, having been allocated to 124 Squadron on 28 November. As Tuck's new aircraft it now proudly wore the initials of the Wing Leader – RS-T. Running up the wing for the first time, Davies also was confronted by the seemingly endless array of black crosses that had been painted onto the fuel tank cowling. There were twenty-eight in total – though Tuck's private tally stood at more than thirty.

Foul Weather Sorties:
The weather for December was not kind to the operations of the Wing, frustrating for the new WingCo and all. Alternating between low cloud, thick overcast, and confounding mist, it was an operational pilot's nightmare. Down at dispersal the flight hut seemed perpetually damp and the one stove gave little heat to make any difference to the cold air (apart from within a couple of feet of it!). Now and again someone would throw down the book they were reading, get up and go to the window to wipe away a little condensation and stare into the murk. At the armoury too, Davies sometimes found himself watching the rivulets of water run down the glass from where he had just wiped, as he looked skywards for any signs of a break in the weather. Still, although the elements were often against them, there was a job to do. So most days continued as if operations were, without question, definitely on. The problem was that sometimes it took the Met boys and HQ until midday to declare that things were definitely 'off' and to stand down one or two of the squadrons. Chances were you'd be the one to continue in the uncertainty of waiting, just in case there was a slim possibility that things would marginally improve, or that some enemy raider would come over to stooge around and make a general nuisance of himself. December '41 was one of those months.

On 12 December, Tuck dropped down to 124 Squadron's dispersal where his aircraft was parked up. The weather was marginal and there were no operations detailed for the Wing. As good a time as any to get acquainted. Spotting the WingCo, Davies made his way across from the peri-track where he had been supping on a large mug of NAAFI tea. Breaking into a quick trot, he caught up with Tuck who nodded in recognition.

From the first time I really got to talk with Tuck I knew that he was one of those officers who took the time to know his men, pilots and us ground crew. Some officers were a little distant and you never got to know them really – you got on with your job and there was a sort of class system to it, so you didn't see them apart from during the time when there was a sweep on or something. But a few days after Chiefy Stewart had introduced me and put me on Tuck's aircraft, I was down at dispersal when he [Tuck] arrived to check out his aircraft. The first thing I noticed was that we started chatting about the aircraft and the guns, and he really did want to know the detail. It wasn't as if he was just listening for the sake of it. But before long he was asking me about where I was from, how

long I'd been in [the RAF] and I told him about Nelson, South Wales and he
seemed to know something of the area. I later found out that he'd been with 92 at
Pembrey in 1940 so that was why he was able to chat with some knowledge. He
then got me to show him the cannon fit on the Spit V – he'd been on Hurricanes
and so wanted to know the differences in how they operated in the smaller bays
of the Spit's wing. You see, there was to my knowledge, no real trouble with them
in Hurricanes but because of the Spit's thinner wing we had had more problems.
(LAC Raymond Davies, memoir 2003)

With the Spitfire now all buttoned up, Tuck climbed in and took it away for a brief
forty minutes of local flying. The last time he had flown a Spitfire operationally
was in September and since then had encountered a number of other types ranging
from the faithful Hurricane, the brutish Typhoon and then a number of American
aircraft – Thunderbolts, Lightnings, P40s and even the Airacobra. So it was in that
unsettled December sky above Biggin that Tuck got back in the saddle and felt he
was on familiar and homely territory.

Still the weather confounded opportunities to have a crack at the enemy. The
following day, Tuck went up on a reconnaissance of the sector but returned after
fifteen minutes having stooged around in the gloom. Having received one of those
calls from 'ops' about the chances of getting something up, he, rather frustratedly,
felt his way into the blanket of mist and low cloud on a weather test (as if you
really needed to test the obvious!). After five minutes he declared it 'absolutely
bloody' and eased his way down to the safety of Biggin's terra firma. And when
the weather cleared in the local vicinity, allowing a practice Wing Balbo or two,
conditions dictated that there would be no 'ops' across the Channel. Attempts
to put up standing or investigative patrols could also be counterproductive: On
the 13th, 400 Squadron lost two of its Army Co-op Tomahawks over the Somme
estuary – intercepted by Fw190s of II/JG2; one Defiant of 151 Squadron crashed
into the sea on a morning patrol on the 14th; on the 15th one of two Beaufighters
scrambled in bad weather ditched off Plymouth after an engagement with a Ju88
– both pilot and observer being lost. There were other losses, every one of them
someone's son, husband, boyfriend or father.

It was the 16th when Tuck got his first opportunity to lead the Wing on an
operation – a shipping reconnaissance near Dunkirk. Uneventful, frustrating for
men like Tuck, it was without incident. The squadrons returned without result.
The following day, Tuck joined Duke-Woolley's 124 Squadron on a 'flotsam'
patrol, once again scouting for enemy aircraft that had been making use of the
dicey weather conditions to conduct sneak raids. Such patrols tested one's
patience at the best of times. Flying through heavily-laden cumulus and patches of

rain that seemed to seek out that one place where the canopy was ill-fitting, they were just about to turn for home when the controller warned of an approaching bandit. Duke-Woolley was first to spot it, a thousand feet below and making for the protection of cloud. Diving down, he chased it down to below a thousand feet, exchanging fire with the rear gunner. With multiple bursts of cannon, he set the enemy aircraft's port engine alight and saw a few crew members take to their parachutes. Not all were able to escape before the aircraft – a Ju88 – crashed into the sea. Tuck, too, had managed an inauspicious squirt at it, but it was nothing to write home about. It was 'the Duke's' claim and turned out to be the last combat of the year for the Wing.

A Stroke of Genius:
The New Year brought very little respite from the poor conditions that had plagued the final days of 1941. Yet truth be known, such adverse weather conditions were a welcome relief for both air and ground crew. Good flying conditions were not always that welcome as they brought with them chances to mix it with the enemy. As the last few months of 1941 had shown, it was an enemy of renewed confidence and aggression that lay in wait across the Channel. Although many would not show it in public and would not want to let the side down, in reality living with a constant fear of being killed or wounded played on one's nerves. Perhaps for most, it was not really a fear of dying. Most had reconciled themselves to the fact that death was an inevitability, in spite of their youth and bravado. More concerning was being maimed; to have a slow lingering death, perhaps from a fatal wound; and most of all being burned, trapped in a blazing inferno of a cockpit from which there was no escape. So although the poor weather that prevailed for most of December and January was frustrating in the greater scheme of waging a war, there was a quiet thankful prayer for its continuation.

With the celebrations of Christmas and New Year fading into memory, Davies, Campbell and a few others decided to make their way round to the Old Jail. There was a dusting of snow on the ground that made the footing a little less confident, to the extent that Davies had even entertained the idea of keeping his gumboots on. They were certainly not getting much use on the flight these days. The past few weeks had seen little more than the odd Rhubarb and some searchlight co-op flying. It was during these times of inactivity that Davies and Tuck had started to have more involved conversations, these mainly being concerned with the details of the work that had been carried out on the Hispanos.

Now Tuck was very interested in the work that had been done on the 20mm and wanted to know everything about our system right from when we positioned the ammunition to the modifications we'd done on the guns themselves. One day at Biggin I remember sitting with him on the wing of his kite with the cannon bay open and taking him through the procedures we had adopted through working with Stewart, talking about the modifications to the gas vent to increase the recoil and so on. I showed him where the main problems of stoppages had been and how we'd managed to solve the problems with them, and he then helped me re-arm. I remember him as being one of those commanding officers that was approachable and that you could make easy conversation, and he was genuinely interested in the work me did whether you were an armourer such as myself or a fitter, a rigger etc. (LAC Raymond Davies, compiled from interviews, 2001)

It was around the second week of January that Bob had turned up while Davies and Campbell had been working on RS-T and they had shared a warming char and wads around a wood-burning brazier that they had set up to one side of a blast-pen. Talk had come round to the problem of estimating, during the heat of battle, how much ammunition one had left and Tuck had said that it was pretty much the sound of compressed air that told you that you were completely out and this was really the only indication one had! In truth it was impossible, and Tuck talked about how frustrating it was to get caught up in a fight, carefully manoeuvring for the best firing position only to find that you didn't have enough ammunition to finish the job.

The conversation had been playing on Davies' mind and so now, holed up by the pub's open fire, he started to chat to Cammie about it. 'Yer know, Cam,' said Davies, 'there must be some way to get to know how many rounds have been fired! Why hasn't anyone done anything about it?' Campbell shrugged his shoulders and supped on his half-pint before answering. 'Taff, you don't half pick your times to talk shop. Here we are, we've hardly done much recently and you would rather have brought a musket out to the pub with you to work out some problem!' He was grinning, knowing full well that when his pal got something into his head – a problem to solve – there was no shifting it until there was some solution to be tried. 'Now, Cam, you know there are no such things as problems,' replied Davies, 'only solutions!' It was one of Davies' sayings, to which the assembled crowd would moan. 'You asked for that one,' laughed Harry Woods, playfully whacking his forage cap across the back of Campbell's head. As the conversation moved on to other things, Pete Long, Davies' instrument basher friend, said quietly to Davies, 'you'd need some sort of counter in the cockpit, would you, Taff? It wouldn't be too hard to cobble together some sort of counter, a bit like the ones they use for cameras.' With this phrase, the seed of a solution started to germinate in Davies' mind. The two of them sat in a huddle, like a couple of mad boffins, and now oblivious to the rest of the group, had borrowed a pencil from behind the bar and were sketching on the back of a ripped open packet of Player's Weights.

It was early the next morning when Davies and Long got down to the Armoury full of enthusiasm for their latest idea. On Davies' workbench, using a cannon that was in for a 120-hour inspection, they busied themselves taking measurements, moving the cannon mechanism through its sequence of actions. Under particular scrutiny came the rearward movement of the breech block. As Davies explained:

Pete Long and myself had this idea of how we could rig up a system in the Spitfire that allowed the pilot to see how many rounds had been fired from the 20mm drums. These only had sixty rounds each which was very limited and in the heat of a dogfight they had no way of knowing how much ammunition they had used up. Pete, he was an instrument fitter electrician and he thought he would be able to wire up a counter in the cockpit that would count off the rounds as they were fired. The thing was he had no knowledge of the operation of the guns and so I had the idea of putting a couple of electrical contacts at the back of the breech. When the block came back after firing a round, it would touch these two contacts and complete the circuit. Pete then got a small counter, the sort we had been using for counting camera gun footage, and connected this to the other end of the wiring.
(LAC Raymond Davies, compiled from interviews, 2001)

After spending the best part of a dreary-looking morning testing out the principle, Davies ran out to find Chiefy Stewart who was down on at dispersal with 124 Squadron. Finding Chiefy in conference with the WingCo, Davies tried desperately to curb some of his eagerness as he stood waiting for a natural break in the conversation. It was Tuck who looked across first, and sensing that there was something of a personal flap on for Davies, alerted Stewart to Davies' thinly veiled need to consult his senior. His explanation couldn't have been too garbled, because before Davies could recollect what he had actually blurted out, he was aware that the three of them were walking together, Tuck was eagerly agreeing to have his own aircraft pulled off the line to be the guinea pig, and both were firing questions at him about the finer details of the idea.

For most of the afternoon Davies spent his time wiring up the two contacts on the cannons, firstly just laying the cable across the upper faces of the wings and into the cockpit where Pete Long was busy fitting the counter instrument. After they were happy that both cannons would 'talk' to the counter, they brought in a rigger to properly route the cable internally through the mainplane and up into the cockpit. Tuck put in an appearance to check on progress, climbing up to see where Long had fitted the counter and inspecting the modification that Davies had made to the cannons. As it was late, and they were losing the light, they decided to push RS-T into the firing butts the following morning.

With the aircraft up on trestles and in the firing position, Davies climbed up into the cockpit and did some preliminary checks before firing. Anxiously, Long stood at the wing root with Chiefy Stewart and Tuck. Looking down at the assembled gaggle, Davies smiled and made a fingers-crossed sign to them before checking everything was clear.

We set the aircraft up on trestles in the usual position in the butts … I was up in the cockpit to do the firing. I can't remember who was out on the cannon, that was usually my job but Stewart, Tuck and Pete Long were all there, waiting in anticipation. I fired off a short burst with the Hispanos with just a slight touch on the gun button. You only needed to just touch it, it wasn't really like pushing a switch or something. And Boy, off went the cannons … brrrrrr … and I checked the counter had worked and by Christ it had! I fired off another burst and was concentrating so hard and was so excited that I forgot Pete and the rest of them. The next thing I knew was Pete was leaning into the cockpit and grinning! I then jumped out and Tuck was asking me questions as he lowered himself into the seat. I knelt down on the wing by the side of him and gave him a tap on the shoulder when he was to fire. So Bob let off a few bursts and was very excited, seeing the counter register the rounds that had been fired. This of course was before we had the belt-feed and I think we fired off a whole drum on this test. (LAC Raymond Davies, memoirs 2001–3)

The ingenuity of Davies and Long had brought a further refinement to the 20mm cannon armament and though it was an unofficial modification, Tuck was eager to test it further. On 21 January, after a more meticulous pre-flight check than usual, he left Davies, Long and Chiefy Stewart waiting at 124 Squadron's dispersal, while he climbed RS-T away from Biggin to test the guns and their ammunition counter system. Taking the aircraft out to sea, Tuck flew around for twenty minutes or so, firing the cannons into the water and taking great pleasure in seeing the little counter ticking away as it quickly measured the movement of the breech blocks as they rattled backwards and forwards. After what had seemed like an age to Davies – in fact only thirty minutes – Tuck dropped back into Biggin and practically leapt out of the cockpit as soon as the propeller had milled to a stop. There was much hand-shaking as Tuck offered his congratulations.

Tuck was so excited and impressed by the system we rigged up to count the rounds being fired from the drums. He said it was just what we needed and that he was

*going to contact Group HQ and the Air Ministry to tell them of our invention
and recommend that it be adopted as a proper modification for all cannon-armed
fighters.* (LAC Raymond Davies, memoirs 2001–3)

Unfortunately, Davies never got to know whether Bob was able to make that call.
One week later, he saw Tuck off from Biggin for the last time.

Failed to Return:
January 28th was a cold, overcast day. Davies barely considered looking up as he
trudged down to 124 Squadron's dispersal. It was almost midday and yet solid
grey clouds continued to drift ominously across the monochrome sky, like a
grand fleet of aerial battleships. 'Stand down, chaps,' Davies muttered to himself,
thinking of how much time it would take for the orderly to issue the inevitable
communiqué after putting down the blower! He had been up since 5 am, having
grabbed a breakfast with Campbell and Harry Woods before helping some of
401's armourers to pull a few cannons out of a couple of the squadron's Spits. He
walked up to Tuck's aircraft and stepped up on the port wing, reaching to adjust
the cockpit cover with a hope of keeping out some of the drizzle that took every
opportunity to seep past the join between the sliding canopy and the windscreen.
Stepping down he noticed how the rainwater ran off the trailing edge of the wing,
and how it now ran in rivulets down the fuselage sides, where he had touched it
to steady himself. Walking round to the leading edge, Davies looked out down the
valley, surveying the mist and rolling cumuli. 'Well, better get to it,' he thought as
he started his ritual with the quick check for his screwdriver and cocking spanner
in the side of his gumboot. While one of 124 Squadron's armourers tended to the
.303s, Davies set about his D.I. on Tuck's cannons, glancing deep into the bay to
check where they had, a few days earlier, routed the wiring for the ammunition
counter. The sound of a taxiing aircraft caught his attention. It was one of 401's
and he watched as the fitter swung it round and parked up the other side of RS-T
before shutting it down.

Tuck appeared soon after lunch with Pilot Officer Harley of 401 Squadron and
another Wing Commander who Davies did not recognise (it was Peter 'Cowboy'
Blatchford, leader of the Digby Wing and one of Tuck's old friends). The drizzle
had somewhat abated, and if you tried hard you could even convince yourself that
the cloud base had lifted to a degree. He imagined this to be what Tuck, Harley and
Blatchford were in conversation about as the three cast evaluative glances towards
the sky. Davies cupped his mug of NAAFI tea, taking a sip as he watched the
bowser pull away from Harley's kite. Tuck must have made his mind up, turning to
stub out his cigarette before tying the tapes of his Mae West. Harley was up on his

aircraft, standing on the wing as a fitter helped him adjust his parachute harness. Tuck walked out with Blatchford, catching sight of Davies on the way.

> *I'd finished everything that needed to be done [on the aircraft] and Tuck spotted me as he got near the aircraft and asked me if everything was OK. Of course I reported that it was and that all the guns were armed up. He nodded and said 'very well, Davies. See you when we get back.' But this was the time he was shot down and became a prisoner of war, so I didn't get to see him again. The last thing I did was run round and cock the guns for him and salute him off.* (LAC Raymond Davies, memoir 2003)

So began Tuck's last flight. Less than an hour later, Tuck's cannons spat one last note of defiance as they wreaked deadly revenge on one of the flak guns that had moments before punched a number of shells into the Spitfire's Merlin. As Tuck recalled:

> *As we went through the steam [from the train they had just attacked], just for a moment I lost sight of Harley, so I made a quick turn to get out of his way. As I came into the clear again at about seventy or eighty feet, I think everything in the Boulogne area opened up on me. I saw right away that Jerry had his guns at the foot of the hills on either side of me, and they were shooting more or less horizontally across the valley. I was caught in their cross-fire, and at this low altitude with a forty-five degree bank on, they just couldn't miss.*
>
> *Several shots smacked into the belly. One shell came right up through the sump, through the cooling system, and everything stopped dead. She started to belch black smoke, glycol and all sorts of filth. The windscreen was covered in oil, so I had to slam back the canopy and stick my head outside. I still had a bit of speed on – about 250 – so I could stay in the air for perhaps a minute. But I knew that if I tried to pull up to bale-out, they'd blast me clean out of the sky. My only chance was to stay very close to the deck, and try to find a space to put her down in. I turned up the valley and kept weaving her from side to side, but I couldn't see the smallest patch of open ground.*
>
> *When they kept pouring shells at me, I had a terrific temptation to climb her before the speed fell too low, but I knew the moment I got on to the skyline they'd have me like a box of birds.*
>
> *At this point I happened to glance over my shoulder, and there was Harley following right on my tail. It looked as if he was going to get the daylights shot out of him, too. I called him up and said: 'Get out quick! I've had it.'* (Wing Commander Bob Stanford-Tuck, quoted in Forrester, 1956, p. 19–20)

Tuck's luck held out long enough for him to set the aircraft down on its belly in what seemed to be the only available field amongst the dozens of flak batteries that had been firing at him. This area around Boulogne was notoriously thick with flak. There was no use in trying to analyse what had happened for some reckoning of contributing factors. In common fighter pilot parlance, Tuck knew he'd 'just got caught'.

Back at Biggin, with the lone return of Harley, news travelled quickly. It was hard to put into words what people were thinking. It seemed that everyone received the news with the same incredulity. The immortal Tuck? Some of the ground crew around Davies tried to be optimistic: 'He'll be back. He's bin shot down before an' got back,' some echelon fitter chirped. Though Davies found it difficult to comprehend as much as the next man, it was 'a cert' as he called it. Harley had said that there was really no way. Too low to bale out; engine belching black smoke; flak still coming from all sides; Tuck's own assessment, shouted over the R/t. Harley had not seen him belly it in, but quietly Davies and others hoped that for a pilot as skilled and experienced as Bob, this would have been his saving grace. A few days later, Tuck was characteristically in the news. This time it was to report him as prisoner of war. Geoffrey Wellum, one of Bob's comrades from those heady days of 1940 with 92 Squadron, made the following assessment of Tuck:

> *It was quite close to the day he was shot down and I don't know what I was doing but I was at Biggin for something, and he took me round in the car and we had lunch together. Bob was very flamboyant. He was a bloody good-looking bloke, mind you. A brilliant pilot, absolutely brilliant and always dashing about, you know, full of energy, never taking it easy. And he did not tolerate fools easily because I think he was apt to judge people by his own high standards and when I say high standards I don't mean of behaviour necessarily but ability to fly a Spitfire and that sort of thing. He was well-known; he played to publicity ... oh bloody hell, yes! Well, you know he was always to be seen in the forefront of anything, if there were any pictures going around. He was a brilliant pilot and a very good shot, and he just got stuck in.* (Flight Lieutenant Geoffrey Wellum, interview 2006)

That Tuck did survive on that day, picking his way between the relentless barrage of flak to make a forced landing, was very much down to his skill and experience. Lesser pilots would have possibly been tempted to gain height with what airspeed they had left, only to be caught in the cross-fire and blown out of the sky. For Davies, the loss of one so skilled was difficult to come to terms with. He had been at dispersal the day when Tuck had put on one of his aerobatic displays, and as

Davies stood there on top of a blast-pen laughing at the sheer flamboyance and daring of Tuck's manoeuvres – watching him pulling the aircraft round below the height of the buildings – he had puzzled at how such creativity and prowess could be used to deadly effect. War was truly exciting, but it was no game, no sport. Worst of all, it diverted people's talents to destructive purposes. And it cut short so many talented young lives.

Still, there was nothing to be gained in dwelling on such matters, not here and now. He had felt privileged to know Tuck, albeit only briefly. Their conversations had always given him the sense of being part of a well-oiled machine, a team. A memory from back home flashed into his mind: his father, Charlie, had the job of a pit-prop man in the coal mines, constructing and installing the wooden supports for the mile upon mile of underground galleries. Fellow miners always said that you knew you could get on with your own job when you were safe in the knowledge that Charlie Davies had prepared the way. Behind every pilot, there was an army of Charlie Davieses, and Tuck had made Raymond feel that he too was preparing the way – for Tuck and men like him. As January '42 slipped by, there were other young men stepping up to the front line.

Chapter Fifteen

Channel Dash

Fog and Fizzers:

If the loss of Bob Stanford-Tuck as Wing Commander Flying had not been enough to sink Biggin into a feeling of gloom that matched the weather, February got off on the wrong foot. The snow and mist of December and January continued, confining what operations that were attempted to rather dicey Rhubarbs across the Channel. With rolling grey cloud, mist, and rain turning to sleet, the only thing that was clear around the camp was the general feeling of frustration and boredom. In an attempt to fill in the time, Barwell and 'Spy' de la Torre impressed upon all personnel the need for good aircraft recognition skills and so implemented a series of lectures and tests. The only ones that were of vague interest were the little silhouettes and models of the Luftwaffe's latest fighter the Focke Wulf Fw190. Having entered front-line service only in October, its superior performance to the Spitfire V was of real concern. Now it had started to appear in greater numbers, thus becoming a real thorn in Fighter Command's side.

As Davies sat half-listening to one of these talks, Campbell nudged his 'oppo' and whispered, 'you on for the King's tonight?' Davies took a sideways glance at his grinning companion and scribbled something on the corner of his notebook to the effect that it was a top-notch idea. In the past few days, Davies had not been able to shake a personal depression following Tuck being shot down. It was not that he had been personally any closer to Tuck, though there was no doubt that he and the team had earned Tuck's respect and recognition of their work and initiative. Yet Bob's flamboyance and constant busyness, Davies had found infectious and motivating. To lose such a charismatic and effective leader was hard-felt and unnerving. So getting the usual throng together for the short trip to the King's Arms was indeed much welcomed – not that they had a pass for being out of camp between them!

Chiefy Stewart released them from duties after yet another uneventful day. As they hurried away to their respective billets, Campbell shouted after Davies, 'quick scrub up, Taff. See you at the usual rendezvous!' Davies waved recognition before scurrying off for a quick shower and change of clothes. Within half an hour he was making his way back towards dispersal, catching hold of Harry Woods and Eddie Healey on the way. It was dark now, in fact in these winter months they rarely were off the camp during daylight hours. Still, this cloak of darkness suited their purpose on this night – no passes meant the now customary hole in the fence was to be utilised once again! Grinning like naughty schoolboys, they eased their way through, Healey always the last, taking greatest care not to snag his uniform. 'A lot of damn fuss and palaver for a beverage or two,' murmured Eddie, dusting himself down and straightening his collar. The others giggled. 'Officer passing the front … Watch for that bit of barbed wire, Eddie … bit o' muck on yer trouser there, Boyo,' came the teasing remarks, as they waited for Healey to stop preening.

The King's Arms was rather busy but Campbell – eager as ever – had got down there double-time and was propping up one end of the bar. A few of 124's armourers were out, along with a number of 3034 echelon, including 'Titch' Thornton. It was a good crowd and Davies felt happy to be in their company. It was almost a year since they had left the rolling hills around Bridgnorth for war-torn Biggin Hill. For Davies, it seemed only yesterday that their Corporal had uttered those prophetic words, 'from now on, you'll be at war'. And how right he had been. Twelve months on and there was no doubt about it, they were now veterans of the conflict – 'old hands' that had pretty much seen it all. Davies was five months past twenty-one years old. There seemed to have been very little time to stop and think about all that had occurred since February 1941. The year had literally flown past, with the rapid escalation of Fighter Command's offensive strategy. Biggin had really been in the thick of the action and it felt that not a day had gone by without something happening that caught your attention. Lying in his bed Davies had on most nights thought through the events of the day, the week, the last month; had struggled to remember the name of some young pilot that had been posted in and lost in a matter of days; and he had reminisced through the letters he sent home, along with a proportion of his pay. As they stood half-pints for each other – they never seemed to drink pints – they all seemed in a reflective mood. It was most probably the weather and the operational inactivity that prompted this retrospective atmosphere.

So perhaps too many old stories of the short, tall and long variety were told and retold. And perhaps a few too many halves of bitter passed their lips. The landlord rang last orders and shoulders bumped shoulders as the trickle of RAF blue slowly wended its way out into the cold night air. Outside it was freezing and the ground was hard underfoot. Davies buried himself deeper into the protective warmth of his service overcoat – that is as soon as Harry Woods had helped his arms navigate the difficult twists and turns of the sleeves. Yes, he, like the others, was rather the worse for wear! With each other acting as mutual support, Campbell, Davies and Woods managed to remain upright and steady enough to keep with the crowd of airmen that were now making their way round the corner of the pub and up the main Bromley Road. They passed the picket post at the Leaves Green end of the road, waved on by the attendant and somewhat amused guard. 'Not far now,' thought Davies as they stumbled their way up to the main gate. 'The main gate,' a voice was shouting in his head! But he was too far gone to respond effectively. There was a group of them now and he could hear some of the others from the pub arguing with a member of the Service Police. 'Passes, gentlemen, please,' came a voice. He raised his head in Campbell's direction, who was checking his pockets in a vain attempt to delay the inevitable. All of a sudden there was a commotion: an SP was hit and, together with Davies and Campbell, they fell to the ground in a tangle of arms and legs. Over-reacting, the other SPs on duty grabbed them all and frogmarched them in the direction of the guardhouse. In the confusion the SP's assailant made his escape, though Campbell, Davies and Woods all knew his identity.

In the sobering light of day, Davies and three others including Campbell found themselves facing being put on a charge of drunkenness, one that usually carried serious penalties – a real fizzer! It was not so much the fact that he had been caught out that worried Davies. They were clearly guilty and deserved to face the consequences. No, what was more difficult to face up to was that he felt he had let the side down, he had let Biggin down. The thought of going up in front of Groupie Barwell filled him with fear and shame. Barwell, he had utmost respect for. To a man, everyone at Biggin would do anything for Dickie Barwell. He was that sort of commanding officer. And just as Barwell took a great interest in those under his charge, Davies felt that he had almost let Barwell down personally. 'Prize idiot,' he thought to himself, and sensed that the others felt pretty much the same. They were also very much aware of the reputation of RAF disciplinary procedures. As Davies recalled the experiences of another airman that was billeted with him:

There was this dirty sod of an airman. He had detention for pinching from the cook-house and you know he'd done a twelve-month detention in the glasshouse and when he came back he was a bloody wreck. And he went straight down to the cook-house to pinch some more bloody food! He really wanted building up. And we said to him 'you bloody fool [name], you'll have another two or three years,' and he'd a had a bloody beating there because those buggers [in the glasshouse], everything was 'on the double', you know. You had a job getting him to talk about it, but when he did, cor … [it was harsh], and you knew he wasn't exaggerating. But he started bloody pinching again – he brought back a bloody great ham! (LAC Raymond Davies, interview 1999)

So if such severe punishments had been dealt out for theft, what would they be for being drunk in charge of the King's uniform? Still, there was some sense that help was at hand, and in preparation to see Barwell, Davies and Campbell got word to plead as being 'under the influence of alcohol', rather than being drunk. Apparently, it was a lesser offence and thus carried with it more moderate penalties. Where the advice came from, Davies was never sure but it seemed pukka gen. Nevertheless, the prospect of being in front of Barwell was not appealing.

One after the other they were marched into Barwell's office, saluted and then stood at attention while the charge was read. Across the desk, Barwell sat listening before he started to question Davies about his version of events and whether he knew anything about what had led to the service policeman being assaulted. He replied honestly that the first thing he had known about the assault was when he was knocked to the ground, along with the SP and Campbell (who until then had been helping maintain a vertical posture). He omitted the last bit, as it tended to suggest he was significantly under the influence! Neither Campbell, nor himself would admit that they were sure who the assailant had been and this 'keeping mum' was not to Barwell's liking. However, once he had directed an uninterrupted barrage of observations of how the service would not tolerate behaviour of this kind and how serious the offence had been, he reached across the desk to some papers and consulted them for what seemed like an age.

I was shaking with fear when I was up in front of Dickie Barwell, and he really did give us all a right bollocking! It was just before he had his plaster-cast removed after crash-landing in the valley down from Biggin and breaking his back. He'd been in the cast for six months but it hadn't stopped him flying, though he was not allowed to fly on ops because of the restrictions of the plaster-cast. Anyhow, I felt so ashamed, not really for being caught – we all liked a drink and it was our way to unwind, to let off steam. The ground crew and the aircrew were much the same in this way, you know. And I'd been on [active service], dawn till dusk for nearly a twelve month now and believe you me I was tired. Now because they were also investigating this SP being assaulted by [name] … we all knew who it was but didn't want to be the one telling tales … so Barwell saw us individually. So after he had given me a real bollocking, you know, he then looked through my records and said that he was surprised at my conduct because I had had a clean sheet up till then, and had been putting the work in. He knew about my work with Mr Stewart's team and so said that he was going to consider the charge and that I would be informed as to the punishment I would receive. I was then dismissed and gave him a smart salute before being marched out. I felt so ashamed and he'd made me feel that small and that I'd let the side down, as well as myself. Boy, I was glad to get out of the room! (LAC Raymond Davies, memoir 2004)

It was not long before Davies heard the outcome of his meeting with Barwell, though the punishment proved somewhat surprising in its leniency. In fact, after Davies had been dismissed, Barwell had summoned Chiefy Stewart in order to discuss the matter of Davies' record and the threat of disciplinary action associated with his recent inebriation. It was clear to all that Davies was a good worker, an example of diligence and commitment to all of his trade. The exemplary work of the team, including Davies' contributions, was well known to Barwell and it was through his actions, supported by Rankin, that Chiefy Stewart and his group of specialists had been kept at Biggin rather than have them posted away with 92 Squadron. The punishment for Davies' being caught 'under the influence' and out of camp without permission, Barwell left for Chiefy Stewart to determine.

Stewart called me into his office and told me that Barwell had said that if I accepted a punishment to be decided by himself – by Chiefy Stewart – then Barwell would make sure that the charge would be dropped and that I could stay at Biggin, rather than spend time in the glasshouse. Of course, I said 'yes, Chiefy. I'll accept any punishment that you feel is fit.' There was no use trying it on, I was guilty of being out without a pass and being drunk – under the influence. So Chiefy said then that he was going to take me off the flight, and I was going to spend my time doing all the backlog of amendments, all the paperwork we had outstanding for the work on the cannons! That was to be my punishment. It was crafty of Stewart as he hated this paperwork and it had been lying around for some months. Time and again we'd make a start when there was no ops, but we'd always find something else to do 'cos none of us liked filling in the forms, we'd much rather be down on the Squadron where we were part of the action' (LAC Raymond Davies, memoir 2004)

However lenient Chiefy's punishment, Davies was not at all happy to be away from the squadrons and the work he found so exciting. Driving a desk and pushing a pencil was not his kind of war! As he sat there, day-in day-out, it seemed that they'd never done any of the paperwork ever before. There seemed to be mountains of the stuff: filling out job sheets from notes; documenting amendments to manuals and servicing procedures; updating reports on the cannon modifications; and endless amounts of filing! Periodically Stewart would pop his head round the door and ask how things were doing, and one of the lads would bring him a mug of tea. But it was monotonous and the only thing that stopped Davies from staring out of the window too much was the prospect of being back on the Squadron, back down at dispersal working on the aircraft. Even a draughty blister hanger in February was better than this. 'By God, Chiefy's a hard man,' he'd mutter under his breath. Sometimes, he thought Stewart had heard him and caught him looking over.

'OK, Davies?'

'Yes, Chiefy. Everything's fine apart from doing this paperwork!'

'Well, it'll be over quicker if you'd spend less time looking out of the window, wouldn't it?'

'Sorry, Chiefy. Just wondering when I can …'

'I know, get back on the Squadron. I think it should be about the same time that you finish doing these amendments, Davies.'

And so it went on. A week passed and there was still no real end in sight. As he had also been confined to camp for the duration of Stewart's disciplinary duties, Davies had elected to stay working into the evening, sometimes into the early hours. The evening work did not bother him too much – there was nothing else to do and no distractions. But during the days, the sight of a couple of bicycles being ridden down along the peri-track, the sound of a Merlin being run up, or catching a bit of dispersal gossip on his way to the cook-house was enough to make him reflect on what a bloody fool he had been.

Get Cracking, There's a Real Flap On!

The 12th of February started off much like any other foul-weather day. The squadrons had been stood down and the pilots released. There was still some encouragement to attend one of the usual lectures that were put on at such time, but few could muster any excitement for them. Even the wing commander and Barwell had decided to go off-camp. Those ground crew unfortunate to be on duty looked forward to routine maintenance, conducting the odd 150-hour check – having first wrestled with the canvas awnings of the blister hangars. Heavy and laden with water that hid amongst their folds, taming one of these coverings in a stiff wind was not anyone's idea of entertainment or exercise!

Having walked down to the armoury, Davies settled behind the desk that had been his home for nearly ten days. The pile of amendments seemed not to be reducing and he was quietly suspicious that Warrant Officer Stewart was sneaking a few more files into the 'to do' tray when he was not paying attention. At least there was nothing doing at dispersal. There had been some of the usual weather checks in the morning, but patrols over the Channel had found the visibility to be not far off the minimum, and practically right down on the deck past Dieppe. So after this initial activity, for the 'Jim Crow' pilots of 91 Squadron and any others still hanging around Biggin, it looked like all operations were off. Over at Gravesend, Brian Kingcome, now commanding 72 Squadron after a spell at OTU, had been catching up on some sleep in the luxurious surroundings of Cobham Hall. Others lay around reading. The picture across 11 Group was pretty much the same – dreary weather, 'ops' off, one of those loose-ended soporific days. Davies rocked the Armoury rubber stamp in the ink pad and impressed it into the top corner of another of the amendment records, signed it and placed it in the 'completed' pile.

Over at Biggin's ops room the senior controller, Bill Igoe, was however getting rather concerned as he watched a growing number of plots appear in the Channel. They were staying mainly in one place, just north of the Somme estuary. Whatever the weather was doing down there, there was significant aerial activity. The Luftwaffe was up in force, but for what reason? Puzzling at reports coming in he put a call out to 91 Squadron's CO, Bobby Oxspring, asking if perhaps he could venture out to see what all the commotion was about. He did so, with a warning: *'be damned careful as there were a lot of Huns about'* (Oxspring, 1984, p. 101). With Sergeant Beaumont as his No.2, Oxspring pointed the nose of his Spitfire into the gloom and within minutes of taking off was skirting the underside of the thick overcast that hung like an old grey blanket at 1,200ft. Though seriously dicey weather conditions, at least this cloud layer would give them some cover should they encounter the massive congregations of enemy aircraft that Igoe had seen on the plotting screens. Characteristically it was flak that gave them the first indication that 'Jerry' was around.

> *Following the coast past Le Touquet towards the Somme estuary we suddenly ran into some bursts of heavy flak. Banking into a turn we peered down through the rain and sighted a large oval of destroyers and smaller escorts in the middle of which were three much larger ships in line astern; all were leaving creamy wakes indicating that the force was moving fast. My first reaction that the Royal Navy was a bit off course was soon dispelled when we saw flak guns on the deck firing at us. Calling Beaumont to break off we climbed up to the cloud base again.*
> (Squadron Leader R.W. Oxspring, 91 Squadron, quoted in Oxspring, 1984, p. 101)

Oxspring and Beaumont were not the only ones from 11 Group in the air over the flotilla of ships. Unknown to Biggin's controller, the irrepressible Victor Beamish and Finlay Boyd – respectively Kenley's Station Commander and Wing Leader – had been getting a bit twitchy and decided to take a chance on some excitement by organising a rhubarb. Chance had certainly thrown them more excitement than they had bargained for as they stumbled upon the German fleet. From their slightly higher altitude, Oxspring and Beaumont spotted this second pair of aircraft but were unable to positively identify them as Spitfires. It was only after diving down and closing to 500 yards that Oxspring was able see enough of them through the rain-covered windscreen to identify them as 'friendlies'. Imperative now was to get back to raise the alarm. After attacking a number of E-boats that were lurking on the peripheries of the flotilla, Beamish and Boyd decided to do the same.

Of course, the strategists at High Command had anticipated such a scenario, having been very much preoccupied with possible breakout of the German capital ships *Scharnhorst*, *Gneisenau* and *Prinz Eugen* from Brest harbour. It was a most audacious gamble on the part of the enemy. Rather than taking the longer way round Ireland and into the North Sea, running the gauntlet of the Channel under the noses of the ever-curious Royal Navy and Royal Air Force may have seemed to many as being suicidal. Yet with an enormous Luftwaffe fighter presence masterminded by Adolf Galland, the ships had slipped out of Brest under the cover of darkness and the appalling visibility. To counter any possible activity of this kind, the Royal Navy and RAF had put together operation code-named 'Fuller'.

Unfortunately, the details of this counter-operation and its code name had become bogged down in the chain of command, and had clearly not filtered down to many squadrons in 11 Group. With this lack of information, neither Oxspring nor Beamish nor their wingmen were able to transmit the code name to set 'Fuller' in motion. Frustrated and conscious of the significance of what he had seen, Oxspring decided to break strict radio silence and put out a call to Biggin.

I was still not sure of the identity of the big ships, but after we landed Sergeant Beaumont was convinced that one of them was the Scharnhorst. *Before becoming a pilot he had served in the RAF Marine Section at Gosport and had seen the* Scharnhorst *at a pre-war Naval review. When I telephoned my report Bill Igoe listened in and cranked me straight through to the incredulous 11 Group controller. Unfortunately the AOC, Sir Trafford Leigh-Mallory, was always at Northolt and I got nowhere in conveying the seriousness of the situation. Thirty minutes later the two Spitfires which Beaumont and I had seen over the German convoy landed at Kenley ... They had maintained R/t silence and, since they hadn't called it, were as ignorant of 'Fuller' as we were. But their report married up with ours; obviously the representations of a Group Captain and a Wing Commander carried more weight than those of a Squadron Leader and Sergeant Pilot.* (Squadron Leader R.W. Oxspring, 91 Squadron, quoted in Oxspring, 1984, p. 102)

It was midday before anything managed to filter down to squadron level, and as a result it was rather panicked and garbled. Still at Gravesend, Brian Kingcome was summoned to the phone and ordered to put the squadron onto a state of immediate readiness. The awaiting transport delivered the pilots to the dispersal, already a hive of activity with fitters, riggers and armourers all seemingly at double-time. Yet, there was still much uncertainty of the plan of action.

> *No sooner had we arrived than we were called to cockpit standby. Hardly had I strapped myself in before I was ordered to report to the control tower and had to unstrap myself again. There was, it appeared, some as yet undefined surface activity off Dover involving the Navy, who were very probably going to need our support. Meanwhile it was back to the cockpit to resume strapping myself in before, yet again, being called to the control tower. During the next quarter of an hour I must have been summoned four times between cockpit and control tower, each time fastening and unfastening the straps and each time been given a set of different instructions, each set more confusing than the one preceding it. It was obvious that not a soul, from Fighter Command downwards, had a clue as to what was afoot in the English Channel.* (Squadron Leader Brian Kingcome, quoted in Kingcome, 1999, p. 117)

At Biggin, Davies tried to ignore some commotion that was going on outside the armoury and reached for another batch of papers from his 'to do' pile. He noted a few smudged oil marks on the top sheet and was just about to undo the string that bound this particular group together when there was a sound of someone running followed by a crash as the office door burst open. It was Chiefy, looking uncharacteristically flustered. Before Davies had a chance to offer the usual 'what's up, Chiefy', Stewart exclaimed:

> 'Davies, get yourself off to 124 Squadron, now!'
> 'But Chiefy, what about me being …'
> 'Forget that for now, look lively. Get yourself off, that's an order!'

In the course of their working relationship, it had been rare for Stewart to ever really look flustered. Concerned, yes – flustered, no. Rarer still was it for him to directly say '… and that's an order' unless there was something very serious indeed. Davies needed no second telling, and he was out of the hut as fast as he could, grabbing the nearest bicycle and pedalling like mad to get round to where 124's aircraft were dispersed. A wagon sped past carrying what seemed to be a mixture of pilots and ground crew and someone shouted, 'C'mon Taff, get weaving!' Too quick to see who it was, much too quick to raise the customary grin and two-fingered response! He practically jumped off the bike, making some half-conscious attempt to prop it against an E-pen wall. Campbell was there, carrying some .303 – unusual as both of them were almost exclusively 'cannon boys' these days. Clearly, everything was in a right old state!

As had been the situation at Gravesend – and probably across the whole of 11 Group – 124 Squadron were as much in the dark about what was happening as the next squadron. The experiences of the commanding officer, Squadron Leader Raymond Duke-Woolley, mirrored those of Brian Kingcome.

We were released that day because the weather was so bad and I said we'd spend the morning in the intelligence section and catch up on the reading we hadn't done. I'd been chatting to the other squadron CO – he and his pilots were doing the same thing. The Station Commander and the Wing Commander were off the Station when the telephone rang. Nobody was about so I answered it and [heard] a panic-stricken voice squeakily yelling 'scramble, scramble!!', followed by a word – then 'click' [as the receiver went down]. I thought I'd heard the word somewhere but could not place it. So I walked into the intelligence section and said to the boys that there seemed to be some panic on. Get down to dispersal, someone phone the hangars and tell them to get the a/c ready while I try to find out what it's all about.

I went back into the I/O's office and rang back 11 Group HQ and the same squeaky voice came on. I tried to calm him down, but all I got was 'scramble, scramble' – this codeword and again 'click'. So I put the phone down and rang him back and before he could say anything I cut in and asked 'Scramble where?' He said, 'North Foreland, 12.30!' – then 'click'. It was now ten to twelve. (Squadron Leader Raymond Duke-Woolley, 124 Squadron, letter, 1990)

As 124 Squadron got off from Biggin, Davies stood wondering what it was all about. Many stood around, really not knowing what had just gone on. Yes, of course there had been scrambles before. There had been times that seemed like the almightiest of flaps was on somewhere. But into that clag of mist and rolling cloud they had put up two of Biggin's squadrons – 124 and 401 – in double-quick time. For what purpose? Nobody seemed the wiser, even after the usual congregation and pooling of a smattering of 'gen' from everyone. Davies tried hard to hold back on the excitement he felt at being back on the flight, knowing that it was but a temporary 'blip' in his 'fizzer' of indeterminate length. No, Chiefy wasn't about to let him off. Feeling his way in amongst the overcast, Duke-Woolley suddenly repeated to himself the word that had been blurted to him down the telephone:

So we got airborne and … it suddenly clicked! The code word 'Fuller' was the signal that the German battleships were out of Brest and sailing up the Channel! I quickly briefed the chaps over the radio, but said that was all I knew. So we were going to help to give some cover to a handful of Fairey Swordfish who would endeavour to attack three large German warships at 12.30 – and I'd only been in the office of the I/O at about 10 minutes to 12!

As I recall, we'd taken off at about 5 or 10 past, which, considering we'd been released for the day, was pretty good going. But now we had to get to North Foreland and I seem to remember we arrived about 2 minutes past the half-hour. In between times I had got hold of my old squadron at Redhill and they rendezvoused with us, seeing them arrive a couple of minutes ahead of me. (Squadron Leader Raymond Duke-Woolley, letter, 1990)

Kingcome and 72 Squadron had finally got airborne and hot-footed it to Manston where Brian had been instructed that he would pick up another five squadrons as escorts to the gaggle of Fairey Swordfish torpedo bombers. That such antiquated aircraft would be thrown at the might of the German Navy seemed futile in itself. The task of keeping from them the swarms of enemy fighter aircraft that had been reported by Oxspring and Beamish exercised the imagination still further. The weather and the prevailing sense of panic resulted in further departures from what Kingcome had been briefed as being 'the plan'.

[On arrival at Manston] There the six Swordfish were already airborne and orbiting the airfield, but we could see no more Spitfires anywhere in view. How long the Swordfish had been waiting was impossible to tell, but they were making their impatience obvious. The instant they saw us they straightened up and set course without hanging about for the rest of the escort to show up. With hindsight I realised that their impatience sprang from the fear that the painfully slow speeds of their 'Stringbags' could allow their targets to get clean beyond range before they could catch them. Yet the most immediate surprise they gave me was that, instead of flying south towards Dover, as I expected, they turned due east and, at zero altitude, headed out across the North Sea, the surface of which was uninviting and threatening beneath a swirling cover of low cloud and rain. Undaunted, I took up station above and behind, deploying the ten aircraft to which the promised five-squadron wing had eventually been reduced. Considering the atrocious weather, this depletion was probably just as well. Five squadrons could easily have become unworkable with visibility fluctuating between zero and a few hundred yards. We also had to maintain a low altitude to avoid losing visual contact. Because the maximum speed of a Swordfish equalled the stalling speed of a Spitfire, the only

way to hold them in view without spinning into the sea ourselves was to sweep behind them in large loose figures of eight. Trying to co-ordinate the movements of more than ten aircraft in those conditions might well have got us all into an untimely tangle. (Squadron Leader Brian Kingcome, 72 Squadron, quoted in Kingcome, 1999, p. 118–9)

Valour and Desperation:
There is perhaps a fine line drawn between valour and desperation, between courageous acts and those that seem reckless, foolhardy, even pointless. Yet it is always with hindsight that we make these judgements, sometimes without being true to the context in which these actions occurred. Yes, 'Fuller' was turning out to be an absolute shambles. Fighter Command, the Royal Navy and those operating shoreline defences were completely unprepared for the realities of the German breakout from Brest. Perhaps in good visibility, with clear intelligence operating from the moment the ships left harbour, then it may have been an effective and realistic plan. But the enemy is rarely compliant, and it must be acknowledged that the decision to put the breakout plan into operation under such poor conditions was a masterstroke. On 5 June 1944 Eisenhower would make a similar decision to 'go' under equally challenging circumstances.

Not long after leaving the coast contact was made with the enemy. As swarms of Me109s and Fw190s came to intercept the attacking force, it was all that Kingcome and 72 Squadron could do to turn into them, fire off some discouraging shots and return to keeping the Swordfish in view. In the confusion, Kingcome found himself face-to-face with a sleek grey battleship that greatly impressed him, and for a moment he was relieved that the Royal Navy seemed at last to be at hand. The intense flak barrage that the ship put up made him turn smartly away, and he was still not wholly certain that the ship was not one of His Majesty's. In Brian's experience, it was not unknown for the Royal Navy to shoot first and ask questions later (maybe even to swot up on their aircraft recognition!). Yet, there was certainty in the actions of the Swordfish crews, now at wave-top height and making a bee-line for the ship.

Approaching this maelstrom of flak and fighters was Duke-Woolley's 124 Squadron, who although having missed the intended rendezvous, had nevertheless persevered, flying almost blindly in the direction they had last been given.

By now the Swordfish had gone on. I had no idea where the ships were – nobody had bothered to tell me that, probably they didn't know. We headed out to sea, with viz down to 3 or 4 miles, cloud base down to perhaps 1,200ft. I didn't know what else to do. Then, some miles out, I suddenly saw, off to my right, that the area between the cloud base and the sea was black with flak. And in the middle was what I took to be the six Swordfish, in the biggest concentration of flak I'd ever seen in my life. I cut round in front of this lot, went up into the cloud, on the basis that we might be able to find the odd German a/c scudding about above. There was certainly no future in going into the flak with my Spitfires.

Coming out, we flew around, saw a couple of Me109s but they smartly disappeared when they saw us. Then, finally, I let down and breaking through found myself slap on top of the funnel of the Scharnhorst*! I quickly turned towards France thinking it safer to fly south than north at that moment.* (Squadron Leader Raymond Duke-Woolley, letter, 1990)

Before long, there was nothing more that the Spitfire squadrons of Fighter Command could do. They had protected the Swordfish to the best of their ability, but there was little they could do to counter the big guns and relentless flak of the German Navy. As Kingcome recalled:

[The German ship] lowered her big guns and fired salvos into the sea ahead of the approaching Swordfish. As the colossal walls of water and spray rose directly into their paths, I had the impression that one was brought down by the deluge. Somehow the others seemed to survive, however, and then the battleship raised her sights and let fly directly at the Swordfish with a fiery inferno. The brave 'Stringbags' never faltered, but just kept on driving steadily on at wave-top height, straight and level as though on a practice run. They made perfect targets as they held back from firing their missiles before closing to torpedo range. They were flying unswerving to certain destruction, and all we as their escort could do was sit helplessly in the air above them and watch them die…. There was not a split second free for speculation. We turned in towards the attacking fighters and did our utmost to intercept between them and the vulnerable Swordfish. The battle was short, sharp and violent, and it probably lasted only a few minutes before the German fighters melted away. Of the Swordfish no trace remained, apart from floating wreckage and one or two life-rafts. There had been six aircraft and eighteen crew. Five survivors were later picked out of the water. (Squadron Leader Brian Kingcome, 72 Squadron, quoted in Kingcome, 1999, p. 120)

All five survivors received awards for their acts of courage, four the DSO, the other the Conspicuous Gallantry Medal. For his unwavering leadership and courage in the face of almost certain death, the leader of the Swordfish attack, Lieutenant-Commander Eugene Esmonde DSO, RN, received a posthumous Victoria Cross. The citation read as follows:

For valour and resolution in action against the Enemy. On the morning of Thursday, 12th February, 1942, Lieutenant-Commander Esmonde, in command of a Squadron of the Fleet Air Arm, was told that the German battle-cruisers Scharnhorst *and* Gneisenau *and the Cruiser* Prinz Eugen, *strongly escorted by some thirty surface craft, were entering the Straits of Dover, and that his Squadron must attack before they reached the sand-banks North East of Calais.*

Lieutenant-Commander Esmonde knew well that his enterprise was desperate. Soon after noon he and his squadron of six Swordfish set course for the Enemy, and after ten minutes flight, were attacked by a strong force of Enemy fighters. Touch was lost with his fighter escort, and in the action which followed all his aircraft were damaged. He flew on, cool and resolute, serenely challenging hopeless odds, to encounter the deadly fire of the Battle-Cruisers and their Escort, which shattered the port wing of his aircraft. Undismayed, he led his Squadron on, straight through this inferno of fire, in steady flight towards their target. Almost at once he was shot down; but his Squadron went on to launch a gallant attack, in which at least one torpedo is believed to have struck the German Battle-Cruisers, and from which not one of the six aircraft returned.

His high courage and splendid resolution will live in the traditions of the Royal Navy, and remain for many generations a fine and stirring memory. (VC citation, gazetted 3 March 1942, quoted in Laffin, 2000, p. 37–8)

It could have been a citation written for all those gallant crew that had gone against the German Navy that day, as much for those Swordfish crews that made the ultimate sacrifice as those that had looked death squarely in the face and had by some fortune escaped. Equally so, the fighter escort had battled against overwhelming circumstances and odds to enable the Swordfish to get as close as they did. Characteristically for Kingcome, there was no doubt where credit lay:

With guns empty, the Spitfires of 72 Squadron made their way back to base together, many shot up but none shot down. We had been in the air little more than an hour since take-off, but it had been time enough to witness the highest heroism and its toll; time enough for lives to be ended and family ties shattered. An epic of sacrifice and tragedy had been squeezed into sixty fleeting minutes, the time you might take over a hurried lunch. (Squadron Leader Brian Kingcome, 72 Squadron, quoted in Kingcome, 1999, p121)

A Set of Props:
'Friday the thirteenth,' thought Davies as he made his way down the Armoury the next day. He was not known to be overly superstitious, but his luck certainly

hadn't been forthcoming in recent weeks. The thought of being back at that desk with those amendments punctuated his every step. It was perhaps more painful considering the excitement of yesterday and being back on the flight. 'God, you could die of amendments,' he muttered as he passed a few Echelon lads working on one of 124's aircraft. By all accounts there was not a small amount of tin-bashing to be had this morning.

It was freezing in the Armoury, bloody freezing. It did not help that he seemed to be the first down this morning. No Chiefy in sight. Keeping his greatcoat on as some protection against the cold, Davies settled down in his now usual spot at the desk in Warrant Officer Stewart's office. As he sat there, huddled into the thick serge of the coat, blowing into his cupped and still gloved hands, it was still obvious that there was a fair amount still to be done. In an attempt to put off the inevitable, he decided that work could not begin without a mug of tea – as piping hot as possible. It was a ritual enacted every day, and now with steam rising from his regulation platter mug he stood by one of the work benches in the main workshop, toying with a couple of sear buffer springs that had been left wandering without a home. 'Better get on,' he thought, turning back to the office and the paperwork.

He had been there an hour or so when he heard a few armourers come into the workshop with Chiefy. He could make out Stewart passing on some instructions for the day, and the sound of the armourers as they put together the equipment they required. Then there was silence again, and he thought himself alone. Back to the work. He could not have had his head down in the papers long, attempting to decipher someone's scribbled marginal notes on an amendment job sheet, when he became aware of Chiefy standing in the doorway. 'Don't like being away from the flight, do you Davies?' asked Stewart. It was more a statement rather than a question – he knew full well that Raymond counted every laborious hour. Davies tried to put a brave face on it. 'Well, my own fault, Chiefy, and I think I am making some headway with these,' he replied, nodding towards the thickening pile of completed work. 'Yes, you've done OK. You've kept at it,' said Stewart, moving towards the desk. He paused, casting his eye over the meticulously assembled paperwork. 'I think you've learned your lesson,' he said, thumbing through the uppermost sheets, 'perhaps, it's time you went back on the squadron.'

Davies looked up from his work, not wholly certain that he'd heard Stewart correctly. 'Sorry Chiefy, did you say I could go back on the squadron?' he quizzed. Stewart smiled and nodded affirmation, reaching for something in the breast pocket of his tunic. He pulled out a small paper envelope and pushed it across the desk towards Davies. 'But before you get on your way to dispersal, you'd better have these,' said Stewart. Davies opened up the envelope. Inside was a pair of blue-grey cloth insignia, bearing a two-bladed propeller. He could scarcely believe his eyes, and it seemed incomprehensible: Here he was finishing off a right old 'fizzer', and he was being given the rank of Leading Aircraftsman – L.A.C. Those three letters spelt out a promotion and he'd only been at Biggin for just twelve months! 'But Chiefy, I don't understand,' he exclaimed, his brow furrowed in puzzlement as he stood, still staring at these small but highly prized pieces of cloth. 'Well, your promotion was recommended a few weeks ago, just before you put up this black. Now go and get them sewn up before you get off to dispersal – that's unless you'd prefer staying on to finish these amendments,' joked Stewart. He needed no further telling and, shaking Stewart's hand, he hurried off to his billets to get his 'housewife' in order to sew on his newly awarded badges of rank. From 'fizzer' to a set of props! Biggin never failed to be exciting!

Chapter Sixteen

Fledgling Eagles

'Yanks' in Blue:

Despite the great loss of life that was encountered on 7 December 1941, when the Japanese attack on Pearl Harbour brought the American nation into the war, there were many in Europe who were relieved. For two years, the United States had tried its best to sit on the peripheries of the developing conflict. It had adopted a broadly isolationist (and some would feel, characteristic) stance and had 'sat out the game', attempting to play a neutral role. It was amazing how a few thousand miles of ocean could engender such a feeling of safety, and could afford such a great power the luxury of choice. War, until 7 December, was not on its doorstep, perhaps not even at the bottom of the drive! In that act of aggression committed by the Japanese Imperial Navy on that winter morning, the casualties were not only military hardware and personnel, not just civilians and families: a far greater loss was America's sense of security and choice. Pearl Harbor cut deep into the American psyche and made the nation question its ability to make its own decisions of engagement and disengagement in an escalating global conflict.

Although as a nation, and as a military power, America had remained at the sidelines of hostilities, this general feeling of disconnection masked degrees of support that were manifest in terms of finance, fuel and war materiel. For some, there was indeed a special relationship with those British cousins across the pond, and individuals (as well as the US government) went as far as they dared to provide assistance. For the Royal Air Force, help came in the form of supplies of 100 octane aviation fuel, and the lend-lease agreement that saw American aircraft manufacturers supplying a range of US designed and built aircraft for RAF use. Yet, alongside Britain and its European and Commonwealth allies, there was also a small group of Americans already within the RAF who celebrated their nation's entry into the European war in December 1941. Organised into three squadrons – 71, 121 and 133 Squadrons – a band of American volunteer pilots provided the vanguard to the United States contribution to the air war waged over France. By early 1942, the first two Eagle Squadrons as they became known, had grown in their combat experience. It was the third, and youngest, of these Eagle Squadrons – 133 Squadron – that flew into Biggin Hill in May 1942 to start its tour as part of the Wing.

The last of the Eagle Squadrons to be formed, 133 comprised of a greater number of new recruits than the other two squadrons. Thus, in order to ease their way towards combat-ready status, Fighter Command deployed the squadron outside of 11 Group, firstly in 12 Group with postings at Duxford, Fowlmere and Colly Weston. Unlike 121 Squadron that had started with a cadre of veterans, forming a third all-American squadron posed a thorny problem from the start. With 71 and 121 being very much in the thick of it by late 1941, drawing experienced pilots from these squadrons in order to make up the nucleus of another would seriously compromise their combat effectiveness. Similarly, posting 'green' recruits into challenging operational theatres (as past experiences showed) almost guaranteed short flying careers! So it was that 133, after a short spell in 12 Group, were posted out to Eglington, Northern Ireland for patrol and convoy duties that were deemed less hazardous. Ironically, the transit flight to Eglington saw the deaths of a number of pilots, killed in poor visibility while trying to land on the Isle of Man in order to refuel. Amongst those lost was one of 133's few experienced pilots, Andy Mamedoff.

After nearly seven months flying patrols from Eglington and later Kirton-in-Lindsey, north of Lincoln, 133 was considered to be combat-ready for operations in the South East of England and took up their posting at Biggin Hill at the beginning of May. With their arrival there were now three squadrons on 'the Bump'. Still operating from Gravesend, 72 Squadron remained the senior, most experienced unit with the Wing that now comprised four squadrons: 72, 124, 401 and 133. For the next four months, these squadrons would operate largely as a four-squadron Wing, flying most operations together. The first of these was uneventful, as the Squadron diary recorded:

7.5.42: 1840: The Squadron's first sweep from Biggin Hill! Together with Nos. 401, 124 & 72 Squadrons, flying as Biggin Hill Wing, they acted as top cover to 6 Bostons which had been detailed to bomb Ostend. They reached Ostend at 20,000 feet and encountered accurate flak in this area. No enemy aircraft were seen. Fine, sunny day, turning cooler with a fairly strong wind at 2000 hours just as the Wing was circling to land. (133 Squadron, Operational Records Book, 7 May 1942)

The day-to-day servicing of these American squadrons fell to regular RAF personnel, a mixture of ground and administrative personnel posted directly to the squadrons, as well as members of the servicing echelons resident with particular Wings. In line with Chiefy Stewart's strategy, as the newly incoming squadron of the Wing, 133 Squadron was given the special attention of his team. Through such practice he ensured that the particularly effective procedures that they had developed in working with the 20mm cannon armament in the Spitfire Vbs would be cascaded to squadron armament teams. So it was that Davies and his comrades began their association with the Eagle Squadron. It was a partnership that would last until Davies' departure from Biggin Hill.

At first, as for many of the British ground crews, the Americans were something of a novelty. Davies' only experience of Americans was of those that populated those Hollywood cowboy or gangster movies that he had seen in the local picture houses in Treharris and Pontypridd. Hard-drinking, bar-room brawling, fond of the ladies, tough-guy sorts – it was not really anything to place any confident judgement on! He, Campbell and Broomhead found great mileage in pretending to chew tobacco and calling to each other, 'say pardner, hear ya got a maaghty fine set o' pistols on that thare airplane.' For a time they would set their service caps at a jaunty angle and stand with their thumbs hooked round their braces. Davies and his comrades would laugh as they remembered one of 92 Squadron's pilots, Tony Bruce, whose many talents included being able to 'rope' unsuspecting members of air and ground personnel with his lasso! Oh how Tony would have been at home at dispersal with the Americans around!

There were real noticeable changes. Many of the pilots had set about getting their Eagle Squadron shoulder flash emblem and other mascots painted on the cowlings of their new Spitfires. A stars and bars flag of the Union fluttered at dispersal. Now there was a distinct smell of coffee brewing around the flight hut. Sociably, they were an approachable bunch and after operations they seemed perhaps a little more excitable. The grapevine rumours also said they were prone to party hard and be rather individualist, perhaps wary and resistant to RAF discipline. Some of this was probably imagined or exaggerated as many a group of fighter pilots came over as overly animated on their return to Biggin to the safety of *terra firma*. Moreover, if the last year had been in any way typical, then any that joined Biggin's brethren of fighter pilots were deft in the art of enjoying themselves, living in and for the moment. So perhaps this new group was different, yet in many ways similar to those other high-spirited young men who had passed this way before.

Early Skirmishes:
Though a number of enemy aircraft were seen on 10 May, it was not until the 17th that the squadron had a chance to mix it with some Me109s, over Le Treport, during Rodeo No.31. Devoid of the excitement, adrenaline and fear that such combats brought, recording the squadron's activities was a dispassionate affair:

17.05.42: 0930: The Biggin Hill Wing made another Fighter Sweep over the Abbeville area, and this time the Squadron succeeded in stirring up the Hun's nest!

Flight Lieutenant McColpin and Pilot Officer Morris both had combats 5 miles N.W. of Le Treport as a result of which McColpin claimed an Me109F destroyed and another 'probable,' and Morris claimed a 'probable.' Neither they or any of the remaining pilots suffered any damage.' (133 Squadron, Operational Records Book, 17 May 1942)

After providing a number of standing patrols on the morning of the 19th, Davies did a quick once over on an aircraft piloted by a young pilot officer from New Jersey. Eric Doorly was twenty years old, and like many of the younger Eagles was a college graduate. Of thin, wiry build, Davies watched him making himself comfortable on the seat parachute, and waited until the fitter climbed down before signalling that everything was checked out on the cannons. Doorly nodded in recognition before turning back to continue his other pre-flight checks. Davies slid off the wing, did the usual last check of the underside of the aircraft and gave it a now customary pat, as one would a faithful dog, a best friend. Campbell was walking over from another aircraft, wiping his hands on a piece of rag, smiling and shaking his head.

'What's up, Boyo, quizzed Davies?' 'Have a guess, Taff,' replied Campbell, still wiping his hands. 'Dad's been out with his bucket of chip oil?' 'Got it in one, Taff, mi old oppo,' exclaimed Campbell, breaking into a smile. It was another standing joke between them. Ever since they had been at Biggin, despite all training, advice and gentle cajoling, 'Dad' Best had continued to be rather liberal with his application of lubricant to the cannons. The team had joked that if he was given half a chance, he'd be spraying it on with a hose! So, under usual conditions, Davies and the rest of the team would keep a watchful eye on 'Dad', and manage to make sure he eased off on the mixture. Sometimes, however, 'Dad' would have had the 'hose' out before they got to him! The sizzle of a Verey cartridge and the sound of Squadron Leader Eric Thomas's aircraft starting up brought them out of their recall of 'Dad's finest moments'.

Rodeo 42 began at 1425 hours. The Wing climbed out of Biggin, eleven of 133's aircraft gaining height along with 72, 401 and 124 Squadrons. The enemy waited as usual until the fighters were on the way back, juggling with the throttle settings to maintain the fuel economy. The Wing found itself heavily engaged by fighters from JG2 'Richthofen', 133 Squadron being caught up in the whirling maelstrom.

19:05:42: Another sweep was made round the Fecamp – Le Treport area. Pilot Officer Morris, F/Sergeant Harp and Pilot Officer Sperry had combats with Me109s, all of them making claims. Pilot Officer Florance did not return, but it is thought he might have baled out. Pilot Officer Pewitt was seen to go down with

2 e/a on his tail about 10 miles S. of Beachy Head. He was picked up later in the evening, but died from head injuries before reaching hospital. A thorough search was made for Florance at 2030 hours but nothing was reported as having been seen.
(133 Squadron, Operational Records Book, 19 May 1942)

Rain on the 24th limited operations throughout the day, though it was not without contact with the enemy. On a routine patrol over Dungeness, Pilot Officers Taylor and Jackson stumbled across a pair of Me109s, most likely making use of the poor conditions to probe the south coast for targets of opportunity. In a running fight that took them to the French coast, Jackson managed to get a number of hits on one of the enemy aircraft. Claiming it as 'damaged', it was last seen with its undercarriage hanging down.

It was after six o'clock when the Wing was finally sent off on Rodeo 48, a sweep over the Hardelot–St Omer area accompanied by the Kenley Wing. With Dickie Barwell flying as his number two, Rankin brought the Wing round over St Omer, his keen eyes spotting a number of enemy aircraft in the distance. For most of the time the enemy seemed to be keeping out of trouble, and the Wing found it difficult to engage. However as Rankin and Barwell turned in the vicinity of Gris Nez, the WingCo managed to close on an Me109F. As Barwell's combat report detailed:

I was flying No.2 to W/C Rankin and during the engagement off Gris Nez an Me109F was closed by the Wing Commander in a North Easterly direction. After he had fired at it I fired from dead astern from a range of about 350 yards; a 2 second burst with machine gun and cannon and I saw strikes on his mainplane and fuselage. I broke away immediately after, rejoining W/C Rankin and turned to the left. (Group Captain Dickie Barwell, Combat Report, 24/05/42)

As many of those down at dispersal noted, Barwell continued to 'keep his hand in', flying almost daily as part of the Wing. With Jamie back in the driving seat as Wing Leader, it seemed a natural partnership, one that had been forged since Dickie Barwell had taken over at Biggin. It was almost a year now, and despite the continued protestations of the C-in-C, Barwell had continued on 'ops', flying number two to the likes of Malan, Rankin and Duke-Woolley. Perhaps this was the key to his popularity: he really did share in the experiences of those under his command. He put himself under the same operational pressures as those around him. In doing so, the high standards that he expected were also demonstrated by his own example, and thus they were never considered unrealistic. For those flying on 'ops', whether you were a sergeant pilot, a sprog pilot officer or the WingCo, it was a great confidence booster to see 'the old man' climbing into a cockpit, ready to share in the same dangers, to face the same fears and conquer them every time you went up. The operational dangers were clear. Over at Kenley, the station commander, Group Captain R.L.R. Atcherley, was made only too aware of this when he took a Spitfire on a sector reconnaissance.

Richard Atcherley, or 'Batchy' as he was almost universally known, was another of the RAF's charismatic leaders. Recognised as a brilliant aerobatic pilot and member of the RAF's High Speed Flight, he had been part of the Schneider Trophy team in 1929. Along with his identical twin David, 'Batchy' built up a reputation throughout his RAF career as an eccentric senior officer, fond of practical jokes and prone to court martials! In the 1930s, whilst serving in Palestine with 14 Squadron, he took to keeping all manner of exotic animals, including a pet lion cub that often accompanied him into the air. It was just prior to leaving the sector when one of his aerobatic escapades took him over a tennis party attended by – unbeknownst to Atcherley – the AOC, Sir Cyril Newell. Following a court martial, he was reduced in rank and prevented from attending the RAF Staff College. Later still, after his time as Station Commander at Kenley, he was promoted to Acting Air Commodore, commanding AOC, No. 211 Group, Tripoli. Here 'Batchy' found himself once again in trouble, and after he had pranged a new Kittyhawk, AVM Harry Broadhurst sent him packing, back to Blighty as a Group Captain!

Yet all those that came into contact with 'Batchy', held him in great esteem and remembered him with much affection. Whilst at Kenley, he was contacted by Eric Barwell, Dickie's younger brother, to discuss the possibilities of deploying Boulton Paul Defiants in the Middle East. Invited over to Kenley with the intention of travelling over to Bentley Priory to gain the support of the C-in-C, Leigh-Mallory, Eric then found himself at the mercy of Atcherley's devil-may-care driving and his mischievous take on life.

I had discussed with Viscount Clive, a descendant of Clive of India, the idea of making use of the Defiant in the Far East. Although it was outperformed in some respects by the Luftwaffe, employed correctly and using the right tactics, I felt it was still a valuable aircraft with a role to play. With this in mind I thought it a good plan to get the support of a senior commander, so I contacted 'Batchy' having known him from our time at RAF Fairwood Common, and he was the most senior chap I could think of. After a telephone conversation, he seemed convinced and so invited us over to Kenley with the idea of going to see some Air Commodore about it. We flew over to Kenley in a Defiant and, after a phone call to this chap, 'Batchy' said he'd drive us all over to see him that night. So we got into Batchy's huge American car, and off we went at breakneck speed down all these winding roads and through the various towns along the way. He never seemed to take his foot off the accelerator and went through red light after red light. Myself and the CO sat rigid with fear in the back, but when we shouted to him to slow down, he just laughed and carried on as before. After going through a number of sets of red lights, we came to a green one, and as Batchy sailed through it, he turned to us and with a big smile on his face said, 'Oh we were lucky that time!' (Squadron Leader Eric Barwell, interview 27/06/2002)

Similarly, Davies remembered 'Batchy' from Kenley, when on church parade one Sunday morning, Atcherley stopped to talk.

I always went on church parade. With my father a lay preacher, I loved to hear the hymns, so I'd always go. Of course my mates, Campbell and the others would always take the mick when I would get ready for church parade and they'd try to get out of it as best they could. Well one day at Kenley I went on parade and I'd tried to look my best but I'd been in [the service] over two years now and to be honest, my uniform was getting to look a bit threadbare in places, and I'd polished my buttons so much that the crowns and eagles had started to disappear. So I was standing in the line, and Batchy Atcherley was doing his inspection, walking up through the ranks and taking time to talk to a few. As he came to me he stopped and looked me up and down as they would, you know. After a while (in which I was thinking, 'Christ what am I in for now?') he said, 'what's your name, airman?' Of course I snapped out a reply, 'Davies, Sir'. He looked up and down again and then, prodding one of my tunic buttons said, 'well, Davies, I can see that you've tried to make an effort, but the uniform's looking rather shabby, don't you think? How long have you been in the service?' 'Over two years, Sir. Been over at Biggin Hill since February '41.' I thought I was in for it, but Batchy turned to an officer that was standing at his side and said, 'after the parade, can you take Davies over to stores and make sure he gets a full new issue of kit, everything he needs.' He turned back to me and said, 'how does that suit you, Davies?' I came to attention, thanked him and gave him my best salute. Then he smiled and said, 'Good, see you at next parade.' And believe you me I got everything! I was taken off to the stores and was given absolutely everything, double what I needed. I had new best blue, fatigues, shoes, boots, socks, greatcoat, everything. And when I turned up back at my billets and told the lads, they were all then envious so I said, 'well, you should have gone on church parade.' (LAC Raymond Davies, compiled from interviews, 2003)

After the death of Victor Beamish in March 1942, Atcherley had taken up the post of OC Kenley and, like Beamish, had intended to keep up the reputation of senior commanders in the sector being very much on active service in every sense. In the first few days he flew as number two to 'Hawkeye' Wells, Wing Commander Flying, but thereafter confined himself to individual excursions across the Channel, declaring later that '*I was clearly a potential Iron Cross to any German pilot who cared to have a crack at me*' (R.L.R. Atcherley, quoted in Flint, P., 1985, p134). The 26th May 1942 was one such occasion when Atcherley decided to have a go and came very close to getting the chop.

He would occasionally climb into a Spitfire and be off somewhere over the English Channel; his first communication would be when he called up the Operations Room to ask if there was any 'trade' for him. When the reply was negative he was sometimes known to comment on the 'yellow so-and-so's' not coming up to fight. It so happened that [on 26 May] he was out patrolling off the French coast when three of the 'yellow so-and-so's' in Focke-Wulf Fw190s latched on to him and shot him down into the Channel. When 'Hawkeye' Wells learned of his predicament he went out to assist and arrived just in time to photograph his Commanding Officer being picked up, in a wounded and half-drowned condition, by a minesweeper. He was taken to Dover hospital where he was treated for exposure and a wound to his arm caused by a cannon shell. As soon as he was physically able, he arrived back at Kenley giving every outward appearance of being entirely unaffected in spirit by his unpleasant experiences. The bandage on his elbow he removed, then described the effects of the wound on the movement of his arm, finishing with the words 'and now the prettiest W.A.A.F. in the room can bandage it up again'. (Flint, 1985, p. 134–5)

The next day Barwell and Rankin were in action again to claim a shared destroyed. During a sweep in the Dieppe–Étretat area, Jamie spotted several enemy aircraft, although the Wing failed to make contact with the Luftwaffe in any great numbers. As they passed in the vicinity of Fécamp, Rankin and Barwell decided to intercept a lone aircraft.

I was Red 2. Together with W/Cdr Rankin I saw several single E/a in the area of Fecamp, one of which I chased. I closed from 300–200 yds. and gave two bursts of 2 seconds each with cannon and m/g, firing simultaneously with W/Cdr Rankin. I saw strikes hit the E/a which turned over and went into a spin. (Group Captain Dickie Barwell, Combat Report, 27 May 1942)

In the last days of May, the fledgling eagles of 133 Squadron became very much aware of the potency of the Luftwaffe, and in particular the new fighter with which the enemy were beginning to operate with increasing confidence. Flying almost daily patrols and sweeps, there were fleeting chances to nibble at the agile Fw190s as they struck quickly, using their superior speed and rate of roll to best advantage. Squadron Leader Thomas managed to damage one on the 29th. On the evening of the 31st however, the tables were turned: though Pilot Officer Edwin Taylor succeeded in damaging one of the enemy, two of the squadron were lost and a number, including Eric Doorly, had some lucky escapes.

> *Squadron took off with 72 Squadron … for a sweep round Dieppe-Fecamp area. Numbers of enemy aircraft were seen. Pilot Officer Taylor claims 1 FW.190 damaged. Pilot Officer Morris and Flying Officer Ford did not return. P.O Doorly's aircraft had bullet holes through the rudder and fin, but landed safely.*
> (133 Squadron Operational Record Book, 31 May 1942)

Settling into the Routine:

If May had been a kind of awakening to operational life in 11 Group for the Eagles, then June brought with it a realisation that the sector was one where keeping alert was a standing order. Whilst the regularity of patrols, fighter sweeps, bomber escort and scrambles was now being experienced with daily frequency, there was an uneasiness about such activity that made it difficult to settle into. Waiting often seemed the greatest of enemies, certainly to that of a settled stomach. It was better when you were doing something: when the engine was started and you were running through your checks; when you were holding position with your leader, climbing into the blue; when you were switching between scanning your sector of the sky and scanning your instruments. The right hand side of the panel seemed to have the ability to concentrate the mind: oil and radiator temperatures; oil pressure; fuel pressure – that little red warning light that you watched for, praying it would not flick on; and the fuel contents gauge – always with less than you expected, and sometimes a 'sticky' one that showed 'plenty', then nothing!

On the ground, the waiting game started with the last glimpse of the aircraft, wings twitching in the summer thermals coming up the valley, a disappearing dot on the horizon. Like all those down at dispersal, Davies always seemed to wait until the last one disappeared before turning to his 'oppo' with that same look: a mixture of satisfaction for a job well done and a 'wish them luck, pray for them coming back'. Then you would grab some grub or some kip. This was front line stuff; an hour and a half later, two at the most, the kites would be back and the usual rush would be on to turn them round quickly.

So was the way of June. Sometimes, starting at 0400 hours, the morning patrols would usually see sections of 133 Squadron sent aloft to cover convoys or general reconnaissance of a specified area. On such occasions it was rare to encounter the enemy. As the morning came to life, so did the larger of the day's operations with take-offs around 1100 hours, heading out to the French coast, perhaps picking up a formation of Bostons with which to stir up the hornets' nest. Further escorts might also be detailed in the early and late afternoon, sometimes later still in the early evening. Caught off guard one night down at the Old Jail, Healey had commented on how the days seemed to become one, such was the regular pattern of their activities. 'The only things that change are the names and faces,' thought Davies, keeping such a sobering analysis to himself. There were ones that you didn't even get to know their name till after they were a goner. Chiefy would sometimes say, 'you're on this kite today,' and you'd go off, find a new lad climbing aboard (new in all senses of the word) and that would be the last you'd see of him.

In the first two weeks of June, the daily life of a front-line RAF fighter station was becoming all too familiar to 133 Squadron. In relative terms, new boys they were. Yet they now experienced operational life on a par with the other squadrons of the Wing. On the 2nd and 3rd of the month, they flew escort to a number of Hurribombers, vectored on to a target in the Haute Forêt D'Eu. This circus (No.181) brought a number of aircraft losses across the sector, although 133 Squadron escaped unscathed. Some successes were had by 64 Squadron, Flight Lieutenant Don Kingaby managing to damage one of three Fw190s claimed by the squadron – and Don's first claim of his second tour of duty. In addition to the repeat circus to Haute Forêt D'Eu, the Squadron flew a number of convoy patrols on 3 June. One of these patrols was the first operation for one of 133's newcomers, Pilot Officer Ervin Miller. Like many of the Eagles, Miller was a keen aviator, having learned to fly before the outbreak of hostilities in Europe. The day after involved the Wing in supporting a commando raid on an RDF station on the French coast, covering the withdrawal of the ground forces at daybreak. Again, luck was with the squadron and although a couple of enemy aircraft attempted to intercept the formation, there were no combats or casualties.

Mixed fortunes were visited upon the squadron on 5 June. The operations of the morning had failed to engage the Luftwaffe, the enemy seemingly satisfied to sit on the ground. By their reaction to Circus No.188 in the mid-afternoon, many a pilot of the Wing (as well as those in the 'Ops room') thought perhaps the morning had been a ploy to lull the RAF into a false sense of security. Ignoring a smaller formation operating in the vicinity of Ostend, the elite of JG2 and JG26 concentrated their attacks on the five Wings of Spitfires over Abbeville – including

Biggin's squadrons. Leading the Wing with 401 Squadron, Jamie Rankin tore into a large formation of Focke Wulfs.

> *Our a/c dived on ten to fifteen FW-190s right over Abbeville town and a general dogfight took place. F/S Morrison fired a ½ second burst at one FW-190 from astern and saw cannon strikes on the starboard side of the fuselage, followed by a puff of white smoke. He stopped firing as W/C Rankin crossed in front of him, firing at the same e/a. As the e/a started down there was an explosion and it spiralled before it hit the ground. During the combat Pilot Officer Smithers was heard to say on the R/t that he was going down, and did not return.* (401 Squadron War Diary, 5 June 1942, quoted in McIntosh, 1990, p. 101)

Brian Kingcome's 72 Squadron also found themselves in the thick of the action, and on return to Gravesend the I/O scribbled frantically to record the excited descriptions of the many combats and the final claim of three destroyed, one probable and two damaged. For 133 Squadron there were mixed feelings as they were debriefed on the day's events. They too had been heavily engaged and had fought a number of fraught combats with the agile and determined Focke Wulfs. For a moment spirits ran high.

> *The Squadron took off with 72, joining up with Gravesend, and went on a diversionary sweep round Abbeville while Bostons bombed Le Havre. Squadron Leader Thomas and Pilot Officer Kimbro had combats from which one FW.190 was probably destroyed and 2 FW.190s damaged.* (133 Squadron Operational Record Book, 5 June 1942)

Yet somewhere in amongst these gyrating masses of opposing forces, Pilot Officer Hancock was desperately fighting for his life. He was last seen in a dogfight above Cayeux and was now missing, presumed killed. Fletcher Hancock from California was twenty-one years of age. Despite the elation of the squadron's successes over Abbeville on that day, it could not make up for the loss of a comrade. Davies walked back along the peri-track a little before 1700 hours and passed a small group of ground crew: an armourer, a couple of riggers and an engine fitter, all looking rather forlornly out across the valley, searching the sky. He'd seen the same thing many times over before. He marvelled at how these young men could put themselves through such hardships, living with the knowledge that each passing hour could be those of their last day and that each conversation could be their final words to a friend. Were these men from far shores any different? They had volunteered when their homeland was not threatened, nor overrun by Hitler's hoards. To understand the volunteer, was to understand the man. Sometimes uppermost in one's motivations was not the sense of a call to arms, to fight with passion a common cause. Certainly for some, the sheer adventure was the catalyst. As Ervin 'Dusty' Miller reflected on his own enlistment:

I'd not heard of the Eagles until I was posted from my previous squadron at Perranporth. I'd learned to fly privately in the States and I went to work as a civil servant in Sacramento and to keep up my flying time I had to go to the local airport. And I went out there one day and there was this little notice – If you'd like to join the Royal Air Force and have 200 hours flying time, contact this phone number (in Oakland, California). So I called 'em up, made an appointment, went down and talked to them. It was as simple as that. That was in 1940, but I didn't hear from 'em until about February 1941. They told me to get to the airport and there would be a chap there to test fly me in a Waco-F, which was an airplane I'd never flown before, was about twice as powerful as any airplane I'd ever flown, and he was a Flight Lieutenant in the Royal Air Force, but dressed in civvies. I expressed fear with this big airplane and he said not to worry, and I got in the cockpit, went up and did what he asked me to do – except a roll off the top, which I cocked up immensely because I didn't go into it fast enough! About a month later I got my invitation to go to the Spartan School of Aeronautics and that was it: I became a member of the Royal Air Force.

I was in the United States Navy. I joined the Navy to learn to fly but I got 'shot down' 'cos I excelled in the wrong branch of the service. To fly in the Navy you had to have an aviation rating and I got a damn torpedo rating! So I kept trying to get transferred back to the Saratoga *or* Lexington *to get an aircraft torpedo rating – aircraft ordnance man you see. But I was always refused and in the second year, when I was a Third Class Torpedo man, I started to fly myself and when I made Second Class Torpedo man, I could fly some more as I had more money. But then I applied again, refused and so said 'to hell with it' and left the Navy. I got me a job as a civil servant at Sacramento, but I loved flying and kept flying you see and I built up my time. But when I was in the American Navy the* Deutschland *came into San Diego and I was on it as an interpreter because I could speak German. So I had nothing against the Germans – I thought they had a beautiful boat, clean, efficient, all the equipment – but I didn't have any thoughts of war. When I went to Sacramento, I was working on engines such as the Allison engine…. So when I saw that little notice, there was no patriotism or anything involved it was just a hot damn chance to fly a big aeroplane. I was always an aircraft nut – I guess Lindberg caused me to go, 'cos he came to open an airport in the 'Spirit of St Louis!'* (Pilot Officer Ervin 'Dusty' Miller, 133 Squadron, interview 28/6/2002)

An English Summer!

'Turning into a real English summer,' replied Campbell to a comment from one of 133's pilots about the scudding low clouds and fog. In comparison to this time last year on 'the Bump', it was hard to imagine a greater change. These were the vagaries of the English weather, much to the frustration of the Americans whose personal introductions to flying for fun back in the States had been almost constantly blessed with good weather and seemingly endless visibility. On a number of days towards the end of June it was difficult enough to see the other end of the airfield's boundary, let alone attempt to get aloft to spot the enemy!

Yet still there were responsibilities to enact and so wherever possible standing patrols, practice flights and a peppering of 'real' ops across to France continued to keep the air and ground crews busy. On 11 June, Brian Kingcome took the Wing out on a practice sweep, taking off from Biggin at around 1100 hours. It was one of those days when the Luftwaffe seemed not to be all that fussed with doing battle and though the Wing swept the familiar contested territory between Hardelot, St Omer and Gravelines, it was not bait enough. Kingcome brought the Wing back to base at 1220 hours with nothing to report. The evening proved much livelier, as Biggin celebrated Dickie Barwell's anniversary as Station Commander. The nucleus of the party was around the officers' mess, with many of those past associated with Barwell's time at Biggin dropping in to wish him their best. As was often the case, Barwell was in great form and often at the heart of the night's more mischievous goings on. The celebrations were not confined to commissioned ranks. If there was one thing that characterised Barwell's Biggin, it was the sense of community. Thus, for those ground crews working on into the evening, a few crates of beer were sent down to the hangars and dispersals.

Towards the end of the month the Wing was in action, once again flying cover sweeps into the St Omer–Hardelot area. On the 20th, Blue section was bounced by Fw190s and Pilot Officer William Arends from North Dakota was killed. The Focke Wulf was continually proving itself to be superior to the Spitfire Vb, and the advantage seemed to give the pilots of the Luftwaffe the upper hand in choosing whether or not to engage. With heavy armament, superior speed and manoeuvrability, it was a deadly opponent. Three days after Arends was lost, the RAF were able to inspect the Fw190 in detail. After a 10 Group 'ramrod' operation against Morlaix airfield, on the northern Brittany coast, a number of Fw190s of III/JG2 pursued aircraft of the Wing and intercepted them off South Devon. In the ensuing confusion, one of the Luftwaffe pilots, Oberleutnant Arnim Faber, became disorientated and flew inland. After an unsuccessful interception from an aircraft of 310 Squadron, scrambled from Bolt Head, Faber crossed the Bristol Channel and, believing it to be the English Channel, he sought out an airfield and proceeded to land. Still under the misconception that he was at a friendly Luftwaffe airfield in northern France, Faber was shocked when he was arrested climbing out of his aircraft. By mistake, he had landed at RAF Pembrey, near Swansea, South Wales!

In the days that followed, the captured fighter became a much-visited attraction, and it was thus only natural that for a number of Biggin's senior pilots, their inquisitiveness got the better of them. On the 25th, Dickie Barwell and 'Spy' de la Torre were the first to fly over to Pembrey to gather some 'gen'. Taking off at 1030 hours, Squadron Leader Eric Thomas took a Spitfire over to Wales to do his own inspection. It was then left in the hands of a privileged few test pilots at the Air Fighting Development Unit (1426 Flight) at Duxford to make a thorough evaluation. The results made for pessimistic reading: at all heights the Fw190 was faster than the Spitfire Vb, with better acceleration; overall it had a speed advantage of between 20 and 35 mph, especially at around 3,000 feet; in both diving and climbing, the Fw190 easily outpaced the Spitfire; its superior rate of roll allowed the Fw190 to change direction rapidly, this being particularly advantageous when taking evasive action. Thus when caught in a turning fight (the only aspect of performance where the Spitfire was still unsurpassed), Fw190 pilots could quickly roll the aircraft in the opposite direction and then execute a diving turn. From this knowledge Spitfire pilots were advised to operate at high power settings in the combat area, and if at maximum cruise and with some height to play with to put the aircraft into a shallow dive on the way out. Although the Fw190 could eventually catch them, this tactic resulted in a long stern chase that took the enemy further from the safety of its operating base. De la Torre and Barwell were quick to disseminate this information to those operating as part of the Biggin Hill Wing.

It had been a month of mixed fortunes. For the 'Eagles' of 133 Squadron, their second month on the Bump had been a swift introduction to the 11 Group sector, its exciting pace, frustrations and the realities of loss. While the pilots of 133 may have come to England for their own reasons, now there was a growing bond and sense of purpose – one that brought together aircrew, ground crew, service personnel and civilians. For some, like Ervin Miller, these early experiences of England were the beginnings of a long-lasting relationship. That the 'Eagles' gained in combat experience was of course partly owed to the expertise that resided at Biggin. In the air, the likes of Rankin, Kingcome, Duke-Woolley, Dickie Barwell and Eric Thomas ensured that any squadron new to the sector got to know the form, the tricks of the trade that sometimes were able to tilt the balance in your favour. For Davies' continued work with Jimmy Stewart's team of armourers, his contribution to tilting the balance also involved passing on expertise to the squadron's armourers. It was interesting getting to know the 'Yanks' and in later months he would find himself responsible for preparing American ground crew for the task of working with the 20mm Hispano cannon and the Mark Vb Spitfire. Yet the challenge that all at Biggin stepped up to seemed as great as ever. On 29 June, Barwell led what was to be his last sweep from Biggin. His loss on 1 July brought home to all that the comradeship and sheer excitement of war walked side-by-side with tragedy.

Chapter Seventeen

'Dickie'

Barwell's Biggin:

There was no doubt in the mind of anyone who served at Biggin Hill that it was a great station. Proud of its achievements, fiercely protective of its reputation and war record, those that served there all contributed to Biggin being on top form. It was clear that Biggin's successes and its strong identity within Fighter Command and the RAF in general was very much owed to the sense of teamwork, of everyone pulling their weight. This was not unique to Biggin, but the degree to which Biggin had been led from the front was very much in evidence. Strong, strategic, and to an extent charismatic leadership had been present at the level of flight commanders, squadron leaders, and Wing leaders. Biggin had been blessed with some of those that history would consider the most able within the Royal Air Force. As Davies had experienced, one's expertise was valued and using one's initiative was rewarded. From a ground crew viewpoint also, Davies had often felt that senior commanders had taken the time to know the men under their command. On numerous occasions the likes of Rankin, Milne, Stanford-Tuck, Kingcome and Kingaby had shown how they took a great interest in the 'other ranks', and although the proper hierarchy of command was maintained, it was never overburdening and peppered with red tape and 'bull'. What mattered was experience and ability.

In the twelve months that Philip Reginald Barwell had been in post as station commander a strong bond of comradeship and respect had developed. Nothing was more certain than that Barwell led from the front, and that his high expectations were no less than those that he expected of himself. Some would perhaps venture that Barwell *was* Biggin Hill: great ability and experience; strong leadership in the field; disciplined but not punitive or over-zealous in procedural matters; rewarding and respectful of others; high-spirited and charismatic. 'Dickie' and Biggin shared such qualities, and the former had been a key influence in making Biggin the way it was. It was thus inevitable that the loss of Barwell at the beginning of July 1942 would be felt by everyone at Biggin and beyond.

Tip and Run Nuisance Raiders:

By the middle of 1942 there was a real sense that the Luftwaffe had gained the upper hand. Mainly this had been achieved by technological advancements such as those embodied in the Fw190. No longer did the Spitfires of 11 Group, and other groups in Fighter Command, meet the enemy on equal terms. While this raised much concern for those engaged in taking the fight across the Channel, other concerns were brought even closer to home by the persistent and seemingly invulnerable high-flying raiders that the Luftwaffe were now able to employ. Although the scale of bombing raids had been limited since the height of the Blitz in 1940–41, the threat remained. Furthermore, the introduction of the Junkers Ju86P+R series meant that such nightly raids could take place almost with impunity.

Like many of the German aircraft designs, the Ju86 had started its life in the guise of a civil transport aircraft in the 1930s. A succession of modifications, those most significant being the redesign of the wings and the completely reworked cockpit that now included a pressurised crew accommodation, had now given the Luftwaffe a high-altitude bomber. Powered by two Jumo 207A+B series diesel engines, each generating around 2,000 horsepower, the Ju86's main advantage was its operational ceiling upwards of 40,000ft. In answer to these high-flying threats a few squadrons had received Spitfire VIs, the first of these being modified from standard MkVs with the fitting of a pressurised cockpit, an uprated Merlin and a modified, four-bladed propeller. At Biggin, a few of these aircraft were operated by 124 Squadron but in practice it was still almost impossible to get into a favourable position to intercept any of these lone Ju86s before they had dropped their loads and were on the way home.

Nuisance raids also came in the form of low-level 'Jabo' operations, carried out by Me109s and now more commonly the Fw190s. Often with a single bomb slung under the centre-line, these fighter-bombers (or *jagdbomber*) used their speed and low altitude to get under the high-level, long-range radar of Fighter Command, avoiding detection until they were almost over the coast and surrounding hinterland. Standing patrols were a limited defence, and though scrambles were common, it was more by luck than design that a successful interception took place. Moreover, the superior performance of the Fw190 over the Spitfire Vb at medium altitudes further caught the RAF on the back foot when the Focke Wulf was used for such operations.

On 1 July 1942 two Spitfires climbed out of Biggin to conduct a standing patrol. As such operations often resulted in unsuccessful chasings after unidentified plots that were already turning for home, it was perhaps unusual that these Spitfires were piloted by two senior commanders – Dickie Barwell and Bobby Oxspring. Indicative of the high regard that pilots held for Barwell, Oxspring had approached him frustrated at the almost helpless situation they were in where these 'tip and run' raiders were concerned. Barwell's viewpoint mattered to pilots, and in taking some thorny problem to him they knew that they would receive a well-considered response and appropriate action. To the greatest extent this was where Barwell's 'leading from the front' and his continued presence on operations paid off. His position of authority was not an armchair wearing thin from overuse, nor an office ever distant from the front-line experiences of those under his command. Characteristically, Barwell decided that in order to understand the problems that Oxspring had related to him, it was best to see it for himself. With Oxspring flying as his number two, Barwell climbed Spitfire Vb (AB806) away, with Bill Igoe back at Biggin on the other end of the R/t in his role as senior controller.

> *In the Biggin Hill sector these raids concerned 91 Squadron more than others because of our disposition on the south coast. Despite this, our success in intercepting the raids was practically nil and caused much frustration. I flew up to Biggin Hill and took my worries to the sector commander. Dicky Barwell was as concerned as I was and we had a long discussion with the senior controller, Bill Igoe. Ultimately Dicky suggested that with Bill controlling he would accompany me on a standing patrol the same evening to try and assess first-hand what the problems were. We took off from Biggin an hour before sunset and patrolled just off the coast between Dungeness and Beachy Head. There was a very thick haze up to 16,000 feet and we stationed just above it.* (Squadron Leader R.W. Oxspring, quoted in Oxspring, 1984, p. 106–7)

There were other fighters in the area. Scrambled to investigate an unidentified plot, two Spitfires of 129 Squadron from Westhampnett in the Tangmere sector were also in the vicinity. As Oxspring was later to recall, the presence of these other aircraft was communicated to himself and Barwell, though the plot remained unidentified. Presumably, the pair from 129 Squadron was similarly informed of other aircraft being in the vicinity. Whether the visibility being what it was contributed to the tragedy that then unfolded may never be known. But with the sun setting slowly out to the west, the two fighters from Tangmere approached the Biggin pair, still uncertain of their identity. Oxspring saw them at the last moment, but it was too late.

> *As we approached Beachy, Bill [Igoe] warned us of unidentified plots in our vicinity and we peered into the haze for signs of activity. Suddenly I sighted two fighters approaching us out of the glare of the setting sun and gave a warning to Dicky who was abreast of me and nearer to them. The leading fighter, which flew*

close over the top of me, I identified as a Spitfire and called the fact to Dicky. I watched it as it faded to my rear and then turned back to see the second aircraft, another Spit, behind Dicky and already opening fire on him.

Calling an urgent break to Dicky I flew on a collision course at his attacker and succeeded in distracting him enough to force a break-away. I turned back close over the top of Dicky, whose aircraft was flaming from the petrol tank, and I could see him desperately trying to open the canopy to bail out. I glanced back to see the first Spit swinging in behind me and opening fire. I broke hard round and down into the haze to shake him off, but search as I might I could see no sign of Dicky. My frantic calls to him bore no response and I circled down through the murk to the Channel. All I could find was what I took to be an oil slick on the surface, but there was no sign of either a parachute or a dinghy. (Squadron Leader R.W. Oxspring, quoted in Oxspring, 1984, p. 107)

A Brother Lost …:

Over at RAF Fairwood Common, Dickie's brother, Flight Lieutenant Eric Barwell was sleeping late, after having had a frustrating night on operations with 125 Squadron and in combat with a Dornier 217.

Usually we came off duty at six to eight o'clock in the morning and probably got up for lunch. When my brother was killed, I was stationed at Fairwood Common in South Wales, flying Beaufighter MkIIs and that night I found an aircraft (a Dornier) and on the Beaufighter we had six machine guns and four 20mm cannons. Well I thought, I'll fire cannons only … We had a bit of bent bar for a trigger, for the cannons, and an ordinary button for the Brownings. So I tried to fire with this bit of bent brass and it would not go! I pulled and pushed, so then had to contend with firing only with the six Brownings. I could see that I'd hit things a bit and so on but it [the Dornier] peeled off and I lost it. There were quite a lot of aircraft about, attacking Cardiff or something, and so I then pulled about with this bit of bent brass and the cannons went off alright but the vibration upset the AI, the radar, so I was hopeless! (Flight Lieutenant Eric Barwell, interview 27/6/2002)

Mid-morning he awoke to find his wife, Ruth, sitting at his bedside.

I was living out at the time. Got to bed I suppose at six or eight o'clock and I woke up with my wife sitting beside me and she had just been advised, because I think the signal had obviously gone to the Station and someone had telephoned her or something, sort of 'regret to say that your brother is missing.' I was just woken like that from a fairly short night's sleep. I, of course, flew down to Biggin to get detail of it. (Flight Lieutenant Eric Barwell, interview 27/6/2002)

It was the most tragic of circumstances and perhaps cruel irony that 'Dickie' should be the victim of misidentification – he who had instilled in his pilots at Biggin the great importance of aircraft recognition with regular ground lectures. The loss of Barwell was immense at both a personal level for the family, but also for what constituted Dickie's extended family, that of Biggin Hill.

When I got there Biggin Hill was almost in a state of shock. Phil had been such a popular CO, entering into everything, whether work or play. I heard the detail from the chaps at Biggin. I saw Bobby Oxspring. I think one of the pilots (from Tangmere) was very much a newcomer at least and the stupid thing was that I don't think either Tangmere had told Biggin, or Biggin had told Tangmere that they had two aircraft up. The Tangmere chaps saw these two Spitfires, and I think the leader of the pair knew what they were and was going to fly up and have a look at them. But the other bloke, his No.2, thought he was attacking and so went in! And unfortunately he was too good a shot. (Flight Lieutenant Eric Barwell, interview 27/6/2002)

Oxspring too was greatly affected by the loss of Dickie and also commented in later recollections how the pilots from Tangmere had been inexperienced.

I flew despondently back to Biggin to report the tragedy. Despite intensive air sea rescue searches, no trace of Dicky was ever found. I felt awful about it and somehow responsible for losing a gallant officer. No blame could be apportioned to Bill Igoe's control organisation; they did their job. It is significant, however, that the subsequent Court of Inquiry revealed that the two Spitfires which caused the calamity came from an Allied squadron in the Tangmere sector and that, incredibly, one pilot was on his first operational sortie and the leader on his second.

So died a superb commander in most deplorable circumstances. But being the man he was he would have been the first to forgive the trigger-happy Tangmere pilots who, itching to claim their first Hun, couldn't tell the difference between a Messerschmitt and a Spitfire. (Squadron Leader R.W. Oxspring quoted in Oxspring, 1984, p. 107–8)

Others such as ex-92 Squadron commander 'Dickie' Milne penned a personal note in his flying log book that conveyed much of how all those that had known Barwell held him in great regard and affection.

Heard that Group Captain 'Dickie' Barwell, my old station commander at Biggin Hill, has been shot down and killed by a Spitfire. A very fine and courageous man who was loved by all who knew him. (Squadron Leader R.M. Milne, Flying Log Book, 8 July 1942)

Still shocked by the loss of his brother, Eric Barwell flew on from Biggin to RAF Oakington, near to the family home.

I took the [Airspeed] Oxford to Oakington where John [Dickie's eldest son] met me to take me to Swavesey and I could tell the family what I knew of the tragedy. It was rather a difficult time, but one which so many people experienced during the war. (Flight Lieutenant Eric Barwell, biographical note on P.R. Barwell)

For all at Biggin the effect of the loss of Dickie Barwell was perhaps inestimable. On his arrival at Biggin Hill, Eric described a sense of shock that cut to the core. The great contribution that Dickie had made was evident throughout this proudest of Fighter Command's stations. The detail of his loss was quietened down, subjected to rumour and a supposition. It was years after the event that Davies heard that his old Station Commander had been killed not as a result of enemy action but in this most tragic of accidents. A few days after the event, Davies, Campbell and a few others of this close-knit community of 'Chiefy' Stewart's armourers, found themselves off-camp at one of their usual watering holes. It was to Dickie that the first and last of the evening's toasts were drunk.

… And Remembered:
The feeling of bewilderment that pervaded all ranks at Biggin Hill was incomparable to the grief felt by Barwell's family. Recalling his brother with great affection, Eric remembered Phil's great combination of qualities: his sense of purpose; of fun and mischief; his great achievements and abilities; and the care he showed to all.

I'd been on the go from March 1940 and I think it was September 1941 my eldest child, Diana, was being christened up here and my brother flew up for it and my wife told him that I seemed jolly tired and so on and almost immediately he flew down to Fairwood Common, spoke to Batchy Atcherley, our CO. And it meant that in a couple of months' time I was rested. I went to 10 Group Headquarters as Squadron Leader, Night Ops, I think it was. (Flight Lieutenant Eric Barwell, interview 27/6/2002)
I admired him very considerably and I suppose I tried to emulate him. When I left school I wanted to go in the Air Force but my family thought that one in

the Service was quite enough, so I came into the family business. But when it was obvious we were going to have war, the RAF Volunteer Reserve started up in Cambridge and I went in. (Flight Lieutenant Eric Barwell, interview 27/6/2002)

Phil was always high-spirited: a rather typical activity was when at Swavesey we had a tennis party (perhaps for his 21st birthday). Beside the lawn were two large Douglas fir trees and Phil and someone else decided to have a race to the top of each, wearing tennis flannels. Fir trees always exuding gum and otherwise being very dirty, the state of their smart white trousers can be imagined at the finish! The officers of 19 Squadron got very well known around Cambridge – when Ruth, my wife, booked a taxi when we had a house at Fenditton in the latter half of the war, the name Barwell was still remembered, I think with affection, from the Duxford days some 15 years before. (Flight Lieutenant Eric Barwell, unpublished biographical note on P.R. Barwell)

Phil really had just one objective during the war – to see that our side won. At Biggin Hill he was able to make a very successful attempt – to achieve it his personal life had to take a back seat. He persuaded Mary to stay in the house they rented in Lincolnshire, although in fact later he agreed that she could come down to live near Biggin Hill, but she was packing up the house when he was killed. Before, he knew she would worry so much if she knew he was flying on operations and he did not want any distractions during the long hours he chose to be on duty. Mary received a large number of letters of sympathy after his death – many were from officers who had been with him at Biggin Hill and at other units. Each was so emphatic over how wonderful a CO, a fighter and a friend he had been. One letter was from Air Vice Marshall Leigh-Mallory who said he could have got him a bar to his DFC, but he thought it was better to wait until he could recommend Phil for a DSO, and he would not have had to wait long for it. Phil's body was washed up on the French coast and was buried at Le Portel, near Boulogne. Later he was reburied in the Canadian War Cemetery on the road between Calais and Boulogne. This is in a fine position about 3 miles inland, and from it the Kent coast can be seen in clear weather. The Scots pines planted round the cemetery are now large trees, the whole being kept to the usual high standard of the Commonwealth War Graves Commission. (Flight Lieutenant Eric Barwell, unpublished biographical note on P.R. Barwell)

Chapter Eighteen

Eagles in Ascendance

Nothing for it …:

July was just one of those months. As Fighter Command stepped up the offensive yet again, for Biggin's squadrons there seemed little to show for the daily pattern of patrols and sweeps. Out of the twenty or so operations flown by 133 Squadron there had been little contact with the enemy. Every fighter pilot will tell you of the way the sky can be one minute filled with tumbling aircraft, the next you are quiet and alone. At other times it just seemed like you were destined to be a spectator. On 13 July, after two weeks of little activity, the Americans landed back at Biggin after not mixing it with the enemy, only to have to endure the excited chatter of 401 Squadron's pilots, recounting their clashes with Me109s and Fw190s. As 133 Squadron's diary recorded:

> *13.7.42: A Diversionary sweep was made by the Biggin Hill Wing in the Abbeville area while 12 Bostons bombed Boulogne marshalling yards. The Squadron flew at about 12,000 feet and did not encounter any enemy aircraft. These were waiting above, however, and chose to bounce 401 instead! 133, hearing the chatter, orbited over the sea for a while, but still not seeing any e/a turned for home and all landed safely.* (133 Squadron Operational Record Book, 13 July 1942)

Whilst being on the sidelines of the action, perhaps completely remote from it, was frustrating in the extreme, one could not help have some sense of relief that luck had been with you in other ways. On the same day 401 Squadron's operations book recorded the same event with a dry, unemotional comment:

> *July 13: The Squadron lost F/L Tyre and F/S Duff due to a collision over the Somme estuary. One a/c fell in the sea about 300 yards from the shore and the other about a quarter mile inland. They were followed down by F/L Whitham and neither was seen to get out of his machine. The weather was fine over France.* (401 Squadron Operational Record Book, quoted in McIntosh, 1990, p. 101)

On the 26th of the month Davies saw Doorly back into Biggin, flying AB910. Pretty new to the Squadron, the Spitfire was becoming Eric's usual mount and it seemed that the Luftwaffe were helping him and his crew in keeping it like a new pin! Landing in at 1425 hours, the gun patches were still unholed – as pristine as when Davies had put them on earlier in the day. Again, 133 Squadron had missed out, while their fellow squadrons of the Wing had engaged pairs of Fw190s over St Omer.

26.7.42: The Squadron took off for a sweep round St Omer aerodrome, with 72 and 401 Squadrons. They made orbit at 10,000ft. No combats were had by the squadron, but 72 and 401 had combats in which 2 FW190s were destroyed and various others damaged. All 133 landed safely. (133 Squadron Operational Record Book, 26 July 1942)

Again, the clash with the Fw190s was not without loss and from 401 Squadron Pilot Officer Tucker did not return. He had last been seen mid-Channel, climbing up through cloud. The Canadians put up six aircraft to search for him, but they returned without any sightings being made. A 72 Squadron pilot was also posted missing.

On 26 July the Wing attempted to stir up trouble again in the Étretat–Fécamp area, using Rankin's low-level approach and rapid climb tactics. Flying in from Newhaven at sea level, it took 133 Squadron fifteen minutes to cross the Channel, before climbing at maximum boost to 15,000 feet above Étretat. An exciting bit of flying, particularly in Wing strength, but nevertheless unproductive. It seemed that July's bad luck was holding and after patrolling up to Fécamp and back, there was nothing for it but for the Wing to make for home. Five days later – on the 31st – the Squadron's operation (Circus 201) to the familiar hunting ground of Abbeville stood as a good example of how Fighter Command's fortunes navigated the treacherous path between Scylla and Charybdis. Escorting twelve Bostons, bombing the Luftwaffe airfield at Abbeville, the Wing was detailed to provide close cover with 133 Squadron being in the unenviable position as 'bottom squadron' (133, Operational Record Book, 31 July 1942). As always, the enemy waited until the formation had turned for home and were crossing the coast before they attacked. In the vicious exchanges that followed, Pilot Officer Baker destroyed a Fw190, while Flying Officer Edwin Taylor managed to shoot down another Fw190 and damage an Me109F. Taylor, a high school graduate from Oklahoma, later recalled this day:

When we were jumped by the Germans, I immediately latched on to an FW 190 and shot him down. At the same time there evidently was a German on my tail. My wing man, Carter Harp, called to warn me but I never did hear him and he was shot down at the same time. I was hit badly with a bullet grazing my head, which blinded me, one through my foot and others all over the airplane. I pulled up, figuring that I would stall and when I felt [it stall], I would get out. Amazingly my eyesight came back and I went down on the deck after three other Germans. I shot an Me 109 which was having a terrible time staying in the air and I am sure it crashed before getting back to France. Down on the deck I engaged two more FW 190s and, although I did not see them crash, Squadron Leader Thomas and William Baker saw the two crash. By that time I was out of ammunition and I headed for England, was put in the hospital and operated on and that was the end of my Eagle and RAF career. (Flying Officer Edwin Taylor, quoted in Caine, 1993)

Carter Harp, Taylor's wingman, did not return. Along with him, Flight Lieutenant Coburn King from California, and Flight Sergeant Grant Eichar from Iowa were also missing in action, presumed dead. In the aftermath of such encounters, pilots, ground crew and the ever-attendant intelligence and medical officers found it hard to reckon the score and remain optimistic that the outcome represented a winning hand. This was no game.

… Old habits die hard:
At the start of August, Davies got the impression that something was up. Unlike the previous year, when weather allowed, the squadrons at Biggin seemed not to be constantly off on operations across the Channel. Some of the usual 'know-it-all' types and those prone to a bout of 'doom and gloom' suggested that the scourge of the Fw190 over northern France was forcing the RAF to limit their fighter operations. In the pubs around Biggin, Campbell and Davies tried to remain optimistic. It was good for the locals and it was part of an airman's duty to contribute to the good morale of the populace. In one of their usual watering holes, the landlord had a real knack for working the odds in the RAF's favour. As soon as they entered the bar, he would call over, 'how many today, lads?' At first their standard reply would be 'a couple of 109s, I think,' or Campbell would get the locals rolling in laughter at his *double-entendre* about the squadron giving a couple of 'dirty Fockers' a good going over!' Whether they started with one or two claims, by closing time it usually amounted to a half-dozen or more, the rising score helped along by a flow of alcohol and the landlord's sense of keeping other spirits up. It was becoming habitual, and Davies and his comrades felt that it was a morale boost for the civilians that they never corrected their host's exaggerated claims.

There was perhaps another reason for the lull in operations. Though neither of them knew for certain, there was clearly something big in the planning. The squadron had been moved around a bit – not just the usual Gravesend move, Davies and 'A' Flight had been down to RAF Lympne on the south coast in July. There had been some scrambles while he was there, but after a few days it was back to Biggin. Chiefy Stewart now talked of sending some of the team back to Lympne. Rumours and counter-rumours hung around dispersal and the workshops, and passed in amongst the crews on late-night inspections. Yet nothing could be confirmed – just a feeling you'd get. There was nothing for it. As they said, you just had to get on with it.

So in the early days of August things seemed rather quiet around dispersal. One day, when the squadron was away, Davies settled into helping a rigger with a minor job on one of the aircraft – a bit of hangar rash that required a fabric patch on an elevator. One thing he'd noticed more of during his time with the Americans and Canadians, there was a greater sense of being a bit of an all-rounder. Perhaps it was Biggin. Perhaps it was being on a front-line station that made the difference. Whatever the combination of factors, the result was that whilst one knew a 'trade' and an expertise, if a rigger or anyone else needed a second pair of hands, then you 'mucked in'. As Davies was applying a coat of dope to the elevator, he caught sight of Campbell walking towards him from the direction of 133 Squadron's dispersal hut. 'Would you look at this, Taff. Bunch of dirty sods these Yanks,' he muttered, with a grin that betrayed how little seriousness was really in his words. 'It's taken me a bloody hour to get their coffee pot clean,' he said, holding it aloft with pride, turning it so it caught the sun and showed off its renewed brilliance. With words of warning, Davies started to chuckle at the thought of the pilots returning to see their trusty, run-in, taste and aroma-laden pot polished beyond all recognition. Convincing himself that he had perhaps started these 'colonials' on the road to better habits, Campbell wandered back to the pilots' hut to return the coffee pot. When the squadron returned, it took only a little while for one of the pilots to find the pot, standing like a trophy on the stove where Campbell had placed it! Now working together, Davies and his 'oppo' did not need to listen hard to pick up that Campbell's over-zealous cleaning had met with disapproval! Every so often Davies would nudge Campbell in the ribs and say, 'awwh Cammie, you're in for it now,' and Campbell would turn and look in the direction of the flight hut to catch sight of another pilot inspecting his handiwork. 'You can goddamn see yer face in it!'

It seemed like days before the commotion subsided, and even then Davies was certain that he would catch sight of one of the pilots looking at the pot disapprovingly whilst pouring. That was, at least, what he continued to tell Campbell and the team. It became another of their standing jokes, but one that was rarely aired in the presence of the squadron aircrew for obvious reasons!

Excitement at RAF Lympne:
In the third week of August, the squadron were back at Lympne and for ground crews there was a significant amount of activity. Squadron Leader Hodson brought 401 Squadron in to the airfield as well, making a familiar partnership. For Don Blakeslee, his posting over to the 'Eagles' and his experience now found him as acting leader for 133. Davies and the ground crews from 133 and 401 had arrived by road on the 14th and they had already set to the preparations for what was clearly going to be a major operation. There was a general scramble for the best rooms at Sir Philip Sassoon's house, with 133 Squadron's pilots getting the better of 401's, having been billeted there during their previous time at Lympne. There was some good banter between the squadrons as they came to readiness, particularly since 401 had been honoured to be the first of the Biggin squadrons to receive the new Spitfire IX. With its two-stage supercharger and uprated Merlin 60 series engine, this Spitfire had been rushed into service as a temporary stopgap to counteract the Fw190 threat. Comparison tests against Armin Faber's captured Fw190 revealed that Spitfire IX pilots could now meet the Fw190 on broadly equal terms. However the Focke Wulf still possessed a superior rate of roll and in the hands of '*experten*' it was able to escape, quickly reversing its turn by half-rolling and pulling back on the stick. The Canadians were excited to be the first at Biggin to receive the Mark IX (and to date one of only four squadrons in Fighter Command so equipped) and air and ground crews alike did their best to 'rub it in' with the usual sense of camaraderie.

On the 17th the two squadrons climbed out of Lympne to escort a group of twelve B-17 Flying Fortresses sent to bomb Rouen. This was the first time that the USAAF Eighth Air Force had operated Fortresses in the European theatre, and thus somewhat auspicious for 133 Squadron to be involved in seeing them safe. Targeting the Rouen-Sotteville marshalling yards, eleven Fortresses from the 342nd and 414th Bomb Squadrons and a single B-17 from the 340th, took off from Grafton Underwood. Aboard the lead aircraft of the main force was Major Paul Tibbetts as co-pilot to Colonel Frank Armstrong. With the Commander-in-Chief of the 8th Bomber Command, General Ira Eaker, along for the ride (in the second formation's lead aircraft '*Yankee Doodle*'), it was clearly considered a historic moment. Climbing to 27,000 feet over Fécamp, Blakeslee turned 133 Squadron north-east towards St Valery, watching the Fortresses pick up their heading for Rouen. Eric Doorly, flying AB910, spotted a few enemy aircraft down below, but the squadron were not in a position to intercept.

The main force of the engagement fell on the Canadians who, at the end of much bitter fighting, claimed one enemy aircraft destroyed, four probables and one damaged. Flight Lieutenant Whitham's confirmed kill and the other successes were somewhat overshadowed by the loss of one of 401's most experienced 'old hands'. As the squadron diarist wrote in hope:

> *Pilot Officer Ferguson is missing. No one saw him go down. Fergie is the oldest timer in the Squadron, having done over seventy sweeps. We all hope he is a prisoner of war.* (401 Squadron Operational Record Book, quoted in McIntosh, 1990)

As the squadrons returned to Lympne, 401 were to incur a further casualty as a result of combat damage. Flight Sergeant Rowthorn had brought his Spitfire back into the vicinity of the airfield and seemed home and safe as he let down into the circuit. But as he executed a gentle turn, the port aileron jammed in the up position, having received a stray bullet. At 400 feet, with little height to recover, the aircraft went into a spin.

> *He managed to level off just before hitting the ground in a field adjoining the north side of the aerodrome, but the port wing hit and the a/c was strewn many yards and caught fire. F/S Rowthorn was thrown out with his seat and was dragged away from the burning wreckage by a farmer and a constable who were fortunately near the scene. He was conscious when picked up and had sustained wounds of the forehead and multiple injuries to legs, hands and face. Condition serious. Before taking off on the do, F/S Reesor and Rowthorn tossed to see who would go. Rowthorn won and said 'I keep the penny for luck.' We do hope his luck holds and he pulls through. He is a spunky chap, full of fight.* (401 Squadron Operational Record Book, quoted in McIntosh, 1990)

Sadly, Rowthorn was not destined to survive, and he died of his injuries three days later. Whitham's successes, too, were short-lived. In another fiercely contested escort operation on 28 August, Flight Lieutenant Whitham in Spitfire BR628 and the rest of the squadron ran into a strong, determined force of forty plus Fw190s. 'Jimmie' Whitham was last seen in combat over Amiens. On 30 August the squadron received notification that he had been awarded the DFC, and in vain they hoped that he would one day turn up to wear it. His citation read:

> *This officer has completed a large number of sorties over enemy-occupied territory. He is an excellent flight commander whose fine fighting qualities have been well illustrated when leading his section in attacks on the enemy's targets. Besides his*

good work in the air, Flight Lieutenant Whitham is a tireless worker on the ground and has proved a source of inspiration to all. (Flight Lieutenant Whitham, DFC citation, *London Gazette*, 18 September 1942)

'Every dog has his day …' The Eagles at Dieppe:
Certainly this time 133's and 401's visit to Lympne was proving to be a busy one – this was no sojourn to the coast. Whilst the actions of 17 and indeed the 18 August had developed into a number of hotly contested running battles with the Luftwaffe, nothing prepared either squadron for the 19th. Davies had been right to wonder whether something big was on the cards after the last trip to Lympne had seemed so much of an anticlimax. When they had returned last time he and Campbell had tried to wheedle out any 'gen' from Chiefy Stewart but without success. The appearance of Group Captain Halling-Potts and Wing Commander Eric Thomas on the 18th confirmed that this time whatever was on was on. All crews were called to an extensive briefing that detailed the general purpose of the air operations for the following day, for Fighter Command to provide an air umbrella over the area of 'Jubilee' so as to deny enemy aircraft any response to a major seaborne operation in that area and its immediate vicinity. 'Jubilee' was the code name for the port of Dieppe.

There had been successful raids on the French coast before. Earlier in the year, when Davies had been detailed to 'look after' Duke-Woolley's kite, 124 Squadron had flown in support of a commando raid on the radar station at Bruneval. This sort of operation provided a real sense that, with the right conditions, the Allies could conduct limited, pinpoint raids on the Atlantic coast and give the enemy some sleepless nights worrying about the integrity of its defences. Maintaining such a broad defensive front was a constant headache, particularly when resources were stretched in North Africa, Russia and now the Balkans. 'Jubilee' was something more than Bruneval, more ambitious than Operation Chariot – the St Nazaire raid of March. Campbell, Davies and a number of the ground crews had noticed the large convoy movements in the area and had watched lorries, packed mainly with Canadians, pass through surrounding villages. This was going to be something big. At Lympne, energies and rumour were running high amongst the crews. Now, in the early hours of 19 August everything was just about ready. It was getting near 4.00 am when Davies finished up on some last-minute hitch – a pneumatic leak on one of the Spits. Harry Woods, too, was lending a hand with gun-camera film loading. A few riggers and fitters had made a sterling effort and worked through the night to get a couple more aircraft ready for the forthcoming operations – ones that had developed faults over the last few days.

With some changes in orders, the squadron lifted away from Lympne at 0720 hours, Blakeslee leading his twelve Spitfires away to the south with orders to provide cover patrol at 7,000 feet over Dieppe. On the ground, the battle was raging and thick palls of smoke drifted up from the main beach areas and from the other landing sites at Petit-Berneval, Pourville and Varengeville. Having landed at 0450 hours, there had been great success at Varengeville (Orange sector) by No.4 Commando, having silenced a coastal gun battery that threatened the naval vessels operating off the main landing beaches. Elsewhere, the movement off the beaches had been checked by heavy enemy resistance and a tangle of complex defence works that engineers had failed to breach. Tanks landed in support of the operation were consequently stranded on the beaches and penetration inland was, in the main, impossible. From the air, the situation looked desperate but there was little time to be spectators. The Luftwaffe were now responding in force and 133 Squadron found themselves in the thick of it. As the squadron diarist summarised:

Every dog has its day – and on the 19th August No. 133 was the Dog! ... The Squadron finally took off at 0720 with orders to orbit Dieppe at 7,000 feet. The target was reached without incident, but the fun began soon after! Flt/Lt Blakeslee DFC, Pilot Officer Baker and Sergeant Alexander all had combats, as a result of which 2 Fw190s, were destroyed, and another probably destroyed. (133 Squadron Operational Record Book, 19 August 1942)

Sergeant Richard 'Dixie' Alexander, of Grant Park Illinois, having sighted Fw190s carrying bombs approaching Dieppe from the North, followed Eric Doorly into attack on Blakeslee's order.

Suddenly I observed two more 190s to the left and slightly below me. I closed on them, and fired one burst at long range ... I was able to close to within about 3 or 4 hundred yards, and by then was well lined up. I gave him two more bursts, and we both passed directly over the entire convoy in the harbour, at about 300 feet ... I was still firing, and observed good strikes in the fuselage, and on his port wing. Suddenly his wing seemed to fall off, the aircraft exploded, and went directly into the water. (Sergeant Richard 'Dixie' Alexander, quoted in Caine, 1991, p. 256)

Alexander flew south and came across three Ju88s heading for the harbour. After putting in a full deflection burst and then a further burst from a better position, he ran out of ammunition and turned for home.

At Lympne, the atmosphere was buzzing. Davies spotted Doorly's aircraft in the circuit and shouted an alert to Campbell who was unloading crates of .303 that had been delivered to dispersal. Doorly was down and a rigger was waving him in. Davies, like other armourers, had spent the time, whilst the squadron were away, preparing drums of 20mm and had them stacked on a trolley. Campbell caught him up as Davies ran out to meet the aircraft. As Doorly slid back the hood and pulled off his flying helmet, Davies was already on the wing, removing the upper blister panel from the cannon bay. 'Any joy,' shouted Campbell, as he reached up to grab the partially spent magazine. Doorly shrugged his shoulders and looked skywards in a frustrated kind of way. 'Lot of aircraft around. Dixie's got one I think,' replied Doorly as he climbed down. Davies did a quick check around before dropping the new drum into place, recocking the magazine release trigger and reconnecting the securing strap. With the blister panel all buttoned up, he slid over the tank cowling to check on the other cannon. Looking across the dispersal, it seemed that the ground crew were almost throwing themselves at the aircraft. Everyone was in a state of busyness. Each knew their trade and all had the same sense of purpose. This was a well-oiled thoroughbred of a military machine. Whilst knowing your trade was an imperative, being another pair of hands was also expected. As fitter Ted Hayes recalled:

Everybody helped everybody else and if a rigger wasn't handy then you worked with somebody else's rigger. It was whatever happened … tyre change, rear wheel, things like that. We had the [engine] cowlings off to make sure there were no bullet holes or leaks or anything like that and fit them back quick. You were refuelling at the same time, rearming at the same time. It was a hectic day. (LAC Ted Hayes, Fitter, 133 Squadron, interview)

Along with the resident squadron aircraft, there were all manner of other aircraft of different squadrons landing in. These all had to be dealt with, although 'ops' were trying their best to send the most badly damaged on to West Malling – Lympne was just too operationally congested. For Ted Hayes, the diversion of aircraft resulted in his own deployment to West Malling for a number of days after the Dieppe operation.

Any aircraft that was too badly shot up, they couldn't land on Lympne because it was too operational. They sent them to West Malling and it was there that I had to go, after everything was over. That was at least two, three days at Lympne and then I had to help any of the fitters or riggers that had aircraft at West Malling, helping them to get away. These were of different squadrons where they needed help. There were a couple of aircraft there from 71 Squadron. It was so hectic for at least a month. (LAC Ted Hayes, Fitter, 133 Squadron, interview)

The squadron were again ordered off for their second patrol of Dieppe. Davies did a last-minute check on Doorly's oxygen connection, as this time they were ordered to provide top cover. Eric tapped his oxygen mask and gave a thumbs-up to indicate that everything was OK. As the engine idled and Doorly waited for the signal to move, Davies took his usual last opportunity to check the extractors on the two cannons. As the sound of the Merlins increased, he took a step back, checked around and waved Doorly off. A few moments later Doorly pulled gently back on the stick and eased AB910 into the air for its second operation of the day. It was a quarter past ten in the morning.

In no time, they were 12,000 feet over the French coast. Below, Dieppe seemed to be embroiled in all manner of corruption. On the shoreline, there were many burning landing craft and associated assault vessels, while further inland there were many other fires from ammunition dumps and the likes. Debris of tanks and other vehicles littered the beaches, sending black, caustic smoke into the morning sky. Everywhere the flak from both the assaulting and defending forces was intense and a real nightmare for those in the air. Blakeslee led his twelve into this boiling cauldron: Bob Smith, 22 from District of Columbia; Charles Cook, 24, from California; Ryerson, from Massachusetts, aged 30; Dick Beaty, a college graduate from New York; Don Lambert, another Californian, of 25; Bill Baker, a 21-year-old from Texas; Gill Wright, a former policeman from Pennsylvania; Don Gentile, from Ohio; Doorly, from New Jersey; Dick Gudmundsen, looking conspicuous flying an MX-K coded Spitfire of the 307th Fighter Squadron of the US 8th Air Force; and Gordon Brettell, ex-92 Squadron and the only Englishman in the formation.

Along with Pete Brothers' 602 Squadron, combat for 133 was immediate. The Luftwaffe presence was perhaps at its height during these hours, with masses of Dorniers, Ju88s and Focke Wulfs joining the battle. Blakeslee, Beatty, Gentile, Wright, Brettell, Gudmundsen and Eric Doorly all had combats, claiming one Ju88 and two Fw190s destroyed, and a further four Focke Wulfs and three Dornier 217s damaged. There seemed to be Focke Wulfs everywhere, and often it was impossible to confirm the results of any hits. Turning into them and firing was sometimes the only thing you could do. Around 1030 hours, 401 Squadron had escorted a large formation of Flying Fortresses to the aerodrome at Abbeville in an attempt to stem the Luftwaffe's operations. Yet more and more enemy aircraft were being vectored into the area from the North and from bases in Brittany. As the ground forces began to withdraw around 1050 hours, the RAF kept up the air umbrella of Spitfire Wings, whilst a mixture of light bombers and Hurricane fighter-bombers targeted the defences and laid covering smokescreens. Miraculously, 133 Squadron turned for home without sustaining a single casualty, although Gil Wright's aircraft

(BL773, borrowed from 'Dixie' Alexander) was badly shot up and would take no further part in the day's operations.

The severity of the battles on the ground was evident to those RAF ground personnel at the forward airfields such as Lympne. The roads coming up from the coast were heavily congested with all manner of vehicles, over which the many ambulances had priority. Dakotas were also flying into these front-line aerodromes to help evacuate the wounded. Though many of those on the ground had wondered whether this could have been the start of the invasion of France (and were geared up for it), it was clear that Dieppe was fast becoming a costly affair. Maintaining air cover was a huge undertaking and showed significant losses, but the ground assault seemed to have little to offer by way of success. As the assault ships began the rescue operation, Davies 'fastened up' AB910 once again, this time with 'Dixie' Alexander in the 'office', and watched her climb back into the air for a third patrol. It was now 1225 hours.

The withdrawal from Dieppe was now in full swing but the enemy were keen to harass the retreating troops and the flotilla of ships and rescue craft. Dorniers and Ju88s continued to pour in, turning their attention to bombing the assembled shipping. Around them a swirling mass of fighters continued their deadly exchanges, each side trying to gain the upper hand. More enemy fighters were coming into the area and attacking from height, and following such reports on this change of tactics, RAF command, ably informed by Group Captain Harry Broadhurst's armed reconnaissance operations, called on as many squadrons operating Spitfire IXs as it could muster. In one of these, 64 Squadron, was one of Davies' old drinking pals, Don Kingaby. Now a Flight Lieutenant and flight commander, Don was to claim his 19th victory on this day.

Squadron Leader Hodson, having returned from the escort operation to Abbeville, led 401's MkIXs into the fray. At height they encountered many Focke Wulfs and a frantic battle ensued, as 401 attempted to keep them from intercepting other squadrons lower down that were busying themselves with waves of Dorniers. The squadron's diarist made the following summary:

The Squadron then put up a patrol over Dieppe at 23,000 feet. Ground troops had withdrawn when we arrived over Dieppe and the convoy had travelled some forty miles from the French coast. Flight Lieutenant Whitham reports: Five miles off the coast at Dieppe we were at 15,000 feet. S/P Morton Buckley failed to climb steeply enough and I saw two FW-190s attack him. I called him to break, he did a gentle weave and the FWs overshot him. Two more FW-190s attacked him and I warned him to break again. He did not take violent enough evasive action. I dove on the rear FW-190 attacking Buckley but the e/a had fired on him. He went down and crashed in the sea without bailing out. We were then at 4,000 feet. I went into a steep right turn using full top rudder and throttle and the two FW-190s turned as tightly as I did and then they broke and I pounced on the tail of one FW-190 and opened fire from fifty yards, giving the e/a a seven-second burst, saw strikes all down the port side and wings and into the engine, also cannon flashes, pieces came off the fuselage and the engine poured black smoke. E/a went into a shallow dive toward the sea, two miles off shore. This e/a is claimed as a probably destroyed. Flight Sergeant Reesor reports: S/P L. Armstrong got hit and went into a spin, baled out and got into his dinghy. I came down low and circled S/P Armstrong. He appeared to be uninjured as he waved. (401 Squadron Operational Record Book, 19 August 1942)

At a lower altitude, 133 Squadron waded into swarms of enemy aircraft, a mixed bag of Dorniers and Fw190s.

Combats ensued in this patrol in which Flying Officer Nelson probably destroyed a Do217, F/Sergeant Alexander claimed a Do217 destroyed and Flight Lieutenant Blakeslee claimed a Fw190 as damaged. It was also noticed that the evacuation of troops was now in fairly full process. Bombers were dive-bombing both small and large boats, and two ships, one a destroyer, were seen to receive direct hits. All our aircraft landed safely at 1345. (133 Squadron ORB, 19 August 1942)

A similar commotion set in at Lympne on the squadron's return, but again 133 had been fortunate in sustaining no casualties. There was no time to stop and think of the almost superhuman effort that the ground crews had been putting in to the day's operations, but their immense contribution was clearly evident. Dispersal was full of chatter about how things seemed to be going on the ground and here and there the many combats were being replayed by the pilots to their crews. The squadron had certainly kept the Intelligence Officer in work over the last few hours! After rearming AB910 (MD-J) following 'Dixie' Alexander's successful combat with the Dorniers, Davies and the team set about checking with the other armourers and conducting a few quick inspections on the 20mm cannons. Overall, Davies was pleased that he could report to Stewart at Biggin that they had received few problems with the cannons for the sorties of the day. Though all at Lympne remained excited and keyed up for what other operations might be required, none materialised for the rest of the afternoon. That was not to say that the ground crews were not without something to do; with the airfield being close to the coast, it was the focus of many aircraft returning from Dieppe, either damaged or short on juice. Davies and Campbell worked on a number of aircraft from other squadrons and found themselves helping out with many tasks, not just those associated with an armourer's 'bread and butter' trade.

It was early evening when the squadron was required again. As the aircraft started to taxi out, Davies waved down one pilot and ran under the wing. It was one of those moments when doubt had crept in. In response to Davies' quick question of 'all OK, boy?' a young armourer, new to the echelon, had exclaimed, 'damn, I can't remember cocking 'em!' With his cocking wire hook, Davies was quick under the wings and, 'job's a good 'un', he signalled to the pilot with a thumbs-up and off he went. The young lad was apologetic but Davies just replied, 'Not to worry. Everything's an education. I'm sure it'll be the last time you do it.'

It was 1955 hours when the squadron took off on what was to be its last patrol of the day. As the sun started to lower to the west, Blakeslee brought them over the convoy of ships that were now well on their way back to the safety of the English coast. At various altitudes other aircraft were seen heading home. Eric Doorly was again in AB910, flying its fourth sortie. In comparison to the rest of the day's patrols, this one was quiet, and no engagements with the enemy occurred. With a mixture of feelings – excitement, relief, and fatigue – the pilots turned for Lympne. The day's reckoning saw 133 Eagle Squadron as flying four patrols. Of all the squadrons operational that day, it was the last to land. It had been most successful, and was the highest claiming squadron of Fighter Command. Perhaps most significant, it had achieved all of these successes without loss.

Chapter Nineteen

Morlaix

A Forty-eight in London:

A week or so after Dieppe, Davies was granted a forty-eight hour leave. It was indeed timely what with the squadron being on a high after the successes of the 19th and for the fact that Davies' second birthday in the RAF fell on Friday the 28th. Boy, the year had gone quickly! It seemed only yesterday that he'd been home to Nelson after Rankin had granted him a week's leave on the eve of his 21st. One year on, he was now an LAC and had the privilege of a sleeping-out pass, which expanded the possibilities for his forty-eight. This time home was too far away to have any quality time with the family, though the thought of seeing Dad, Mam and Leighton and being back in the comforts of the Wern represented real 'leave'. The Americans had other ideas. It seemed like a gesture of goodwill, a reward for the job well done. Whatever the reason, as Davies sat on the end of his bed, he thumbed a card he'd been given with his leave pass. He'd been told that accommodation at the famous Eagle Club on Charing Cross Road was at his disposal. All he needed to do was give his details at the desk and hand in the card, the squadron adjutant had let them know. Working for the yanks sure had its benefits! He got a call through to his brother, Ron, who was up at RAF Police headquarters.

He met Ron near Marble Arch. 'How you been, boyo,' said Ron, catching hold of Ray's arm. Before he could reply, Ron was in full swing – always full of ideas, always ready to entertain. 'Now I thought we'd go off to the Lyons Corner House on Oxford Street first, and then we'll get us off to the Eagle Club, did you say?' 'Not far is it, Ron?' quizzed Ray, as they started to walk. He was conscious that they'd already passed Maison Lyon's, but Ron kept up the pace. 'Not that one. If we go along to the one on the corner of Oxford Street and Tottenham Court Road, then we can walk down Charing Cross to the Eagle Club,' said Ron. Ray was used to this – his brother always had a good itinerary planned out – Ray's own sense of direction was never something to rely on!

The walk along Oxford Street went quickly and, before he was really aware, Ron was ushering him along the line at the counter service of the café. They found a table, dressed with a check-patterned cloth, and pulled up a couple of studded-back upholstered chairs. It was a busy place, as all Lyon's cafés and restaurants in London tended to be. It was about four months since they had last seen each other and, of course, talk turned to the family. They swapped news and compiled their collective knowledge of how things were back at home from the different letters they had received from Dad and Mam, and from Howard and Eric in Wolverhampton. Howard and Eric had joined the local fire-watching service in Wednesfield, feeling that they were making more of a contribution to the war effort (as if spending long shifts underground digging coal didn't count). Late one evening a German bomber had dropped a stick of bombs in the fields over the back of the house – the usual bad shot, Ray had thought to himself. One incendiary device had failed to explode so Eric and Howard had gallantly raced up the field with a stirrup pump and hose! Whilst Howard pumped the pump furiously, Eric stood directing the resultant trickle of water from the brass hose nozzle at the offending object. All of this was accompanied by howls of laughter and shouts of encouragement from their wives, Rhoda and Kitty, as they stood in the back garden! 'In these moments, wars are won,' laughed Ron as he recounted the version of the story he'd received through Eric's letter.

From the Lyon's Corner House, they walked along to Charing Cross Road and down in the direction of Trafalgar Square. The Eagle Club, at number 28, was run by two Americans, Mrs Francis Dexter and Barbara Blake. Here the Eagle squadrons could catch up on news from US newspapers and have something of a taste of home. Ray handed over the card he had been given and sure enough was shown where they could sleep, where the bar was, and were asked if they wanted any food. He signed in the guest book and was handed an envelope containing two theatre tickets.

I told Ron that I had this weekend, long weekend it was. Ron was stationed with the RAF Police up near Grosvenor Square – he was a driver, mechanic. He came up with me to the club and they gave me a couple of tickets to a show, 'Ramsbottom, Enoch and Me'. I think it was at the Palladium. We had top, front-row seats from the American Eagle Club. (LAC Raymond Davies, interview 2002)

The show was really a showcase of different acts, its origins being in music hall. Later, in 1943, it acquired a loose plot of sorts and was made into a film. It was light entertainment: a bit of sing-along, comedians and double-acts, all strung together in the story of a run-down music hall. 'Our Eric would have loved that,' said Ray, as he and Ron left the theatre.

It was late when he left Ron near Regent Street. His elder brother had given him easy instructions to get back on to Charing Cross Road and to the Eagle Club. When Ray got to the club there were still a lot of service personnel sitting around talking, laying back in the comfy leather sofas that were dotted around the room.

There were piles of American magazines and newspapers, and Ray flicked through a few pages of one. He was the only non-American in the place. Yet for Ray, it didn't seem unfamiliar; after all he had been with 133 Squadron since June and had grown accustomed to the Americans, their easy hospitality and informality. He spotted a sculpted eagle above the fireplace and thought of the various squadron mascots that he had seen liberated from hotels by 92 and 609 Squadrons! That seemed a lifetime ago. He got chatting to a group from 121 Squadron and there was much talk about Dieppe. The drinks flowed freely and it seemed to be getting lighter outside when he finally made it to bed. It was a great night, one that he would remember as one of the best.

'Gen Wallah' and Other New Names:
The end of August had seen the squadron over at RAF Martlesham Heath for gunnery practice. The squadron's new Mark IX Spitfires had started to arrive and the time at Martlesham gave them a 'breather' after Dieppe, as well as the opportunity to become accustomed to the new aircraft. When Davies returned to Biggin on the 31st, the squadron were just returning and he was given the task of looking after a group of new armourers, fresh from the USA, that would be servicing the American squadrons. As a temporary expedient, these all-American squadrons were being equipped with Spitfires and so their ground crews needed to 'gen up' on the aircraft. With most of Stewart's specialist team returning from Martlesham, it was Davies who was assigned the task of bringing the US armourers up to speed regarding the 20mm Hispano cannon, as fitted to their Mark Vb Spitfires. His time with Stewart's team had gotten him used to instructing and taking such responsibility. Campbell and Pete Long had taken to calling him 'Gen Wallah', marking his lofty position as the all-knowing sage on anything to do with the 20mm armament. There was some variation: sometimes 'cannon wallah' and other times 'musket wallah'. He took it all in good humour.

Sitting on the port wing of one of the Mark Vbs, he first spent some time talking to the assembled crowd about the general principles of the Hispano and its fitment in the Spitfire. He talked about the care and preparation of the ammunition and the procedures they had adopted to minimise stoppages. Two armourers had removed the cannon bay panels. 'Right-O, now let's first show you how to do a few jobs with the cannon still in the bay,' said Davies, 'then I'll show you how to remove and refit one, and we can break into groups and you can have a go yourselves.' Laying out a number of tools (some of them purposely fashioned in the field for the job at hand), he began to demonstrate to the crews the sort of work that could be just about carried out with the cannon *in situ* – jobs that could save you the time of having to remove the gun from its mounting. It was tricky stuff and some of the

Americans looked on somewhat bewildered. It was only when he offered them the chance to have a go themselves that he realised why.

> [*With tools*] *we had to improvise a hell of a lot. The Yanks showed us up: some Yank armourers came and I was one who had to show them how to take a cannon out and put it back in. Of course we had a large box spanner and we had to get up on the mainplane to undo the various nuts to get the cannon out. I went right through the method. I took the recoil reducer off – we had this big spanner to do it – and we slid out the cannon, put it on the bench and I pointed out various things to watch for and check. Then we got the cannon back up and I showed them the way of putting it back in, tightened it all up, put the recoil reducer back on, tested the recoil and took the particular number of turns off and I said, 'right, the guns are now ready for operations.' I showed them the safety catch and explained that we always kept the safety catch on 'safe' until the aircraft were on readiness. When the squadron was released, then you'd put the safety catch on – there was a little catch at the back of the gun, that you could get to from underneath [the aircraft]. Anyhow, I did this demonstration of how we did it and when we'd finished I said 'OK, do you want to have a go now?' And they opened their bloody tool box! Christ, where I had to get up onto the deck, they had tools that allowed them to take the panel off, take the gun off, without them getting off the floor! They showed me how to do it! They had better tools, extension tools … Boy was I envious!* (LAC Davies, interview 2003)

For most of the ground personnel, when it came to the operations of the aircraft there were two things that they seemed to want to experience. One of these was to sit in the cockpit and run the engine, to feel the sheer power of the Merlin as it sent ripples of energy through the airframe. The other was to press that small gun-firing button to unleash the great destructive firepower of the cannons and machine guns, and there were eager requests to have a quick squirt when the aircraft was on the firing butts. 'Agh, go on, Taff, think you could let us have a go?' came the chat. 'If I stand you a pint at the King's, do you reckon you might see me have a quick squirt with those cannons, Taff?' One group that Davies gave in to included Fitter, Ted Hayes.

> *Our [squadron] armourers knew nothing about the cannons really. They were all .303 machine-gun type personnel and they could whip those out, whip them back in, clean them, do everything in the space of time of refuelling and rearming. They were very very good. Now we were given the opportunity of sitting up and pressing the button. It was something which, really and truly, everybody wanted to do was to sit*

in a Spitfire when it was up on its jacks and fire the cannon and machine-guns. You could feel yourself moving backwards. The pilots always said that in firing, especially the cannon, the aircraft seemed to stop and then shoot forwards! It couldn't have happened that way, but the point was it felt like that. I did have a go at the cannons. I was given the chance of a couple of seconds burst … just press the button … brrrrm … and away. (LAC Ted Hayes, Fitter, 133 Squadron, interview)

Davies would crouch on the wing with the aircraft on trestles and the side door open. With each of the 'lucky blighters' that got the chance to have a go, he would explain to them, 'Now, no more than a two-second burst, mind you. I'll give you one tap on your shoulder when to fire, and another when to stop. No more than two-seconds, remember!' And just like his own running up of a Spitfire's Merlin, it was one of those experiences that would remain indelibly imprinted on the senses.

Other occurrences left similar lasting impressions. On 6 September Davies had seen Eric Doorly off for the last time. The squadron had been escorting a force of thirty-six Fortresses, bound for the Méaulte factory near Albert but had been intercepted by a group of ten plus Focke Wulf 190s on the way in. Though split up, the squadron, along with the Canadians of 401, gave effective cover to the bombers whilst over the target. On the way back, escort duties took on a greater unpopularity amongst the attendant fighter boys as the Fortress gunners, for no apparent reason, started shooting at their own escort! Having none of this, 133 Squadron dived to a lower level, getting out of harm's way and set a course for home. The Fortresses could find their own way back! Not all of 133 Squadron made it back. At Biggin, Davies waited anxiously with the small group of fitters, riggers and armourers that had seen off Eric Doorly and Dick Gudmundsen.[3] Some in the squadron thought they had seen them when the formation had been thirty miles inland from the coast, but perhaps it had been another pair of Spits. Davies returned to his billets with no news, pretty much convincing himself that Eric had 'bought it'.

---

3. Doorly had managed to evade capture after bailing out. He and Gudmundsen had been caught by the FW190s that had intercepted the formation. With the tail of his aircraft shot away, Doorly managed with some difficulty to extract himself from the gyrating Spitfire. At 20,000ft he got free, pulled the ripcord of his parachute and then took 20 minutes to reach the ground. Although a circling FW190 had perhaps alerted those on the ground to his descent, Doorly was able to conceal himself under piles of leaves, while his would-be captors searched nearby. After dark he made contact with the Resistance and was returned to England via Spain. Gudmundsen, from Burley, Idaho, did not survive the encounter with the Fw190s. He is buried at Poix-de-Picardie, Amiens, France.

A week or so later, during a lull in the day's duties, Davies and his comrades were down at dispersal, taking the weight off with the usual mug of tea and a quick game of cards. Broomhead was particularly pleased with himself as he had managed to secure a 'new' tin mug after weeks of moaning that someone had been discourteous enough to liberate his own from his billets! For the immediate group of friends, they thought that they would not hear the end of it, as Broomhead had bemoaned his loss at every opportunity! Yet, now, he sat opposite Davies, content that he'd acquired a replacement that he'd found abandoned on a window ledge at dispersal. It wasn't until he up-ended the mug to drain the last of its contents that Campbell and Davies fell about in fits of laughter. 'You finished yer tea there, Dooley,' called out Campbell? Davies, grinning from ear to ear, was pointing at the bottom of the mug, where the previous owner had daubed his name in red dope – 'Doorly'. 'Better get yourself another one, Brom,' laughed Davies, taking the mug from his bemused comrade. Though the mug was surrendered – and Davies cleaned and returned it to the pilots' hut where he hoped Eric would come back to retrieve it – for Broomhead the name stuck. From then on, all those 'in the know' called him 'Dooley' and he grew to answer to it!

Just Another Escort – A disaster called Morlaix:
For those serving with 133 Squadron, September 1942 marked their last month in the RAF, before the transfer of all Eagle Squadrons into the United States 8th Army Air Force. As it was, many experienced the month as unsettling and with some uncertainty. It was not, perhaps, the easiest of times for any involved, either on the ground or in the air. In their movement into the USAAF, there were many changes to negotiate and although many of the pilots were eager to join their brethren, they had made the RAF their home and were used to its organisation and leadership. 'Mac' McColpin, now CO, kept a weather eye on the developments and, in an attempt to maintain some stability within the squadron over this transitional period, sent his pilots up to London in ones and twos for their transfer interviews. In this way he made sure that there were still enough aircrew to respond to operational requests.

Davies, too, sensed a feeling of uncertainty. Having spent some time during the last few months occupied with training US ground personnel, there was talk of him leaving Biggin with the Americans, just to ease their transfer. After all, they would be taking the Spitfires with them. Of course the idea of leaving 'the Bump' sat uneasily with him: It had become a second home, and there was a familiarity about the place. He and Campbell pretty much assumed that Warrant Officer Stewart would still want to keep the team together at Biggin and so perhaps it was likely that, when 133 Squadron left the RAF, there would be another squadron to which they would be assigned. Later in the month, news came through that the squadron would be moving up to RAF Debden's satellite airfield at Great Sampford. Here they would become part of the USAAF's 4th Fighter Group along with the other Eagle squadrons. Davies didn't fancy the move. In comparison with Biggin, it was not well equipped and used a sort of metal tracking and mesh arrangement for the runways. He was sure that the pilots wouldn't be very keen either, but as the orders trickled through to start moving the squadron headquarters, Great Sampford became a new name to find on the map. The complete transfer from the RAF would take place on the 29th of the month.

The movement of squadrons in and out of Biggin was, of course, part of its natural rhythm. Davies, himself, had seen many changes during his time there. Yet, September 1942 seemed different in a number of ways. Firstly, the servicing echelon was also set to move across to Kenley, to support the building up of an all-Canadian wing. The Canadians of 401 Squadron were to move down the road to Kenley as part of this arrangement. Secondly, in anticipation of two of Biggin's resident squadrons moving out, other squadrons were to be moved in and the Station seemed to be becoming a little crowded. On the 18th, Davies' old pals from 609 Squadron arrived, this time sporting their awesome Hawker Typhoons. Davies was eager to see one up close and sought out some of 'the old crowd' from 1941. There were many familiar faces in the ground crew and so it was not long before he was up on the wing of one of their 'Tiffies' – and *high* up he felt. Though the big PR codes on the fuselage sides gave him a feeling of familiarity, this was a very different experience to running up onto the low wing of his beloved 'Spit'. He was also pleasantly surprised to see 'Joe' Atkinson down at dispersal again, one of 609 Squadron's long-serving pilots. 'Joe' was rather surprised himself that he was *still* with the squadron as it was coming up for two years that he had been operational with them! On the 20th, 66 Squadron appeared and, three days later, 340 '*Ile de France*' Squadron arrived, the first Free-French squadron that Davies had encountered. Just when it all seemed too much to comprehend, 611 Squadron also joined the Wing on the day that 401 Squadron were moving out.

For McColpin, such transience did not help a sense of nervousness he had about a planned sortie that had been on and off the operations list in the preceding weeks. Postponed mainly for reasons of weather, the operation, to bomb a Luftwaffe and Focke-Wulf maintenance airfield at Morlaix, Brittany, seemed a routine affair. Circus 220, as it was to be listed, consisted of a standard escort operation for the experienced squadrons of 11 Group Fighter Command. A formation of Flying Fortresses was to be picked up at a predetermined rendezvous point, mid-Channel, and escorted south to the northern coast of Brittany. The target was less than 150 miles from the designated take-off point – the small coastal airfield of Bolt Head, Devon. It was, in RAF parlance, 'a piece of cake'. Whilst the operational details seemed pretty straightforward, even to those squadrons and personnel far less experienced than Biggin's and Kenley's elite, it was the weather that was proving itself the fickle partner in the relationship. For days, weather conditions had been unpredictable. On the 23rd, gathering cumulo–nimbus had stretched vertically through the day to cause localised thunderstorms. Rain and thunderstorms persisted into the next day, with winds varying in both direction and strength. Cycling down through dispersal, Davies watched a couple of pilots who were hoping for some circuit and bumps, looking skywards with furrowed brows as pilots do. Then he caught sight of the wind sock, which seemed equally unable to make up its mind what to do. On the day before Circus 220 actually took place, 401 Squadron's diarist summarised another day frustrated by poor weather.

0542 hours, 'B' Flight readiness, 'A' Flight 15 minutes available, till 0830 hours, then Squadron 30 minutes available. Weather: Ground fog persistent all morning, no wind. A scramble came through for Red Section, but the weather made it impossible to take off. At 1500 hours, 8 a/c on readiness, at 1645, Squadron released. (401 Squadron, Operational Record Book, 25 September 1942).

Sometimes the weather seemed the greatest enemy. Earlier in the year, in March, 317 (Polish) Squadron at Exeter had taken off on a bomber escort and had met with weather that brought about the tragic death of their squadron leader and the near loss of all aircraft. As their operational records documented:

More rain in the morning clearing to fair weather with low cloud. Although the weather was still bad instructions were received for the squadron accompanied by No. 306 squadron to provide bomber escort to five bombers and to proceed towards the French coast in search of shipping. Both squadrons took off from Exeter at 15.40 hours and rendezvoused with bombers over base and course was set on a vector of 200º. The ships were seen about 5 to 10 miles from the French Coast in the vicinity of Tregastel but no attack was seen by our pilots owing to the state of the weather i.e. 10/10 cloud at 200 feet. At approx. 16.30 hours the fighters turned for home and when in the vicinity of Falmouth at 17.10 hours where the weather was the same as over the French Coast they steered course for Predannack where they intended to land. On arrival in the vicinity the cloud and mist being so low they searched for 15 minutes in an effort to find the drome, but without success. It was decided to proceed to Bolthead although the pilots were now losing sight of each other owing to the poor visibility. On arrival in the vicinity conditions were very bad the drome being completely covered with thick cloud. In fact one pilot, Flying

Officer Koc, with the aid of instruments flew over the drome at 20 feet but was unable to see it. The pilot although his gauge indicated that he had only 7 gallons of fuel left decided to make for Exeter where he made a successful landing at 18.04 hours. All aircraft were now very short of fuel; the result was that they had to crash-land in the vicinity of Bolthead. The only other successful landing was made by F/Sergeant Brzeski at Newquay. The remaining 10 aircraft all crash-landed in the Bolthead area. In the course of landing all 10 aircraft were damaged six being Cat. E., four Cat. B. The Squadron Commander, S/Ldr Brzezinski struck the side of a cliff and was killed instantly. Other casualties were Flying Officers Kratke and Hrycak slightly injured and admitted to R.A.F. Hospital Torquay and Flight Lieutenant Niemiec slightly injured, but not admitted to hospital. (317 Polish Squadron, Operational Record Book, 15 March 1942)

Perhaps therein lay an omen of what was to transpire on 26 September 1942. Superstition aside, a number of factors would recur on this day to deal 133 Squadron a greater tragedy – one that would be forever remembered as one of Fighter Command's darkest hours.

An Uncertain Start:

When Exeter control read the Met Officer's reports for the day, it seemed that Saturday, 26 September, would provide more favourable conditions for Circus 220 than the previous few days. Given as 6/10ths cloud cover, varying up to 15,000 feet, it was estimated that the cloud would be broken up at higher levels allowing the formation to proceed to the target at 22,000 feet. The three squadrons to provide escort would rendezvous with the Fortresses at 17,000 feet over the Channel before beginning the climb to altitude. All flying Mk IX Spitfires, 401, 64 and 133 squadrons, were to make their way to forward airfields on the South Devon coast to enable a better operational range. Their relatively new Spitfires would also be equipped with equally new additional fuel tanks, slung under the centre-line of the aircraft and with the facility to be jettisoned once the fuel was expended. This would provide a further 30-gallon supplement to the 85-gallon internal tank capacity of the Mk IX.

In the early hours of the morning, Davies and other attendant ground crew diligently prepared the aircraft for the squadrons' departures for Bolt Head and Harrowbeer. It had been a bit of a rush in some respects as the operation had been cancelled then rescheduled a number of times. It was the sort of last-minute job that the crews were accustomed to, yet none liked. As Davies buttoned up one of 133's Spits ready for the early take-off, over at RAF Fairlop his old pal Don Kingaby was climbing into his 64 Squadron Spitfire to lead a flight down to

Harrowbeer for their part in the operation. Now with rain set in and a cold, stiff wind blowing, the sky looked uninviting for any sort of solo aerial endeavour, let alone an attempt to rendezvous with a whole bunch of other aircraft feeling their way through the solid overcast. When the squadrons finally took off, the cloud base was down to an unhealthy 300 feet. Perhaps someone would see sense and abort again? For Kingaby and 64 Squadron, it seemed uncertain conditions under which to conduct the operation. Taking off from Fairlop, the squadron attempted to cut their way through the grey wall of cloud, to gain height so as to fly above it. Yet it was decidedly dicey to say the least. Calling up on the R/t, Squadron Leader Tony Gaze decided it was too bad and ordered a return to base. It was a less than auspicious start. His squadron would spend a couple of hours on the ground at Fairlop before starting out again at 1210 hours. Kingaby, Gaze and the rest of 64 Squadron would finally make it down to Harrowbeer at 1330 hours.

The Kenley Wing Leader, Brian Kingcome, was scheduled to lead the operation to Morlaix, but he too experienced delays in getting down to Bolt Head.

The first snag occurred when Batchy [Group Captain 'Batchy' Atcherley, OC RAF Kenley] sent for me just as I was about to take off with No. 401 Squadron. I told Keith Hodson, the tall Canadian squadron leader, to make his way to Devon without me, and I would follow as soon as I could. But Batchy held me up for longer than expected, and by the time I was in the air and hot-footing it to Devon the three squadrons were already briefed and waiting to take off from Bolt Head. Tony Gaze, the leader of the third squadron, No.64 from Hornchurch, was an experienced and competent pilot. I therefore told him that he had better take over from me as wing leader, since there was no time left for me to be briefed. I would then take over the leadership of the Canadian squadron to act as 'top cover', with the Eagle squadron in the middle. (Wing Commander Brian Kingcome, quoted in Kingcome, 1992, p. 130–1)

Kingcome was not alone in missing the briefing at Bolt Head. Very few of 133 Squadron attended the briefing, many considering it pretty much a routine job. The target was less than 150 miles from Bolt Head and the squadron would be operating its high-performance Spitfire IXs in force. It was perhaps with some overconfidence that the Eagles gathered their kit together for the operation. As Pilot Officer Charles Cook would later reflect:

We didn't go to the briefing because there was no point to it. We had been doing this kind of flying for a year. Every one of us had flown 50 or 60 missions. It was a real quick thing, a hurry-up do. That mission wasn't supposed to get underway until the next day. If we had known what we were getting into – well, we would have been thinking ahead. (Pilot Officer Charles Cook, 133 Squadron, quoted in Haughland, 1979, p. 171–2)

In actual fact, only two members of the squadron attended the briefing, Pilot Officer George Sperry and Flight Lieutenant Gordon Brettell. Yet, the meeting itself was, according to Sperry, somewhat casual with perhaps insufficient attention to detail. It was, after all, going to be an uncomplicated type of operation. Wing Commander Brian Kingcome would later describe that:

Our orders were straightforward [and] the operation would give the Eagle pilots a chance to baptise their Spitfire IXs at minimum risk – a fitting farewell gesture. (Wing Commander Brian Kingcome, quoted in Kingcome, 1992, p. 130)

With 'Mac' McColpin ordered to London to undergo his transfer to the USAAF, the Eagles would be led by their English flight commander, Flight Lieutenant Gordon Brettell. Edward Gordon Brettell was twenty-seven and an experienced fighter pilot, having spent most of his operational service in 11 Group Fighter Command. Along with Neville Duke, fellow graduate of 58 OTU at Grangemouth, Brettell had joined 92 (East India) Squadron in April 1941. On Gordon's arrival at the squadron, Duke penned the following entry in his diary:

A word for Gordon Brettell – the quiet, the incredible, the likeable Gordon. A person as deep as the very ocean itself, who I am sure I shall never quite understand. I'm very glad to have him here with me. We were together in my week at Hatfield (although I did not come into contact with him till later at Ternhill), at Sealand and Ternhill and very much together at Grangemouth. He arrived at Biggin just after dinner, much to my relief as he had all my flying kit with him, and we were taken by the chaps down to the White Hart (Brasted), a good spot, the other side of Westerham. We suitably consumed a quantity of liquor and in due course removed ourselves to bed. (Pilot Officer Neville Duke, quoted in Franks, 1995, p. 11)

Pre-war, Brettell had graduated from Clare College, Cambridge in 1937 and had been the secretary of the university's automobile club. His interest in motor racing continued after his time at Cambridge and he made a name for himself as a racing driver, doing particularly well by winning the Five Lap Road Handicap in his favourite Austin Seven Ulster Single during the Short Handicap meeting at Brooklands racing circuit in March 1938. His achievements at Brooklands in 1938 were, perhaps, even more remarkable in light of the serious injuries he had sustained the previous year when he had, infamously, crashed through the barriers on one of the circuit's steeply banked sections and gone 'over the top'.

Flying continuously throughout 1941 with 92 Squadron, there was no doubt of Brettell's experience. The citation for his DFC read:

> *This officer has taken part in 111 sorties over enemy territory. He has always displayed great keenness to engage the enemy. On one occasion he was wounded in combat and on recovery, he resumed operational flying with renewed zest. He is an excellent Flight Commander.* (Flight Lieutenant Edward Gordon Brettell, DFC citation, *London Gazette*, 1942)

His exuberance whilst off duty had also brought some attention from the authorities and one particular incident had put him in front of a court martial inquiry. During his time at Biggin Hill, he had taken the opportunity to fly a WAAF back from a party in a Spitfire. Dispensing with a parachute, Brettell had piloted the aircraft with the WAAF sitting on his lap! He was court martialled and received a severe reprimand. He was not the only fighter pilot to have done this. Tony Bartley, his fellow ex-92 Squadron friend, openly admitted to doing the same. Davies too, remembered waving in an aircraft at Biggin that had just landed. Holding up his arms, he had indicated to the pilot that there was a spare bay at dispersal and attempted to marshal him in. With the cockpit hood fully back, the pilot waved in recognition but proceeded to taxi up past flying control to park there for all to see! It was only then that Davies realised that there were two people in the cockpit: one being a rather pretty blonde WAAF!

While severely reprimanded following the findings of the official inquiry, Brettell was not grounded and thus continued to fly operations from Biggin as a member of the Wing. Posted in to 133 Squadron as a flight commander in August 1942, he had been with them at the time of Dieppe, having flown three operational patrols. With McColpin in London, it was Brettell that climbed into one of the squadron's Mark IX Spitfires (BS313) to lead them off from Bolt Head.

Even here there was a less than confident start: facilities at Bolt Head were not in abundance. Ground crews found themselves dealing with the challenge of starting a whole squadron with only three trolley-accumulators between them. These heavy wooden carts, containing batteries, provided a means of auxiliary electrical power for start-up. Sitting up in their cockpits, the pilots looked on as teams of fitters, riggers and armourers raced to get these trolley-acs from one aircraft to another. Earlier, they had encountered another problem in that the airfield did not seem to possess the correct refuelling equipment required for the under-belly jettison tanks. Thus, any pilots who might have used a little from this tank on the way down to Bolt Head, could not have it topped up. Boy, this was not Biggin!

Then, as the squadron's aircraft started to pick their way around to the take-off point, the Gremlins struck again! While taxiing around the peri-track, Brettell's aircraft suffered a burst tyre. Quickly changing aircraft with George Sperry, Brettell led the squadron off with little delay. Always at hand, members of the ground crew managed to change the tyre to allow Sperry to join the formation mid-Channel.

It was 1600 hours, wet and windy with a Met forecast of 6/10ths cloud varying up to 15,000 feet. At 133 Squadron's operational height of 28,000 feet, the wind was expected to be around thirty-five knots and blowing towards the south-west. With Morlaix being approximately 112 miles due south of Bolt Head, this estimation gave the squadrons a moderate tail-wind component to figure into their navigational calculations.

Clouds, Wind and Missing Fortresses:
Leading the Wing, 64 Squadron's Tony Gaze climbed the formation through almost solid cloud towards the expected rendezvous point at 17,000 feet, high above the Channel. With the greater than forecast cloud density, the close escort squadrons were unable to make visual contact with the bombers. Recent escort operations with the USAAF bomber squadrons did not give much confidence in their keeping to schedule: sometimes they were early and would elect to proceed on towards the target without the fighters; other times they were rather late, requiring the fuel-conscious fighters to stooge around waiting. Mindful of the need to protect their charges over the target, the close escort of 64, 133 and 401 squadrons decided to press on to Morlaix above the overcast. Working with the Met information they had available to them at briefing, they would let down through the clouds over the target after a given elapsed time. Having calculated what they thought was their true air speed (TAS) and ground speed, accounting for the thirty-five knot wind, the formation continued south. All things considered, the Fortresses of the 301st Bomb Group would also be approaching the target as the Spitfires arrived on their ETA. Yet for now, above cloud and with no visual reference of the ground, the squadrons flew on with still no sign of the bombers.

As they continued south, one of 133 Squadron's aircraft, Gene Neville's BS140, started to experience engine trouble. Gene was Dusty Miller's roommate and it was Miller who had flown BS140 down to Bolt Head. At the last minute, as Miller was walking out to the aircraft, he had been informed that he was going to be one of two 'spare' pilots this time round – the other being Don Gentile. With that news, Miller removed his parachute from the Spitfire, now relegated to wait for the squadron's return. Now with the engine running rough, Neville called up Brettell to inform him that he was going to have to turn back. Acknowledging this, Brettell ordered Dick Beaty (in BS148) to escort Neville home, as was the proper procedure. Turning onto a reciprocal heading, Neville and Beaty left the formation and struck out for Bolt Head.

Back at 10 Group's Exeter HQ, the operation's controllers sat watching the WAAF plotters pushing the small marker further south, updating the formation's position on the large map below. Fighter Command HQ at Stanmore was also watching the radar plots coming in and there was growing concern as the formation seemed to be going too far to the south, out of range. In the operations room at Stanmore, Squadron Leader 'Laddie' Lucas DFC reached for the telephone.

You could see the radar plots being placed down and I can remember seeing them going miles down south and eventually they disappeared off our board. I rang up the Sector Controller at Exeter and asked what was happening to these fellows, we can't see them, can you? But he said, no, they'd gone off their board too! I said, 'They'll never get back from there,' but the Controller said that they were now out of radio touch and had been for the last 20 minutes. (Squadron Leader P.B. Lucas, Fighter Command HQ, Bentley Priory, quoted in Goodson & Franks, 1991, p. 68)

High above the French coast, at the head of 401 Squadron, Brian Kingcome was becoming equally unnerved. As they had approached what they thought would be the target area, still high above a great, unending carpet of cumulo-stratus, his keen eyes had spotted a formation of Fortresses way off in the distance and much further to the south. Curious to see them so far beyond the target area, the Wing held its position as the bombers wheeled back round onto a north–easterly heading. With the cloud cover being what it was, it seemed that the Fortresses had abandoned all possibility of bombing successfully and were turning for home. So much for that then! Time to make tracks.

The three escort squadrons took up their positions, with 133 and 64 Squadrons close by the bombers and 401 Squadron as top cover. While there was still no visual contact with the ground, dead reckoning on the information they had suggested that the formation was over the northern coast of Brittany, with the English coast and Bolt Head only 100 or so miles due north. The Spitfires would stick with the Fortresses until near the Devon coast and then land back at Harrowbeer and Bolt Head. At this point it all seemed routine, apart from the continued lack of response from Exeter Control. Kingcome was completely baffled by this. Operational procedures dictated the need for radio silence so as not to alert the enemy via their many listening stations monitoring radio frequencies. Now, however, they were near enough to home and yet repeated calls were met with obstinate silence from the controllers at Exeter HQ. His operational experience working like a sixth sense, Kingcome was also uneasy with the pattern of weather systems that the Wing was encountering.

> *Weather can be changeable, clouds can build up quickly, but the junction of two weather systems is generally a well-defined, recognisable area. There is a slow change of character from clear skies to wisps of low stratus cloud, and these thicken and build into towering cumulus only gradually. It was just such a junction of weather systems that we had flown through on our outward journey. By now we should have been able to see it again if we were anywhere near the English coast. There was something more to this than a niggling instinct; my reason told me decisively what we ought to have been finding and the home skies should still have been clear. In the hour or so we had been airborne it would have been quite impossible for the weather to change so dramatically in character, or for it to have moved so far.* (Wing Commander Brian Kingcome, quoted in Kingcome, 1992, p. 131)

At Exeter HQ, the formation was still off the map and with it out of radio range it was impossible to inform Tony Gaze of his Wing's actual position. The reality was not easy to contemplate. Being out of sight of the ground, they had relied wholly on dead reckoning to bring the formation over the target area and to estimate progress. The key factor in these calculations was wind speed and, while the Met had forecast this to be thirty or so miles per hour at the operational height required, in reality a tail wind in excess of 100 mph had blown the formation way south of the Brittany peninsular. Both bomber and fighter formations had been equally affected, with the Fortresses being far south into the Bay of Biscay before it was decided to abandon the operation. Now turned back and facing into a headwind of over 100mph, the fighters, with their rapidly diminishing fuel reserves, were in a dire position.

A Gap in the Cloud – Sighting Land:
Unaware of their predicament, Tony Gaze led the Wing north, still thinking that they were over the English Channel and not far from the friendly coastal airfields from where they had taken off. With Exeter HQ continuing in its silence, there was no other information to hand to suggest otherwise. There was no response to requests for a fix, a positional update, or a vector to steer for home. As the three squadrons pressed on, their concentration alternated between watching their fuel

gauges, keeping a sharp lookout for any land that might appear to suggest their position, and scanning the sky for any sign of the enemy. The latter was pretty unlikely, being so near to the English coast, but many a lapse in respect for one's enemy could lead to an early demise. It was then, momentarily, that a small gap in the clouds appeared and revealed a rugged, south-facing coastline.

It *had* to be England. What little had been visible seemed characteristic of the Cornish/Devon coast. All of the evidence seemed to add up: the nature of the coastline and its south-facing aspect; the time elapsed on their northerly heading; the amount of fuel expended. The only issue still worrying Kingcome and others was the still silent Exeter Control. Yet, even this could be explained by a technical problem, a gremlin in the system somewhere. Fuel for the fighters was now uncomfortably low and it was imperative that the Wing should find some forward airfield at which to land. For Brettell and 133 Squadron their fuel situation had perhaps been worsened by their position as close support cover: joining with the ponderously slow bomber formation had required some degree of zigzagging to avoid overtaking the Fortresses. A decision had to be made and so Brettell called up Bill Baker, his experienced flight commander, to discuss the options. As Pilot Officer Charles Cook, flying BR640 (a Mk V Spitfire converted to Mk IX), recalled:

> *It was getting to be a long mission – we had been in the air two hours and fifteen minutes – but I was not worried at all … I thought our commander knew where we were. I heard Baker say, 'I think we're supposed to go down.' Soon we could see a hole in the clouds, and Baker repeated, 'Gordon, I think we should go down.' Brettell said, 'Okay'.* (Pilot Officer Charles Cook, 133 Squadron, quoted in Haughland, 1979, p. 176)

The navigators of the USAAF's 301st BG, sitting up in the noses of their Flying Fortresses, seemed certain of their position. As 401 Squadron's operational diary recorded:

> *The bombers then saw land on the right and evidently thought they had reached the English coast at Falmouth and the bombers turned right. 133 and 64 Squadrons broke away from the formation and 133 went down to land.* (401 Squadron, Operational Record Book, 26 September 1942).

With 133 Squadron's responsibilities as close escort now completed, Brettell weighed up the evidence and asked permission of the Wing Leader to descend. Convinced of their location near Falmouth, the formation of Fortresses turned onto an easterly course, heading home to their bases. The visibility was still poor and so Brettell, as was standard practice, ordered the formation to close up so as to not lose any of the squadron as they dropped down through the dense layer of cloud. The challenge now was to find suitable landmarks to fix their position, before plotting a course back towards Bolt Head. If the navigators of the 301st BG had been correct about Falmouth, then Bolt Head would lie to the west of their current, estimated position. There was still no word from Exeter.

The Canadians of 401 Squadron, who as high cover to the bombers had maintained altitude and course, remained uncertain of their position. With Squadron Leader Hodson, Wing Commander Kingcome was still bothered that they had no confirmation of their location from Exeter Control. With the advantage of height, Keith Hodson, though unsure, had thought that he had seen an expanse of water, north of the south-facing coastline they had caught a glimpse of earlier. If Hodson was right, then their landfall could not be the south coast near Falmouth. They might have been blown much further west than their intended course. As fuel was now desperately low, Kingcome and 401 Squadron decided to stay tracking north, in hope that the position would become clearer.

No Welcome Committee: Flak, Focke Wulfs and Out of Fuel!
Just after Brettell had turned 133 Squadron onto a westerly course, one of the squadron caught sight of a city off to starboard. With visibility still marginal and still uncertain of their whereabouts, Brettell decided to reverse course and to overfly the area; they would be sure to pick up an identifying feature to confirm their location. The cloud base had pushed the formation down below 3,000 feet, but with the urgency of finding somewhere to land being uppermost in their thoughts, their lowering altitude was of little concern.

Suddenly, the sky around them seemed to explode! Everywhere, there was the unmistakable smell of cordite, flashes from multiple detonations and the black stain of smoke lingering in the air. The tight formation instinctively broke into a scatter of individual aircraft, as their pilots searched frantically for some place to hide. There seemed nowhere to go: it was as if every anti-aircraft gun in the world had bracketed them! Amidst the confusion, Charlie Cook shouted down the R/t, 'tell those bastards to stop shooting at us!' It was an appeal to the Royal Navy, the Army – whoever the idiots might be – to put aside their trigger-happy tendencies and take a moment to recognise a squadron of returning Spitfires. In fact those on the ground that continued to throw all manner of corruption up at them had recognised them as Spitfires. But this was not Falmouth, Southampton, Plymouth or Portsmouth: this was Brest, one of the most heavily defended ports on the Brittany peninsular!

For 133 Squadron, there was no time to wonder how it had come to be that they were still over enemy-occupied France. Bemused, many of them were unable to contemplate what was happening. Pilot Officer (2nd Lieutenant) Middleton heard nothing of the R/t chatter and exclamations from his comrades. Since take-off he had assumed that his radio was dead but had kept with the formation since he had returned from the previous operation with a similar problem and felt the need to press on regardless. Having not attended the briefing, he had not been informed of a last-minute radio frequency change over from channel C to B.

> *It seemed that every anti-aircraft battery in the German army was stationed there that day, and they were all shooting at us. It was obviously an every-man-for-himself situation. We all scattered, some back into the clouds, some out to sea, some just blundering around trying to figure out what the hell had happened. I looked at the petrol gauge, which had stopped even wiggling by now, and that rainy, wind-whipped ocean – it was getting dark too – and decided to go as far into France as I could, and when the gas ran out I'd bail out.* (Pilot Officer George Middleton, 133 Squadron, quoted in Haughland, 1979, p. 177)

Pilot Officer (2nd Lt) George Sperry, flying in Red Section, saw Brettell catch a packet of 40mm flak in the starboard wing root. As he spun in with one wing gone, passing underneath Sperry's aircraft, there seemed little chance at this low altitude that Brettell would survive. Miraculously, Brettell did crawl from the wreckage of his Spitfire, though badly injured and requiring hospitalisation for many months. Sperry himself was similarly caught by 40mm fire, losing his canopy, a portion of the windscreen, and much of his engine coolant. After passing between two Focke Wulf 190s that were in the process of taking off from Brest airfield, Sperry sought refuge in the clouds, knowing that with coolant gone and temperatures rocketing off the clock it was only a matter of time before he would have to take to his parachute.

The parachute saved many a life that day: Charlie Cook had managed to spot a field that he thought he could just get the Spitfire into, but before he was able to do so an Fw190 seemed to come out of nowhere. Numerous 20mm cannon shells tore into Cook's aircraft. Cook jettisoned the hood, undid his Sutton harness, and rolled out. Being very low, his parachute had little time to deploy, but it still did enough to decelerate his fall. Pilot Officer (2nd Lt) Bob Smith's aircraft (BS447) was caught by flak, fragments of which perforated the cooling system. Before the engine seized, he managed to turn it on its back and drop out before deploying his 'chute.

Having set a south-easterly course away from the commotion of Brest, George Middleton checked his maps hoping for some inspiration as to where to go. Amazingly, the engine was still running, even though the fuel gauge was reading nothing. Spotted by two Fw190s, Middleton was then intercepted but succeeded in turning into the attack at the last minute, a stream of cannon shells passing underneath him. His luck was holding. Escaping into cloud, he continued on for another ten minutes or so before deciding to chance dropping down again to check his whereabouts. Unfortunately, he had inadvertently popped out of the cloud-cover right above an enemy airfield. The reception from the flak defences was, as Middleton later reported, *'like an explosion in a red ping-pong ball factory'*. Once again the cloud provided brief sanctuary and after a few more minutes he let down over a peaceful stretch of French countryside, where farmers seemed only intent on going about their daily business. Comforted that no-one now seemed interested in him (at least interested enough to shoot at him), Middleton decided that this would be as good a place as any to bail out.

His first attempt to do so was unsuccessful, as the aircraft was still doing 230mph and the slipstream thwarted any effort to extricate himself from the cockpit. Dropping back into his seat, Middleton executed a wide turn with the throttle fully back, gradually slowing the Spitfire to a more acceptable 160mph. This time he managed to get out, pulled the ripcord and breathed a sigh of relief as the 'chute opened. The aircraft crashed half a mile away, seemingly drawing the attention of the farm workers he had spotted earlier. On landing he discarded and buried his parachute. There started a six-week period in which he was able to evade capture, aided by the French. Like Brettell, Sperry, Cook, Marion Jackson and Gill Wright, Middleton would eventually end up as a PoW.

Pilot Officer (2nd Lt) Len Ryerson from Massachusetts and Pilot Officer (2nd Lt) Dennis Smith from California were killed. Nothing more was seen of Pilot Officer (2nd Lt) Bill Baker, though George Sperry had last heard him over the R/t saying he was too low and was going to ditch in the sea. Gene Neville was also dead. After turning back with Dick Beaty as escort, he had nursed his failing engine for thirty minutes. Heading north until he and Beaty estimated they must be over England, they let down through cloud, only to be caught in a barrage of flak. Neville's aircraft was hit and he crashed near Guingamp, forty miles east of Morlaix. Gene Neville, Ryerson and Dennis Smith were all buried in the same cemetery.

Counting the Cost:
Of 133 Squadron, only Dick Beaty made it back to England. When Gene Neville was shot down, Beaty had managed to slip back into the overcast and, realising

that he must still be over France, he set a northerly course with the leanest of mixtures. Eventually, the engine finally drained the tank of its last drop and he decided to bail out, rather than risk ditching the aircraft. But at the last moment, as he undid his seat straps, some of the mist and cloud cleared and Beaty could see the English coast. Still with some altitude, he elected to attempt a forced landing, putting the Spitfire into a gentle glide. Beaty just about made it, crash-landing above the cliffs near Kingsbridge. Suffering multiple injuries, Beaty was rushed to hospital where he remained in a critical condition. In the confusion following the operation, word got round that it was Dennis Smith, rather than Beaty, who had managed to return. Beaty survived.

Having elected to continue on a northerly course, Kingcome and the two remaining escort squadrons set the leanest of mixtures to conserve fuel. Not long after 133 Squadron had separated, Kingcome's repeated calls to Exeter HQ were finally answered. Barely audible through the interference, Kingcome inquired as to where 'Ops' had been for the last two hours! As he later recalled, their information about the formation's current position and advice to 'watch your fuel' were less than encouraging.

> As if I needed telling! But eighty miles south! What on earth had been going on here? It was no time for rumination, but at least we knew our direction now. The crucial task was to get everyone home intact if I could. Luckily we still had plenty of altitude, so we throttled back to the minimum of revs needed to keep airborne, and in due course let down slowly in long, powered glides towards Bolt Head. The airfield was laid out at the edge of quite sheer granite cliffs, and an off-shore wind meant we had to land towards them. As I came in on my final approach I expected each second to hear the engine cut and anticipated ending as an ephemeral scar on those impervious granite walls. (Wing Commander Brian Kingcome, quoted in Kingcome, 1992, p. 131)

While the decision to remain at altitude had proved to be the marginal advantage that 133 Squadron had lost when they descended to protect the Fortresses, 401 and 64 Squadrons' return was still a close run thing. As 401 Squadron's diaries wrote:

> After the Wing had been airborne for 1½ hours, ops finally gave the position as 100 miles south of the English coast, and gave a homing vector of 020 degrees. Calls were then heard from 133 Squadron, some having been hit by a/a and some pilots out of petrol. 401 continued on course 020 which was later changed to 030 and seven of our a/c landed at Bolt Head at 18.20 hours, and three landed

at Harrowbeer at 18.20 hours. Pilot Officer L.E. Hokan, forty miles south of
the English coast, reported, 'Out of petrol, bailing out, so long boys, will see you
tomorrow.' He was last seen in a gradual dive and had not been picked up. S/P
(Sergeant Pilot) D. Wright missed the landing ground and crashed at Torquay and
is in hospital seriously injured. Squadron Leader Hodson asked permission to do
ASR but was not allowed. Until sighting the English coast on the return journey
all pilots were of the opinion that they would have to bale out. (401 Squadron,
Operational Record Book, 26 September 1942).

Pilots of Tony Gaze's 64 Squadron had a similar experience, draining their tanks very nearly dry as they crawled north against the wind. Thankfully, all but one made it back to Harrowbeer, having been airborne for two hours and twenty minutes. When the ground crews dipped the tanks to check contents, they found many had less than a gallon remaining. The only casualty was Pilot Officer Calder who managed to force-land in a field bear Wembury, writing off his aircraft (Spitfire IX BR603). Calder suffered severe abdominal and head injuries and was rushed to the Royal Naval Hospital at Plymouth, but survived.

All told, this 'cinch' of an operation to the French coast turned out to be a costly affair. The losses to aircraft and personnel were:

133 (Eagle) Squadron:
Flight Lieutenant E.G. Brettell DFC. Spitfire IX (BS313) Shot down, Prisoner
   of War.
Pilot Officer L.T. Ryerson. Spitfire IX (BS275) Missing, presumed killed.
Pilot Officer W.H. Baker. Spitfire IX (BS446) Missing, presumed killed.
Pilot Officer D.D. Smith. Spitfire IX (BS294) Missing, presumed killed.
Pilot Officer G.B. Sperry. Spitfire IX (BS638) Shot down, Prisoner of War.
Pilot Officer G.G. Wright. Spitfire IX (BS138) Shot down, Prisoner of War.
Flight Lieutenant M.E. Jackson. Spitfire IX (BS279) Shot down, Prisoner of War.
Pilot Officer R.E. Smith. Spitfire IX (BS447) Shot down, evaded capture.
Pilot Officer C.A. Cook. Spitfire IX (BS640) Shot down, Prisoner of War.
Pilot Officer R.N. Beaty. Spitfire IX (BS418) Returned, force-landed in England.
Pilot Officer G.H. Middleton. Spitfire IX (BS301) Shot down, Prisoner of War.
Pilot Officer G.P. Neville. Spitfire IX (BS140) Missing, presumed killed.

64 Squadron:
Pilot Officer K.V. Calder. Spitfire IX (BR603) Returned, force-landed in England.

401 (Canadian) Squadron:
Pilot Officer J.L.E. Hokan. Spitfire IX (BR981) Returned, force-landed in England.

The Blackest of Days & Biggin Farewell:
For those ground crew that had seen 133 Squadron off that day, it was the worst of times. There was no clear news as to what had happened. However, the old service grapevine – or 'bush telegraph' as some called it – was quick to garner what information was to hand.

Davies was helping out with a fifty-hour inspection on Spitfire BS137 when Campbell came into the hangar. 'What's the gen, Boyo?' Davies light-heartedly called out, not really expecting any real news. For once Campbell's face did not break into a smile. Instead, he walked slowly over to the aircraft, slumped down on a nearby packing crate and muttered something unintelligible. Davies slid off the wing and walked over to his friend, wiping some oil from his hands as he did so. He sat down next to Campbell, giving him a playful nudge. 'C'mon Cammie, what's up?' As Campbell lifted his face from his hands, Davies could see he was on the verge of tears, and in that moment he could feel himself starting to lose his composure.

'We've lost the lot,' said Campbell, his voice trembling as he tried to form the words. 'All twelve of them, all bloody twelve of them, Taff,' he exclaimed. 'What was that?' called out another of the ground crew. 'Whaddya mean, all twelve,' said another in disbelief. Davies cut the others short, grabbing hold of Campbell's arm. 'How?' he asked. Campbell had very little more information. He had been walking past 'ops' when he'd bumped into a couple of WAAFs coming out of the door, one clearly distraught. That's how he'd heard of it but all he could get was rather sketchy accounts. Apparently McColpin was also back on the station, having returned from London, and was trying to piece together what had happened to 133. There was little of which to be certain.

Davies found little comfort in rumour and conjecture, best guesses, 'tittle-tattle', as he called it. After a few hours, it was all too much and he quietly made his way back to his billets, walking slowly in the rain, not really noticing that his uniform was soaked through. Then it was as if a great silence descended on the whole station, everyone deep in their own thoughts.

… ground crew and everyone became anxious, still wondering whether they [the Squadron] had landed somewhere else … but then the tragic news came that only one had survived. That was the first instance, the first news we had. Then we heard that they had run into a freak storm … and then no-one wanted to speak to

each other. We had gotten to know the pilots and oh God, this was such a tragedy. Awful! (LAC Raymond Davies, interview 2003)

Returning to his billets, Davies pulled off his boots and lay back on the bed. In the far corner, a young rigger, still in his working overalls, slouched on his bed, just staring silently at the wall. The sounds of another airman sobbing drifted across the corridor from one of the other rooms. Lying there, Davies made a mental note: 26 September 1942, 133 American Eagle Squadron, twelve aircraft lost, the blackest of days.

After the initial trickle of information that had made its way through the usual unofficial channels, it seemed certain that someone 'at the top' had decided it was necessary to minimise the damage to morale that such news would bring. Already at Bolt Head, there was an immediate clampdown on information and the two reserve pilots of 133 Squadron, Miller and Gentile, were confined to camp. The official line wending its way back to Biggin and Great Sampford was that the squadron would not be returning from Bolt Head. There was some truth in this as the weather was still awful: it was forty-eight hours or so before 64 Squadron was able to make it back to Fairlop because of poor visibility and torrential rain.

In the following days, it seemed to many that a strategy of dispersion had been put in place to lessen the psychological blow that came with the loss of a whole squadron. The machinery of war quickened its pace and within days the majority of those personnel associated with 133 Squadron were posted out, not as a unit, but in groups. As LAC Ted Hayes (Fitter) remembered:

… when the Squadron was transferred to the US Army Air Forces at Debden, there were only a few of us … most of the Squadron had been posted quickly because they wanted to get rid of us really after the mishap, because it did upset a lot of the blokes, a lot of the chaps, pilots missing and that. It really did. It upset the ground crew losing just one pilot let alone a complete squadron … the Squadron was really upset, ground crew, ground staff, riggers, fitters, anybody that belonged to it. I never forgot the shock of knowing that we had lost a complete squadron. (LAC Ted Hayes, Fitter, 133 Squadron, interview)

A few, like Hayes, went up to Debden, where the nucleus of the 4th Fighter Group was being gathered together. Some were posted to neighbouring RAF stations or even further afield. It was as part of these quick post-Morlaix postings that Davies, Campbell and the majority of 'Jimmy' Stewart's specialist team left Biggin Hill. With 401 Squadron and 3034 Servicing Echelon moving across to Kenley to begin forming a new all-Canadian Wing, it seemed natural for Davies and the team to follow them. After all, there were new armourers to train, new squadrons to look after.

As the wagon skirted the suburbs of Croydon and passed down through Purley and Whyteleaf on its way to Kenley, Davies felt sad to be leaving Biggin. He thought about all those he had known there: Don Kingaby, Johnnie Johnston, Rankin, Milne, Sailor Malan. So many he had had the honour of serving with. Dickie Barwell, Boy Wellum and Bob Tuck; Duke-Woolley, Brian Kingcome and good old Nobby Lund. They were names that would stay with him forever.

Epilogue

4 June 1944, 183 Squadron, 136/123 Wing, Thorney Island:
It was 3am and there seemed little point of trying to sleep now, thought Davies, at the end of another restless night. Over the past few days they had become commonplace for him along with most, if not all of the crews. OK, some managed to shrug off this feeling of apprehension to get their head down for a few hours, but it was a brief and partial respite. 'Taff?' It was Campbell – his voice cut through the damp air that clung to the inside of the canvas of the tent. 'What?' said Davies, now sure that the morning was upon him. 'Can't you sleep?' queried Campbell. 'No,' he replied, 'how could I when all I could hear was you thinkin' all damn night!' In the half-light of the morning Davies could make out Campbell grinning. He knew what was coming next. 'Do you think it's on, Taff?' quizzed Campbell. 'Don't know. Do you think it's today, Boyo?' replied Davies with a laugh.

They had kept this banter going over the past few weeks, ever since the squadron had returned with the rest of the Wing from the armament practice camp at Llanbedr, North Wales. Here the Typhoons had been carrying out rocket firing against old tanks. They had even hit a few! Though little was being said to anyone to confirm their excited suspicions, both air and ground crew were convinced that, even it wasn't today, it was close. Invasion – the Allied return to France – was close. It had to be. There were millions like them, all waiting, all straining at the leash like some gargantuan mastiff ready to make the greatest assault on Fortress Europe. At Thorney, 123 Airfield was a microcosm of the alliance that had brought so many together from far-flung corners of the Commonwealth in partnership against a common foe. In just an hour's tour of the dispersals one could find Scots, Welsh, English, Canadians, Australians, Mauritians and New Zealanders. Then there were those from France, from Belgium, and Holland. Over in 609 Squadron, Klaus Hugo Adam flew every operation with the added worry that he was a Jewish German national. Such a cosmopolitan mixture of nations was replicated across the whole of the RAF with other squadrons and other nationalities, Poles, Czechs, South Africans and Norwegians to name an illustrious few. With the massed might of the American military also in residence, it seemed that this small island might slip beneath the icy waters of the Atlantic under the sheer weight of arms and personnel. For five long years it had borne this increasing responsibility, and now – as many felt – the time had come. Dunkirk seemed such a distant, yet ever reminding memory of the challenges that lay ahead. Dieppe too, remained as a wound still fresh enough to steel hearts and minds as to the price of victory, and the cost of failure.

Could this be it? The beginning of the end?

The Ten Rules of Air Fighting

By Wing Commander A.G. Malan, DSO, DFC

1. Wait until you see the whites of his eyes. Fire short bursts of one to two seconds and only when your sights are definitely 'on'.
2. While shooting think of nothing else, brace the whole of the body, have both hands on the stick, concentrate on your ring sight.
3. Always keep a sharp lookout.
4. Height gives you the initiative.
5. Always turn and face the attack.
6. Make your decisions promptly. It is better to act quickly even if your tactics are not the best.
7. Never fly straight and level for more than thirty seconds in the combat area.
8. When diving to attack always leave a proportion of your formation above to act as top guard.
9. Initiative, aggression, air discipline, and team work are the words that mean something in air fighting.
10. Go in quickly - punch hard - get out!

Bibliography

Bartley, Anthony DFC, *Smoke Trails in the Sky: From the Journals of a Fighter Pilot*, William Kimber (1984).

Bowyer, Chaz, *Fighter Pilots of the RAF, 1939–1945*. William Kimber (1984).

Caine, Philip D., *American Pilots in the RAF: The WWII Eagle Squadrons*, Brassey's, New York (1993).

Caygill, P., *The Darlington Spitfire: A Charmed Life*, Airlife Publishing Ltd, Shrewsbury (1999).

Caygill, P., *Spitfire Mark V in Action: RAF Operations in Northern Europe*, Airlife Publishing Ltd, Shrewsbury (2001).

De Havilland Aircraft Company Ltd., *De Havilland controllable pitch airscrew constant speed control unit: service manual*. De Havilland Aircraft Company, Hatfield (n.d.)

Duke, Neville, *Test Pilot*. Allan Wingate (1953).

Earnshaw, James, D., *609 at War: An Auxiliary Fighter Squadron's 72 Months of Active Service 1939–1945 Recorded in Photographs*, Vector Fine Art, Hailsham (2003).

Foreman, J., *Fighter Command War Diaries: Volume Two, September 1940 to December 1941*, Air Research Publications, Walton-on-Thames (1998).

Foreman, J., *Fighter Command War Diaries: Volume Three, January 1942 to June 1943*, Air Research Publications, Walton-on-Thames (2001).

Flint, P., *R.A.F. Kenley: The Story of the Royal Air Force Station 1917–1974*, Terence Dalton Ltd, Lavenham (1985).

Forrester, L., *Fly for Your Life: The Story of the "Immortal Tuck", Wing Commander Robert Stanford Tuck DSO, DFC and two bars*, Fredrick Muller Ltd, London (1956).

Franks, N., *Sky Tiger: The Story of Sailor Malan*, Crécy Books Ltd, Manchester (1994).

Franks, N. (Ed), *The War Diaries of Neville Duke DSO, OBE, DFC (two bars), AFC, Czech Military Cross, 1941–1944*, Grub Street, London (1995).

Freeman, R.A., *The Mighty Eighth: A History of the U.S. 8th Air Force*, MacDonald and Jane's Publications Ltd, London (1976).

Freeman, R.A., *B-17 Fortress at War*, Ian Allan Ltd, Shepperton (1977).

Goodson, James A. & Franks, N., *Over-Paid, Over-Sexed and Over Here: From RAF Eagles to 4th Fighter Group Hawks*, Wingham Press (1991).

Haughland, V., *The Eagle Squadrons: Yanks in the RAF, 1940–1942*, David & Charles, London (1979).

Johnson, Group Captain J.E., *Wing Leader*, Chatto & Windus (1956)

Kingcome, Brian DSO, DFC and Bar., *A Willingness to Die: Life and Memories from Fighter Command and Beyond*, Tempus Publishing Ltd, Stroud (1999).

Laffin, John., *British VCs of World War 2: A Study in Heroism* (2000).

McIntosh, D., *High Blue Battle: The War Diary of No.1 (401) Fighter Squadron, RCAF*, Spa Books, Stevenage (1990).

Ogley, Bob, *Biggin on the Bump: The Most Famous Fighter Station in the World*, Froglet Publications Ltd, Westerham (1990).

Oxpring, Bobby DFC AFC, *Spitfire Command*, William Kimber, London (1984).

Shores, C. & Williams, C., *Aces High*, Grub Street, London (1994).

Shores, C., *Those Other Eagles: A Companion Volume to Aces High*, Grub Street, London (2004).

Spurdle, Bob DFC and bar, *The Blue Arena*, Crécy Books Ltd, Manchester (1995).

Tanner, J. (Ed), *The Spitfire V Manual: The Official Air Publication for the Spitfire F.VA., F.VB., F.VC., LF.VA., LF.VB., and LF.VC., 1941–1945*, Arms and Armour Press, London (1976).

Tidy, Douglas, *I Fear No Man: The Story of No.74 (Fighter) Squadron, Royal Flying Corps and Royal Air Force (The Tigers)*, MacDonald, London (1972).

Wallace, Graham, RAF Biggin Hill, Putnam, London (1957).

Wellum, Geoffrey, *First Light*, Viking, Penguin, London (2002).

Ziegler, Frank, H., *The Story of 609 Squadron: Under the White Rose*, Crécy Books Ltd, Manchester (1993).

Glossary

Author's note:
The historical account presented within this work was formed over many years of personal connections and conversations with veterans of the conflict, the longest association being of course with my grandfather, Ray Davies. In the process, the language of the time, particularly those 'service slang' terms, became an easy and familiar vernacular for me. It was thus both appropriate and natural for such terms and phrases to become part of the way in which this part of Biggin Hill's story would be told. In my conversation with veterans and their families, it was also a shared language and understanding. The following glossary provides definitions and explanations that the reader may find helpful.

92nd Foot and Mouth: Members of 92 Squadron would affectionately refer to it as the 92nd Foot and Mouth, mimicking the ways in which the Army named its infantry regiments.

a/a: Anti-aircraft

Angels (two-five): RAF code word for altitude (25,000 feet), used in radio communication to indicate the height at which the operation would be conducted, or to alert everyone to the height of an enemy aircraft/ formation.

ASR: Air Sea Rescue. Used to refer to aircraft engaged in such operations or to the operation itself.

Bank: To turn the aircraft. As the pilot pushes the controls to either left or right, the aircraft's wing tilts towards the direction of the turn.

Bead: Technically, this refers to the centre of an early type of gunsight, which had a small round bead as the aiming point. The phrase was used within the RAF to refer to the act of aiming at a target (e.g. 'getting a bead' on the target). Also, he 'made a bead for' the local pub!

Beam (attack): An attacking approach made against an enemy aircraft from the side.

Beehive: A term used to describe the overall formation of aircraft engaged in an operation, stacked up at different altitudes around the bomber formation.

BG: Bomb Group. A unit of the USAAF.

Blast-pen: See E-pen.

Blister panel: A panel with a bulged surface used to cover over internal equipment that was larger than the bay in which it was fitted. For instance, when the 20mm Hispano cannon was adopted as a standard armament for the Spitfire Vb, the original armament bays (designed for the smaller .303 Browning machine gun) could not accommodate the drum-shaped ammunition carrier. When fitted, the drum protruded above and below the wing and so the panels covering the bays were modified to have a teardrop-shaped section to cover over the raised area of the drum.

Break!: An instruction to break formation and take evasive action.

The Bump: Slang for Biggin Hill – 'Biggin on the Bump'. The airfield is located on high ground to the south-east of London. Resembling a spur of ground, the land, particularly to the south, drops steeply away into a valley.

Butts, the: Firing butts. A walled construction, made of brick, earth and sand, used to test the firing of live ammunition. RAF stations normally had two types of firing butts: a smaller one would be used for the practice firing of small arms (rifles, pistols etc). The other would be larger and be situated with access to the perimeter track so that aircraft could be set up in the flying attitude, with the tail on a supporting trestle, so its guns could be test-fired.

Cat.E: Aircraft declared written off or beyond repair on site. These terms are taken from the official system of categorisation for aircraft damage used by the RAF. The categories during the period were as follows:

Cat.U: Aircraft undamaged.
Cat.A: Aircraft can be repaired on site.
Cat.Ac: Repair is beyond the unit capacity (i.e. may be repaired on site by another unit or contractor).
Cat.B: Beyond repair on site (i.e. repairable at a Maintenance Unit or at a contractor's works).
Cat.C: Allocated to Instructional Airframe Duties.
Cat.E: Aircraft is a write-off.
Cat.E1: Aircraft is a write-off but is considered suitable for component recovery.
Cat.E2: Aircraft is a write-off and suitable only for scrap.
Cat.E3: Aircraft is burnt out.
Cat.Em: Aircraft is missing from an operational sortie.

Char and wads: 'Char' means tea, and is a borrowing from the Hindustani word for tea. A significant amount of RAF slang originates from its time involved in the policing of the Empire, particularly during its service in India and Afghanistan in the 1920s. 'Wads' refers to a chunky portion of cake or a bun often served by the mobile NAAFI wagons that would come round to dispersal points when the squadrons were standing by in readiness for operations. Sometimes 'wads' could also be used to refer to a thick-cut bread or sandwich.

Circus: An official code-name for an operation involving a formation of fighter aircraft (normally at Wing strength or greater) and a small group of bombers. The intention of circus operations was to draw the enemy into action.

Cross-over turn: A manoeuvre used to change the direction of a formation. For example, if two squadrons are flying parallel to each other, executing a general turn would mean the squadron on the outside of the turn would have to travel further and thus increase speed in order to maintain its position. The cross-over turn was developed as a better alternative as it was quicker and saved fuel. In this type of turn, if the turn is executed to the left, the right-hand squadron in the parallel formation would turn behind the left-hand squadron and the formation positions would be reversed.

Dead-stick: Often used in reference to making an emergency landing, when the aircraft has experienced an engine failure or has run out of fuel.

Deflection/quarter deflection/full deflection: Deflection is a term used in shooting, referring to the practice of aiming ahead of a target in order to account for the target's speed and direction and the path travelled by the bullets. The angle of deflection refers to the angle at which the attacking aircraft needs to be positioned in relation to the enemy's aircraft in order for the bullets to strike it. Making an attack from dead astern (i.e. your line of travel is exactly that of the target aircraft) would be referred to as a zero degrees or 'no deflection' attack (or shot). Approaching the target aircraft at around 20–30 degrees to its line of travel would generally be considered a 'quarter attack' (or 'quarter deflection' shot). At an approach angle of 40–50 degrees to the target's line of travel, such an attack would be termed as 'half deflection'. 'Full deflection' is used to describe an interception that happens at anything between 60 and 90 degrees to the target's line of travel.

D.I.: Daily Inspection. Aircraft were routinely inspected in rotation to reduce the number of aircraft that were unavailable for operations due to maintenance. Aircraft were thus subject to a general daily inspection and a form (Form 700) was signed to indicate it was fit for operation that day. After a specified numbers of operational hours each aircraft was then taken 'off-line' to conduct more in-depth inspections. In the RAF these would occur when the aircraft had flown 50 hours, 100 hours and 150 hours.

Dispersal: An area on an airfield where a squadron's aircraft would be located. The term refers to the practice of dispersing the aircraft, parking them with distance between them, so as to minimise possible damage to many aircraft from a single attack. Being 'down at dispersal' thus means to be in this area where the aircraft are located in readiness for operations.

E/a: Enemy Aircraft. Often found in pilots' logbooks, combat reports and squadron operational records.

Echelon: A specific group of professionals organised to carry out designated tasks. In this book it refers to a body of aircraftsmen (of various trades) organised to maintain the aircraft (i.e. a Servicing Echelon) at their operational base, rather than at a non-operational maintenance unit. These personnel were different to squadron personnel in that they were not normally posted to a specific squadron and thus worked across a group of squadrons at the same airfield. In Davies' experience, Biggin Hill seemed to use echelon personnel differently. For example, he was officially listed as being with 3034 Servicing Echelon but was quickly assigned to a specialised armament team and then specifically 'loaned' to 92 Squadron. On at least two occasions he was detailed to move posting with a particular squadron (as would be squadron personnel), thus separating from 3034SE. When 92 Squadron's Flight Sergeant Stewart was promoted as Chief Armaments Officer for Biggin Hill, Davies was then allocated to specific senior pilots (including wing leaders and squadron commanders).

E-pen: A brick and earthen construction designed to form a protective barrier around a parked aircraft. On RAF airfields such structures often had space for two aircraft and thus from above looked a little like a letter 'E', with brick and earthen walls to the rear and sides of each aircraft. They were built around the perimeter track of the airfield at a place of dispersal. The rear wall of these structures often contained a shelter to protect personnel.

Erks: Ground personnel. Particularly those 'other ranks' working on the aircraft as ground crew in preparation for operations. According to Squadron Leader Ward-Jackson's (1945) publication of RAF slang, 'erk' referred to any airman below the rank of corporal and possibly originated from the Royal Navy term for a lower deck rating. Such Royal Navy slang entered the RAF via its roots in the Royal Naval Air Service (RNAS) in the First World War and also corresponds to the abbreviation of the rank of 'aircraftsman' (abbreviated as 'airc') that came into existence in the 1920s.

Fix: A term used to describe the position of an aircraft for navigation purposes. One would obtain a 'fix' of position by radio, in contact with a ground controller or perhaps using astro-navigation, using the stars.

Fizzer: RAF slang meaning a disciplinary charge. Its most likely origins are in a slang term for a non-alcoholic drink. Anyone put on a disciplinary charge (and under arrest) was denied access to alcohol and thus restricted to soft drink.

Flap: RAF slang for any sort of operational excitement.

Glycol: A coolant liquid used in aircraft engines such as the Rolls-Royce Merlin. Often a vulnerable part of an aircraft with a liquid-cooled engine, if the coolant system was damaged resulting in the loss of glycol, the engine would quickly overheat.

Grancher: Welsh vernacular for grandfather.

Groupie: Group Captain, most often the Station Commander.

Hangar rash: Any sort of minor accidental damage caused to an aircraft whilst in maintenance hangarage.

Harmonisation (of armament): This technical term refers to the calibration of an aircraft's wing-mounted guns. With the spacing of the guns along the Spitfire's wings, it became essential to set the guns at an inward-facing angle so that the ammunition fired would converge at a given point some distance in front of the aircraft. Early in the war, there was a general belief that setting the guns to achieve a pattern spread of shot was useful in order to ensure that some part of the target could be hit (even by the average pilot). However, combat experience in the Battles of France and Britain showed that with the relatively small calibre of the .303 Browning machine gun, pattern harmonisation often did not achieve a concentration that would deliver enough damage to an enemy aircraft. Some pilots, such as Sailor Malan, started to experiment with harmonisation settings to achieve a greater concentration and a shorter convergence distance. In essence, you needed to get closer to the target and all your guns would be set to converge on a point to achieve a maximum concentration of shot. While it had been standard practice to set the guns to converge at around 400 yards, many of the 'aces' of Fighter Command gave instructions to their armourers to reduce this distance so that their guns would be more effective at a closer range. At Biggin Hill, many of the Wing's experienced pilots had their armourers adjust the harmonisation of their guns to achieve maximum effectiveness at around 250 yards.

High cover: In operations where a group of fighter squadrons were used to support a formation of bombers (i.e. escort operations), individual squadrons were allotted specific positions in the formation. To fly as 'high cover' or 'top cover', meant the squadron was being detailed to fly above the bombers at a higher altitude. Having the advantage of height in aerial combat was of great importance because in diving the aircraft, a pilot could gather speed to intercept the enemy.

I.O.: Intelligence Officer.

Old 'H': Often personnel (pilots and ground crew) would refer to an aircraft by its individual code letter. In the RAF, squadrons operated a two-letter squadron identification code (e.g. 92 Squadron was QJ; 609 Squadron was PR; 74 Squadron was ZP). Individual aircraft of each squadron were then allocated a single letter (appearing after the squadron code, separated by the national roundel marking on the fuselage sides). When pilots managed to stay with a squadron for a length of time, they often flew a regular aircraft (rather than being allocated any available one). For example, in 92 Squadron, Flight Lieutenant Brian Kingcome tended to fly QJ-F (as it bore the initial of his middle name, Fabris). Flight Lieutenant Allan Wright regularly flew QJ-S (that he affectionately named 'Satan'). The exception to this system was the letter codes displayed by Wing Leaders who would have their own initials painted on their personal aircraft. Thus, when Robert Stanford-Tuck became Wing Leader at Biggin Hill, his personal aircraft was coded RS-T.

Oleos: The undercarriage legs of an aircraft that provide some absorption of the forces associated with landing. Oleos were hydraulic shock absorbers carrying the main wheels and tyres of an aircraft. Collectively they were often referred to as 'undercarriage', 'the undercart' or 'landing gear'.

Oppo: A close comrade or working partner. Its origin is probably 'opposite number', used affectionately to refer to the other person of a partnership or marriage.

Peri-track: The airfield's perimeter track, linking dispersal areas with the runways.

Pitot head: A sensor located on the external structure of an aircraft that works by measuring pressure changes. The Spitfire V had a combined Pitot-Static sensor located on the underside of the port wing which was the primary sensor for the measurement of airspeed and altitude.

Prop-wash: The air flowing back from a propeller. To stand in the 'prop-wash' is to put oneself in the passage of this airflow.

RDF station: Radio Direction Finding Station. A forerunner of RADAR.

'Right down on the deck': At zero altitude (or near zero) – flying at minimum height above the ground (often to avoid detection from RADAR or to escape an assailant). Visibility 'right down on the deck' means that the cloud, mist, fog was virtually at ground level.

Roadstead: An operation against enemy shipping, normally carried out at low or medium altitudes.

Roll/half-roll: An aerobatic manoeuvre whereby the aircraft rotates around its longitudinal axis. Executing a roll would have the aircraft rotate 360 degrees around its longitudinal axis to return to its original orientation. A half-roll would see the aircraft execute a similar rotation but only for 180 degrees, thus adopting an inverted position. A 'rate of roll' is a measurement of the speed at which a roll could be executed. Often a smaller wingspan (e.g. of the Focke Wulf Fw190) would mean an aircraft could rotate faster, allowing it to change direction more quickly and gain a tactical advantage against a slower opponent.

Silk: A parachute. Thus 'hitting the silk' or 'taking to the silk' means to bail out.

Started rivet: A loose rivet. Sometimes if an aircraft had been put under excessive strain during combat the flexing of the airframe might result in the rivets starting to stretch, thus loosening the attachment of the metal skin to the framework.

Stringbag: Nickname given to the Fairey Swordfish aircraft, a torpedo-bomber.

Sweep: Any operation that involved fighter aircraft only, more commonly over enemy territory, with the intention of drawing the enemy into combat.

Temperatures and Pressures: Pilots of the time tended to refer to temperatures and pressures in the plural (even in the case of a single-engine aircraft such as the Spitfire). Shortened to 'Ts and Ps' as part of the standard cockpit checks, a pilot would periodically conduct a check across the cockpit instrument panel, from left to right and back. In the Spitfire, the dials and associated warning lights for such vital engine-related readings (e.g. coolant temperature, oil temperature, fuel pressure, oil pressure) were located on the right hand side of the panel.

Tin-bashing: RAF slang for work on an aircraft's structure or aluminium skin.

USAAF: United States Army Air Force.

Wing: A group of aircraft, larger than single squadron strength. In 1941 the 'Wing' organisation at Biggin Hill normally comprised of three operational squadrons. Sometimes all three squadrons would fly together operationally as one formation (i.e. as a Wing). At other times they would fly as individual squadrons.

Wing man: An individual pilot detailed to fly in close support of a leader. The smallest unit of a formation of aircraft was most typically a pair, with one aircraft taking a lead position and the other operating to one side and slightly behind. This secondary position (or number two position) offered protection to the lead aircraft.

Index